FIGHT FOR THE SEA

FIGHT FOR

Naval Adventure

Naval Institute Press
Annapolis, Maryland

THE SEA
from World War II

John Frayn Turner

Naval Institute Press
291 Wood Road
Annapolis, MD 21402

Library of Congress Cataloging-in-Publication Data
Turner, John Frayn.
    Fight for the sea : naval adventures from World War II / John Frayn Turner.
      p. cm.
    ISBN 1-55750-884-4 (alk. paper)
      1. World War, 1939-1945—Naval operations, British. 2. World War, 1939-
1945—Naval operations, American. 3. Naval battles—History—20th century.
4. World War, 1939-1945—Personal narratives, British. 5. World War, 1939-1945—
Personal narratives, Americans. 6. Sailors—Great Britain—Biography. 7. Sailors—
United States—Biography.
I. Title.
D771 .T78 2001
940.54'5941—dc21

                                                              2001031687

Printed in the United States of America on acid-free paper ∞
08 07 06 05 04 03 02 01   9 8 7 6 5 4 3 2
First printing

In fondest memory of my brother,
Lieutenant Commander Philip Turner, RNVR

Contents

Acknowledgments

I have tried to tell this story in human as well as historical terms. In many cases, I have talked to the men—and women—involved in the epic events. Where this was not possible, I have gone back to sources contemporary with the original actions. Prominent among these, I would like to acknowledge and thank the U.S. Department of the Army for access to the files of *Yank Magazine,* and to the U.S. Navy Department for background material. On the British side, I must express my real gratitude to Her Majesty's Stationery Office for accounts of many actions in World War II; to the Ministry of Defence for official information; and to the Public Record Office for access to the hitherto unpublished rescue ships material.

More specifically, I am glad to give credit to Associated Newspapers, London, for allowing me to quote from my feature published in *Weekend Magazine,* which forms the basis for the first chapter. I would like to thank the following for their past help: Cdr. J.G.D. Ouvry, DSO, RN; Capt. G. B. Stanning, DSO, RN; Cdr. Geoffrey Tanner, RN; Johnnie Ferguson; D. J. Lawrence; C.E.T. Warren and James Benson, authors of *Above Us the Waves* (London: Harrap, 1954); R. C. Benetz, author of "Battle Stations Submerged" (U.S. Naval Institute *Proceedings* [Jan. 1948]); and Theodore Roscoe, author of "U.S. Destroyer Operations in World War II" (U.S. Naval Institute *Proceedings* [1953]); and thanks to my meticulous editor, Therese Boyd.

I have also referred to material in several of my own books: *Service Most Silent* (London: Harrap, 1955); *V.C.s of the Royal Navy* (London: Harrap, 1956); *Periscope Patrol* (London: Harrap, 1958) *Invasion '44* (London: Harrap, 1960), *A Girl Called Johnnie* (London: Harrap, 1963); and lastly, *Battle Stations* (New York: Putnam, 1960).

FIGHT FOR THE SEA

September—December 1939

I Went Down with the Royal Oak

It was 13 October 1939—only forty days after the outbreak of war. The 29,000-ton battleship *Royal Oak* lay safe in Scapa Flow, off the north of Scotland. No enemy had ever penetrated these defenses in the whole of World War I—and there seemed no reason why it should be any different in World War II. But before the night was out, a German U-boat, *U-47*, got into Scapa Flow, sank the *Royal Oak* in fourteen fathoms, and escaped. The number of crew lost totaled 833. Sick-berth Attendant Reg Bendell told me how he went down with the *Royal Oak*—and survived.

We had got back to base after a ten-day patrol in the Atlantic and we were all pretty fagged out. I decided to turn in early. I was nearly twenty years old and *Royal Oak* was my first ship. I had signed on as a sick-berth attendant because it was a clean, comfortable job with a "cot" instead of a hammock. I was also ship's photographer. We'd been paid that day and had drawn all our back pay. With my savings I had 120 pounds in my wallet, tucked in the inside pocket of my jacket. All was quiet, so although I was on duty call, I climbed into my cot soon after 2100 with the intention of getting a good night's sleep.

I didn't.

Four hours later someone shook me. "What's the matter?" I grunted. "Wake up, Lofty, I've got a cut knee." I was 6 feet 3 inches tall, hence the nickname. I treated it with some plaster and asked him, "How did you get it?" He replied, "I was blown out of my hammock by the explosion." "What explosion?" "Didn't you hear it?" "Don't be wet," I burst out. "I'm going to turn in again."

I had just dozed off when I was blown out of my cot by the second explosion. The first bang had been at 0104. Now it was 0116. I was half knocked out and came to in darkness on the deck of the sickbay. The deck had already taken a list of 10 degrees. No doubt this time—I'd heard a hell of a bang.

Petty Officer Harry Main shone a torch at me. "Anyone in there?" he asked urgently and then saw me. "Come on quick—the ship's going."

I followed the stabbing beam out of the sickbay. Then I remembered my money. "Wait a tick, will you? I must get my wallet." I groped back into the sickbay and found my serge jacket, put it on, and checked that the wallet was there. Our plan was to get up. The only way was via the ladder outside the sickbay that led to the fo'c's'le. The ladder was tilted but we got to the top. Then we heaved at the hatch, our only escape route upwards, but it would not budge an inch. The list had caused it to stick solid.

We went down again and had to crawl along the deck, clawing aft in the direction of the quarterdeck. It was like climbing up the roof of a house toward the chimney—hand over hand . . . and it was getting steeper. Then ahead of us we saw a big ball of orange flame—a sheet of fire. Men were being burned by cordite, as the explosive spurted up through the safety vents—only they were *not* safe. The fires spread along the starboard side, and the boys' messdeck blew up. The whole ghastly scene stopped us. That and the third explosion. Another torpedo had torn into the ship.

"No good going aft now—let's try the PO's mess." Main said.

This lay across the port side of the ship and he knew it well. As the ship rolled to a 45-degree starboard list, we struggled, slipping, all the way up to the PO's mess. We had lost the torch by then. What with the darkness and everything tipped to a crazy angle we lost each other. Main got out of one of the portholes in the mess, but I floundered about badly. It all had to be by feel now, and I was on my own. No one else was going to save me.

Groping about in the gloom, I realized I was out of the mess and in the little eight-feet-square pantry that led off it. I was vaguely aware of kitchen utensils and a sink. Above the sink I saw a small, dim ring of sky through the porthole. It dawned on me that this was my last link with the outside world, with life. I hadn't time to turn back. Just that speck of sky. A pale, eerie circle of stars. I could still hear men's voices and the trampling of their feet as they raced for life.

The ship was nearly flat on her side by then and so I had to act quickly. I must get through that porthole or perish. Luckily, the ventilator was not in place—hence my seeing the sky. So I shinned up on the sink or its surround and managed to hoist my head through the porthole and actually get my shoulders through, too. Then the fourth and final explosion boomed out—and bumped me back into the pantry. All the pots and pans, cups and saucers clattered all over the place as the ship turned right on her side. The mast ran parallel to the sea. The door of the pantry slammed shut.

As I fell backwards into that dark void, I slipped and was flung against the bulkhead. Then the sea started spewing in through the porthole with the power of a water-jet. As the torrent tore into the

British battleship HMS Royal Oak, *sunk in Scapa Flow, off Scotland, by German U-boat.* Imperial War Museum

pantry, the ship took another list and was beginning to turn turtle. The pantry was filling up quickly and I came to with a jerk to find myself hanging on to the pipes around the bulkhead—floating and breathing.

The pantry was half-full of water. Then three-quarters. Then nine-tenths. My head was just above it as the sea of Scapa Flow sloshed in my face and up to my chin. My head was hitting the ceiling, which was nearly the deck now. But by a fluke, that last precious one-tenth part of air up in one corner of the pantry somehow stayed. Like an airlock in an upturned bottle. That little airlock plus the porthole were all that I clung to for survival. Only the porthole was four feet under water already.

The ship was sinking. She was upside down, her keel uppermost. I dived down into the dark liquid, a blackness you could almost feel, and fingered frantically where I thought the porthole was. But I was losing my bearings and getting more and more agitated. I had no vision to guide me and the whole room had swivelled through 180°. I swam around underwater for a few seconds and then came up for air. Those precious few cubic feet of it. Gasping in some more breaths as my head hit the ceiling, I took a second dive to try and find that small circle of escape. The only way out. I stayed down there, searching, blundering till my lungs were drained and still I could not feel the opening. Up I had to come again, my heart pumping with the strain of holding my breath. Then I prayed. And I really meant it for the first time in my life.

"If there's a God—get me out. Please."

The pantry was nearly fifty feet down by then, as I dived for the last time for that porthole. I was frantic when I couldn't find it. Blind, and almost bursting, I surfaced again—but couldn't find the airlock either.

"This is the end. Better get it over quickly." I was going to die, so I opened my mouth to swallow as much water as I could—as soon as I could. "This is it. I've had it."

I started to swallow the water, but it had filthy oil mixed with it and instinctively I vomited. I emptied my lungs, snapped the last link. I had lost the last gasp in my whole soul. I blacked out. Drowned. Dead.

The next I knew I was shooting up to the surface through a liquid mist. The barnacles on the ship cut my hands and feet but I didn't know it then. The *Royal Oak* went down as I came up. The last man out of her alive.

I was breaking the surface of Scapa Flow, puffing, panting, being sick, scarcely able to believe I was alive. It was too soon for it to mean much. Later I thought of it as a miracle. I couldn't find the porthole when

I was conscious, yet I found it unconsciously. The time was about 0300. But my troubles had not ended—they had just begun.

The sea temperature: 48°F. The average survival time for a man at that level is one hour. The maximum is two. Gradually I made out the cliffs. I called out hopefully:

"Help. Help."

That got me nowhere so I saved my breath. The only ship nearby was the *Daisy II,* which was in fact searching for survivors. I tried to make for the cliffs which I knew were only half a mile off, but then I got clogged in oil. It seemed to cover the sea like black treacle. I dived in an effort to get under it and came up in clear water. But I was soon in it again and becoming smothered. It tasted foul and made my eyes burn. And it got in my ears and nose. I was not moving at all. My limbs were being choked and it felt as if I were being dragged down or back.

I began to get really worried, so I just tried to keep clear of the oil and paddle around in small circles. Someone must rescue me eventually—but would it be in time? A signal projector snapped on out of the darkness from an old seaplane carrier. During one of these light patches I saw the only man I saw all the time I was in the water. But as I swam toward him, he went under at that precise moment.

The oil glued me fast and my jacket got more and more sodden, leaden. I stripped it off but kept the wallet between my teeth. I felt colder and colder. Luckily I was a strong swimmer. I knew I had to keep going, moving. But the water was roughing up and I started to swallow more of it, mixed with oil, as I couldn't close my mouth. After two endless hours, I had to make the awful decision. I let go my teeth-hold on the wallet and watched it sink, with my 120 pounds. A fortune to me.

I paddled on. It was a frightful feeling of being clamped. I thrashed about and wore myself out. Three hours had gone. I was nearer to freezing, nearer to cramp, nearer to death. I had to keep going. But I was nearly all in. But it was the coating of oil that had protected me against the cold.

"There's another one over there."

The voice seemed to come from another world. I was ink-black and almost invisible, but they had spotted me. A boathook poked toward me. I grabbed at it and passed out for the second time that night. They fished me out of the water at about 0530. I had been in it for four hours. I was the last man alive out of the water. They gave me morphine. I never got back that 120 pounds. Too bad. But I was alive.

Conquering the Magnetic Mine

War was declared on Sunday, 3 September 1939. The war at sea started exactly a week later. At 1725 on 10 September the SS *Magdapur* was steaming slowly through the channel between Aldeburgh Napes and Sizewell Bank, up the east coast of England from Harwich. Suddenly an explosion disturbed the calm of the Sabbath afternoon. Coastal villagers who looked eastward saw the ship sinking rapidly, her back broken and boiler burst. It was two hours after low water, and she lay in seventy feet on an even keel, with both masts showing. An eerie sight.

Suspicions were at once around, as this much-used channel had been swept for any normal horn mines with sinkers that the Germans might have laid, or for similar mines that might have strayed from British defensive minefields. But as the *Magdapur* was the first loss, it was possible that she might have been sunk by torpedo from a U-boat. Sweeps for buoyant enemy mines were ordered in the vicinity of the wreck but none came to light.

Six days elapsed without further incident. Then at 2010 on 16 September an external explosion occurred to the west of Aldeburgh Napes which severely shook the SS *City of Paris* as she sailed through. Violently blasted, the ship seemed to be sinking and was abandoned by her crew. But after seeing her still afloat, they returned to find her seaworthy but with her heavy machinery damaged. Next day she managed to make port at Tilbury under her own steam, where a thorough examination revealed that she had not been holed in any part of her hull.

Assuming that mines sank the *Magdapur* and damaged the *City of Paris*, at no time had they come in contact with either vessel. The ships had caused them to fire, but by some other influence than the direct hit of the horn on the old-fashioned floating mine. The new mine menace had shown itself. There was only one thing to do: to find a mine, take it to bits, see how it worked, and devise countermeasures.

The Royal Navy's officer most qualified to deal with enemy mines was Lt. Cdr. John Ouvry. On Tuesday, 19 September, Ouvry was at Harwich. He put a plan into action to try to sweep any further enemy mines that might be lurking on the bottom. Three minesweepers spent ninety minutes in impossible conditions and found nothing. On his return to HMS *Vernon,* his Portsmouth shore base, Ouvry told his senior officer,

> I'm pretty sure that they're noncontact mines. Influence mines, the Americans are calling them. I think that the Germans must have laid a field the day after war broke out—probably from a merchantman steaming across the channel up there. Ground mines could easily be dumped without anyone knowing anything about them.

At that moment, Ouvry's senior, Capt. G. B. Sayer, gave him a précis of a signal just handed to him: "SS *Phryne* was sunk just to eastward of Aldeburgh Napes in 81 feet at 0800 this morning. She took two hours to go down. That's one ship each weekend three times running."

The mine menace spread seriously: off the Thames Estuary and Portland, in the Firth of Forth, and in the Bristol Channel. On 13 November the cruiser-minelayer *Adventure* was seriously damaged by a mine off the *Tongue* light-vessel in the Thames Estuary. The destroyer *Blanche,* in her company, fared worse and was sunk. It was thought that German destroyers laid this field on the previous night. At least six ships succumbed in a straight line. The minesweeper *Mastiff* was mined and sank as she worked with one of the *Vernon* mine-recovery flotilla. Between 18 and 22 November, fifteen merchant ships were mined, including the passenger ships *Simon Bolivar* and the *Terukini Maru*—Dutch and Japanese. In the Firth of Forth, the cruiser *Belfast* actuated another noncontact mine and was put out of action for over a year. Clearly the situation had become critical. Neutrals were endangered as much as British shipping.

The country carried on, unaware of the full force of the drama at sea. The arteries of Britain's sealanes could not be cut for long if the country were to survive. Then on the night of 21–22 November the Luftwaffe laid mines by parachute in the Thames, Humber, and Stour-Orwell Estuaries. All sea traffic stopped; the arteries froze. The destroyer *Gipsy* sank off Harwich.

John Ouvry was sent to London to await further orders. Given a desk in an Admiralty Office, he found that ordinarily august building in the grip of mounting frustration. A senior officer told him, "Lieutenant-Commander Lewis has been down to Southend all day trying to find out if we can get any of last night's batch." Soon afterwards, Roy Lewis returned to the Admiralty and was introduced to Ouvry. They talked things over and were told to stay the night nearby.

Unbeknownst to them, a German seaplane was at that very time steering an unsteady course over the Thames Estuary. It was a moonless night and the pilot peered into the dark and the driving rain, looking for bearings. Dimly he made out the river-mouth and prepared to run in on course. He flew a little lower to be sure: two hundred feet altitude. Then a machine gun recently installed on the end of Southend Pier shattered the night with a series of bursts.

Already tense with the stress of night-flying in filthy conditions, the pilot was shaken by the sudden gunfire. Instinctively he pressed the button on his control panel, and his load was released. Twin bundles dropped through the night air for a very few seconds, and almost before their parachutes had opened Hitler's secret weapon number one was deposited into the shallow water off Shoeburyness. A lucky break at last.

A soldier on sentry duty spotted that the mines had dropped too far inshore and at high tide. It was realized that they could well be uncovered at low water, around 0400. A call was put through to Admiralty. Ouvry and Lewis were soon on their way by car to Southend. They both knew that unless they could do something drastic about the mine menace, victory could conceivably be in jeopardy.

Now it was 0400 and still a vile night. Black and wet. The soldier who had first seen the mines led them, splashing through pools left by the ebbing tide. An Aldis lamp held aloft swayed to and fro with each step, lighting small patches of the rippled, stippled sand.

The soldier waded on. Then he called out, "There it is ahead, sir."

"Don't go any nearer," warned Ouvry. He scanned the intervening yards to where the soldier was pointing. His heart pounded. Ouvry and Lewis, torches in hand, moved toward it for a better look.

There it was . . . the unknown quantity . . . inanimate object . . . one touch might animate it . . . blow them to bits. What was it? Magnetic? Acoustic? Photoelectric? Out of the dark it seemed to edge toward them with each step they took. A black, glistening hippopotamus, sinister, shiny, looming into the torchlight. Half-embedded in sand five hundred yards below high-water mark. A little pool encircling the end in mud. Half a mile out to sea in the before-dawn chill of a late November night. Excitement intensified on the rainswept shore. The war at sea might depend on these next few hours.

More than the length of a man it was. Nearly seven feet. And about two feet in diameter. Cylindrical, made of some aluminum alloy. That much they saw at once. Tubular horns on the rounded, embedded nose attracted their attention. Ouvry moved to the other end. Neither he nor Lewis spoke. An acoustic vibrator could respond to a voice—and anything might be inside.

Ouvry pointed out the tail to Lewis. It was hollow and open, with a massive phosphor-bronze spring sticking out. This was where the parachute had been attached. Now no sign of it could be found. But the mine was the crucial thing, and specifically two devilish devices near the nose. Prominent on top of the mine, one was brass and one aluminum. The brass fitting Ouvry took to be a hydrostatic valve. But the second was different from anything he had been used to, or seen, on our own mines. The aluminum was polished and secured by a screwed ring sealed with tallow. Another encouragement: attached was what seemed to be a tear-off strip, twisted but secure—possibly a safety arrangement.

Somehow Ouvry had to find a way into the mine. These two fittings were the only visible means. Once they were off, it would be up to him to make the thing safe so that its secrets could be unlocked. The first job was to consider what tools he would need. The mysterious second fitting seemed as if it would harbor the primer and detonator, so this would have to be tackled first. But no tools he had ashore came near to matching the ring securing the fitting.

Lt. Cdr. J.G.D. Ouvry, DSO, RN.

Equally terrible from all angles: four views of first German magnetic mine to be recovered and made safe—one of the most hazardous and vital operations of the whole war.

A four-pin spanner was needed, so Ouvry motioned Lewis to take an impression of the aluminum fitting on a sheet of an Admiralty signal pad. He placed the paper gently against the fitting, still more softly pressing it to the shape. Then soldiers passed hemp lines around the mine and lashed them to stakes plunged into the soft mud-sand. Ouvry and Lewis jotted down their final notes before stepping back.

The local naval officer, Maton, said, "You'll want a nonmagnetic spanner made to unscrew the ring. I'll get the workship to fix one in brass by noon. That should be in plenty of time for the tide. Some brass rods of all sizes might come in useful, too."

He added, "Come along to my house and try to get a bit of rest. You can have an hour or so before breakfast." But Ouvry and Lewis felt too excited to do more than doze and at about 0600 the dawn heralded a meal of fried eggs as a special treat. Ouvry felt better after that. He looked out over the town to the sea and the flooding tide. As they made out their preliminary report, they realized the heavy responsibility resting on them. It seemed to outweigh the danger, though they were conscious of that, too.

The phone rang and Maton took it. "Another one? Three hundred yards from the first? We'll be down at once."

In a matter of minutes they were all at the nearest point to the stretch of beach. Drawing on their waders, they lunged into the deepening water, but the tide was on the flood fast now. They decided to wait for the falling tide when both mines would be accessible.

Soon afterwards, Chief Petty Officer C. E. Baldwin and Able Seaman A. L. Vearncombe arrived with the rest of the tools. The chief, utterly loyal, the epitome of all that was best among noncommissioned officers, and young Vearncombe, a tall good-looking two-badge AB (able seaman). It was comforting to have these two with him, Ouvry thought. And Lewis, too, a tower of strength and support. Lewis was responsible for organization, Ouvry for the technical job of tackling the mine. The first one, anyway.

"Now that we've settled the best method of attack," Ouvry said to Lewis, "I think the only possible procedure is to split the four of us into two groups, in case of accidents. That will double the chances and the second pair may be able to profit from any miscalculations. There is the other mine left for them. That's the deciding factor, as I see it."

Lewis yielded grudgingly. Ouvry went on: "Baldwin and I have got the background for this sort of thing—so far as anyone has—so we'll kick off, and you and Vearncombe can wait on the foreshore. I'll signal each move we make and you can tick them off the list, so you'll know how far I've got. I'll wave both hands above my head after each episode." There was no hint of melodrama in his voice.

The time: 1300. Neither of the officers felt like lunch. The tide had fallen clear of both mines. Maton and some of the soldiers took up a sheltered position on the foreshore opposite the mines.

While the military photographer took a series of daylight pictures with long rulers to indicate the length and height of the mine, Ouvry and Lewis strolled over to look at the second specimen. Like number one, its nose was nuzzled down deep into the sand, but the whole thing was on a different slew. This left a large plate exposed which could not be seen on the first mine. The horns, they concluded, were in no way dangerous, merely projections to bury in the seabed and keep the mine steady so that it would not roll with the pressure swell of the water. That was one item less to worry about, but plenty remained. A live acoustic mine might kill at the first touch on its shell. A magnetic mine might equally easily explode, by intent or accident. Both types were liable to have some device incorporated to stop their secrets being shared: a boobytrap that might go off as the first nut was loosened. Many were killed later by them.

1330: Ouvry thought of his wife as he and Baldwin waved to Lewis and Vearncombe. The pair walked quickly over to the mine. They had each other for moral support. A few paces off it, Ouvry saw a little brass ring reclining in the sand.

"That looks as if it may be the missing part to that spindle on the top brass fitting. Yes, it is. Now let's concentrate on the aluminum fitting. You can see the shell's aluminum, too. The black paint has chipped off still more after last night. Now how about that fitting?"

1337: Baldwin handed him the four-pin spanner. Ouvry looked closely into the fitting and saw a small plate, jointed with tallow, an oval-shaped groove filled with black wax, a screwed recess, and the copper tear-off strip he had seen earlier. The strip was masking one of the holes for the spanner. Baldwin went to pull it off, but Ouvry stopped him.

"Don't do that. It may be some safety device. Just turn it back carefully." The chief complied.

Ouvry felt the homemade spanner. "It fits," he whispered. His throat felt parched already. The wind had dried his lips, too. A whining wind.

This was it. The moment had come at last. Moving the spanner unbelievably slowly, he unscrewed the ring a fraction of a turn. Nothing happened. They were still alive. Ten degrees of one turn . . . twenty . . . ninety . . . one-eighty . . . a whole turn. He glanced up at the chief. Another turn. And a few more. And then the ring was free.

"A rod, chief."

Baldwin offered a choice. Ouvry took the smallest. He assumed what he saw inside to be either a detonator or some sort of magnetic-needle device. Either could be dynamite.

Again at a crawl, holding the rod delicately, he lowered it into the opening, with angler-like precision. The hook on the end looped over the fitting, and he withdrew his catch, a fraction of an inch at a time. It slid up smoothly. Ouvry was sweating now. Spray in the wind sprinkled his face. His waders stuck in the mud. Then they squelched free. If this were the detonator he had only to drop it once. Inch by inch it came. Then it was out. Back inshore, Lewis adjusted his binoculars.

"He's got something. Look, the chief has signaled."

1349: Ouvry peered down into the dark void that the fitting had left. Dimly he saw a pocket containing a tubular disc of explosive and a primer. And under the disc, two more solid discs. He fished for these, but they would not come free.

"Never mind, Chief. Let's look at what we've got."

A cylindrical cup was screwed into the underside of the fitting in his hand, which was evidently the detonator or, at least, *a* detonator.

"I think this is it, Chief. If it's the detonator, the worst is over. But we'll have to take a look at the underneath of the mine. Run ashore and fetch the others to help manhandle it. We can't budge it alone."

"Aye, aye, sir."

1404: Ouvry felt suddenly good. He breathed deeply. The strong air reached the lining of his lungs. That must be the detonator. And if it is the firing source, what have we got to worry about? Nothing—much.

Looking southward he saw the end of Southend Pier. No one stirred on it, save the naval gun crew Lewis had organized there. The wind again, gusting in short, blustery bursts over the mudflats. Pools of water left by the tide quivered as the wind whipped at them. Over on the cliffs, he made out a royal-blue trolley bus looking rather like a model. So life was going on normally. Out here it was as if they were marooned in space and time. The chief had reached the others. The three of them were hurrying out now. Ouvry felt quietly confident. But at the back of his mind stuck the suggestion that the day's work was not yet done.

1422: With ropes and brawn they just managed to turn the mine. The underside rolled clear, coated with damp mud-sand. It was now about 120 degrees round from its former position, so that both top and bottom fittings were accessible. Ouvry could collect the loose primer discs he had not been able to reach at the earlier angle. Just as on mine number two, this one had a plate flush with the shell, diametrically opposed to the brass "hydrostatic valve" on top. This was confidently unscrewed. Beneath it appeared a circular screwed bung with four recesses. No spanner seemed suitable to shift it, so some elementary force had to be applied. This took time.

1457: There seemed to be no end to the gadgets—like forcing a way through a jungle. So it was not going to be as easy as Ouvry had hoped. Another screwed plate met the gaze of the little company of men. Two terminals mounted neatly on it had two leads winding away out of sight through a hole into the bowels of the mine. Suddenly it occurred to Ouvry that this was the main detonator circuit and not the other one.

It all had to be gone through again. Still in slowest motion, Ouvry twisted both leads round and round in turn till each strand of each wire snapped under the strain. Then he insulated them. Break an electrical circuit—always a good policy, he thought.

No spanner fitted the screws securing the plate, so a nonmagnetic screwdriver filled the bill. As he took out the plate, Ouvry saw that it was a detonator carrier with an electric detonator similar to that used on German horned mines. Out it came—and he felt on top of the world.

1510: He could not see to get at the primer from this side, so the mine was rolled back, the original brass fitting taking up its position on top. This was the continuation of the detonator-primer pocket. Ouvry undid the cover with a spanner, and the fitting inside leapt out under the force of a strong spring! There was an instinctive surge back, then a chorus of relief. The long phosphor-bronze spring followed it, cascading high into the air before coming to rest in the wash of the incoming tide. The priming charge was easily removed, and then there remained only a large hydrostatic arming-clock.

1527: Triumphant, all four of them signaled to the soldiers inshore for the tractor and crane. The five leads to the clock were cut, and the trophies carted ashore.

1600: It was all over. The mine was hoisted into the lorry and sent away for safe storage overnight under cover. The light was failing, so no attempt was made to get to the second mine; in any case, it was already awash. Up on the beach, they all stretched out in glorious relaxation. Lewis laid the arming clock down. Straightway it started ticking. All four of them hurtled away from it. They were too well aware of boobytraps to risk anything at this late stage.

"Nothing to worry about," Ouvry laughed. "It's only the spindle." And all really was well at last.

1700: A report to the Admiralty informed Their Lordships that Hitler's secret weapon number one was lying harmlessly in a shed, awaiting transport to HMS *Vernon*, Portsmouth, the following morning.

Lewis left for London, summoned to attend a meeting at 2315 that night. A company of almost a hundred awaited him in the largest room at the Admiralty. Lewis felt overwhelmed to find himself seated between Winston Churchill and Admiral Sir Dudley Pound. They were dwelling on his every word, only too conscious of what had been at stake.

"Come on, Lewis, we want the whole story," Mr. Churchill said. He was still First Lord of the Admiralty. Midnight came as Lewis reached the end of his account. Mr. Churchill spoke for everyone there: "Thank you." Then he added, "I'm going to get right through to *Vernon* now and tell them that we want to know exactly what it is without delay—and that work must proceed day and night to this end. Only when we've got their verdict can we put countermeasures into effect, and every hour is beginning to count."

Next morning the mine was transported to *Vernon*, with all its components. The postmortem took place in a nonmagnetic laboratory building where operations went on behind locked doors. Stripping and examination of the mine continued day and night, as Churchill had ordered. Gradually, painstakingly, the whole intricate mechanism began to make sense. By 0200 on 25 November the verdict was pronounced—a magnetic mine.

One-millionth part of the current needed to light a torch was enough to fire the mine, and this was generated by the magnetism of a ship passing over it. By that dawn their report was complete. From this knowledge, steps immediately initiated resulted in the suggested solutions: degaussing or demagnetization of vessels.

As fast as conditions allowed, ships of all kinds were girdled with an electric cable to counteract the effect of their magnetism and the effect it would have on a mine. And an organization was set up to produce positive defense against the mines. Channels were swept by shallow-draught ships towing long lengths of heavy electric cable astern. Through this cable a current was passed so that mines might be actuated at a safe distance from the sweepers. All such measures took time, however, and casualties continued. But at least answers were being applied. On 4 December the battleship *Nelson* was mined as she entered Loch Ewe, but fortunately she was able to make port.

That same month King George VI visited HMS *Vernon* and conferred the Distinguished Service Order on John Ouvry and Roy Lewis, with Baldwin and Vearncombe receiving the Distinguished Service Medal. Baldwin was killed later. At Christmas Mr. Churchill reported that they hoped the danger from magnetic mines would soon be out of the way. And that the crew of the *Vernon* was studying the possible varying forms of mine attack—acoustic, supersonic, or other means. Photoelectric-cell mines were later boobytrapped so that daylight meant death to anyone dismantling them.

Meanwhile, Ouvry and others had to go on tackling enemy mines as and when they came to light. On land, underwater, anywhere. One mine was made safe, apparently, and then transported back to *Vernon* for closer examination. As the last nut was loosened from the rear door of the mine, there was a sudden whirring sound, a flash, a roar, and then blank. The roof was blown out of the mining shed at *Vernon*. Blackened, burned men were helped out. The shed was a shambles. Glass and blood everywhere. Six men were killed. Others perished subsequently while dismantling enemy mines, but John Ouvry survived. And he could claim, in his very modest manner, to have conquered the magnetic mine.

The Battle of the River Plate

The war at sea was already becoming almost global. The story shifts to the South Atlantic. At the start of December 1939, Allied and enemy ships were ranged all around this ocean. The *Exeter* and *Cumberland* lay far south at Port Stanley in the Falklands; the *Achilles* was off Rio de Janeiro; and the *Ajax* sailed on her way from the Falklands toward the River Plate. The *Neptune,* the submarine *Clyde,* and four destroyers covered from Freetown to Brazil, while two French cruisers, assisted by the small aircraft carrier *Hermes,* patrolled from Dakar off the African coast.

On 2 December the *Renown* sank the German merchantman *Watussi,* after she had been intercepted by the cruiser *Sussex.* And on the same day, a distress message was received from the British SS *Doric Star* far to the north, in the hunting ground of the German pocket battleship *Graf Spee.* The *Doric Star* sank some 3,000 miles away from the focal areas guarded by the British Commodore Harwood, whose responsible region included Rio de Janeiro and the River Plate. Harwood considered that sooner or later the *Graf Spee* would be tempted by the traffic in these southern sealanes. So he decided to concentrate his forces accordingly.

Harwood ordered the *Exeter* to leave Port Stanley on 9 December and the *Achilles* to join him aboard the *Ajax* on 10 December. By 0600 on 12 December the three ships were 150 miles off the entrance to the River Plate. The *Graf Spee* found another victim, the SS *Tairoa,* the day after she sank the *Doric Star,* and then steered due west. In mid-ocean, she sank her last ship, the SS *Streonshalh,* on 7 December. Thereafter she steered direct to the estuary where Commodore Harwood's cruisers were waiting.

At 0608 on 13 December the *Ajax* reported smoke to the northwest and the *Exeter* was sent to investigate. Eight minutes later she signaled, "I think it is a pocket battleship." The hunt for the *Graf Spee* was over.

Harwood decided to attack at once in two divisions to give his ships the benefit of being able to report each other's fall of shot. The first phase of the battle lasted from 0614 to 0740. *Ajax* and *Achilles* engaged the enemy from the east, opening fire from about 19,000 yards' range. The *Exeter* left the line and turned west to engage from the south, thus presenting the *Graf Spee* with the problem of either leaving one adversary or dividing her armament to engage both at once. At first she chose the second alternative but soon shifted the fire of all her six 11-inch guns to the *Exeter,* whose 8-inch salvos probably appeared the more dangerous. Moreover, her captain had at first thought that he was facing one cruiser and two destroyers, and to engage the heaviest foe would be his obvious tactic.

The German gunnery was accurate during this phase and remained so throughout the day. Unlike her adversaries the *Graf Spee* had a radar set that could pass its ranges to the guns. The *Exeter* was soon heavily hit, lost one turret, and had her steering gear put out of action temporarily, although her commander, Captain Bell, quickly regained control from the aftersteering position. She then resumed the action and fired her stock of torpedoes, only to receive further hits from 11-inch shells which left her with only a single turret to use. By 0650 she was steering west with a heavy list to starboard but still engaged the enemy with her solitary gun turret. By 0730 she could not keep up any longer and turned to the southeast to repair her damage in safety.

Meanwhile, the *Ajax* and *Achilles* had been engaged alternately by the enemy's secondary armament of eight 5.9-inch guns, but neither had been hit. The two cruisers were firing in concentration, with the *Ajax* controlling, and they closed the range rapidly. Their fire must have proved effective, for the *Graf Spee* shifted an 11-inch turret on to the *Ajax,* which was quickly straddled but not actually hit.

At 0640 the *Achilles* was damaged by a heavy shell that burst on the water line. Some confusion then occurred between the firing of the two cruisers. Both ships lost accuracy for nearly half an hour until after 0700 when they found the range again, which was still at about 16,000 yards. A smokescreen laid by the enemy added to their difficulty of spotting by the fall of shot.

0716: The *Graf Spee* made a large turn to port—to the south—apparently aiming to finish off the *Exeter*. Both the smaller cruisers at once turned to her assistance and fired so well that the pocket battleship abandoned the attempt and turned northwest to re-engage the *Ajax*. She received her first 11-inch hit at 0725 and lost both her after-turrets. The range was then 11,000 yards, but by 0738 it had closed considerably to 8,000. The *Ajax* suffered another hit, which brought down her topmast. The battle appeared to have taken a dangerous turn, as the enemy still seemed to be firing accurately and had sustained little damage. It looked like that, anyway. The total armament remaining to the two British cruisers was scarcely superior to the enemy's secondary weapons. Commodore Harwood on *Ajax* therefore turned to the east under cover of smoke at 0740. In the exact words of the official history: Thus ended the first phase of the action.

The *Graf Spee* did not press her weakened opponents but continued on westerly courses so that, after only six minutes' respite, the British cruisers turned back to the west and followed her. The second phase of this historic action consisted of shadowing the enemy along her obvious course toward the River Plate. The enemy turned periodically and fired a few salvos if the cruisers closed the range sufficiently. Some of these fell close.

2317: Commodore Harwood finally recalled the *Achilles* from her role of shadowing the *Graf Spee* when it had become quite clear that the enemy intended to try to enter Montevideo. Harwood now had to face a problem: he must prevent the enemy from escaping once more into the oceans after refueling or accomplishing whatever purpose lay behind their entrance into neutral waters. And for the time being at least, Harwood had only two small cruisers, one with half her armament out of use.

On the previous morning, when it had become imperative for the *Exeter* to seek port, the commodore had ordered the *Cumberland* to sail immediately from Port Stanley, but she could not join the others until the evening of 14 December. Until this much-needed reinforcement arrived, the two smaller cruisers could only patrol the wide mouth of the River Plate and hope to keep the enemy bottled up inside it. All other naval aid was several thousand miles away. But the enemy made no attempt to escape.

Meanwhile, on 13 December the *Dorsetshire* set sail from the Cape of Good Hope for the River Plate, and the Admiralty ordered the *Shropshire* to follow on 15 December. Both ships were diverted to Port Stanley on 18 December but placed under the orders of Harwood. Other vessels were also churning to the scene. The *Ark Royal* and the *Renown* were told to fuel at Rio de Janeiro and proceed to the Plate at full speed. The *Neptune* was also sent there, while the 3rd Destroyer Division arrived at Pernambuco on 15 December and sailed for Rio within an hour. The *Ark Royal, Renown,* and *Neptune* all reached Rio de Janeiro on 17 December, fueled, and hurried south. But this overwhelming strength could not be concentrated at the Plate before noon on 19 December.

Diplomatic negotiations were meanwhile proceeding in Montevideo. The *Graf Spee*'s Captain Langsdorff obtained a seventy-two-hour extension to the twenty-four-hour stay in port permitted to repair damage. British objections to this were more technical than real, for they had no wish to force the *Graf Spee* to sea before reinforcements had arrived. British merchant ships were sailed from Montevideo at intervals and the Uruguayan government was requested to allow them a day's clear start ahead of the enemy.

The *Graf Spee*'s extension expired at 2000 on 17 December. Langsdorff believed that the *Ark Royal, Renown,* and destroyers were already waiting for him outside. On 16 December Langsdorff reported to Berlin the strength of the concentration that he incorrectly presumed to be awaiting him outside the estuary and that he proposed to try to fight his way through to Buenos Aires. He added a request for the following decision: if the attempt to make such a breakthrough would result in destruction of his ship without causing his adversaries appreciable damage, was it preferred for him to scuttle his ship or allow her to be interned? Admiral Raeder and Hitler discussed the matter urgently. They both agreed that scuttling was preferable to internment, and a reply to that effect was sent from Berlin that evening.

At 1815 on 17 December, the next day, Captain Langsdorff sailed downriver, with the German SS *Tacoma* following in his wake. At 1956 the *Graf Spee* blew herself up. Shortly afterwards, the British blockading squadron,

German battleship Graf Spee *in flames*
after being scuttled off Montevideo,
17 December 1939. Imperial War Museum

still consisting only of the *Cumberland, Ajax,* and *Achilles,* steamed into the estuary and on toward Montevideo. On the way, they passed the blazing wreck of the *Graf Spee.*

Three days later, Captain Langsdorff shot himself. He left behind a letter addressed to the German ambassador in Montevideo but clearly intended for Hitler. In it, Langsdorff explained the reasons that led him to commit his ship to her ignominious end. During a cruise lasting from 26 September until 13 December, the *Graf Spee* sank only nine ships totaling some 50,000 tons. It must stand to the credit of Captain Langsdorff that not one British life was lost through his ship's actions against defenseless merchantmen. But this was in the early days of the war. So ended one of the strangest episodes in the entire conflict at sea.

January—December 1940

One Ship and Two Men

This is the story of a ship and two men—one of them lived, the other died. The Germans invaded Norway in April 1940 and captured the port of Narvik almost at once. British warships were already lying off the Norwegian coast when the Admiralty flashed orders to Capt. Bernard Warburton-Lee of the destroyer HMS *Hardy:* "Take three ships and attack Narvik." The youthful Warburton-Lee, or "Wash" as he was always known, chose the fast H-class destroyers *Hotspur, Havock,* and *Hunter* to help him.

The *Hardy* arrived off Trancy by Vest Fjord and Wash sent a boat ashore to ask local Norwegians what they knew of the enemy. The locals told him that German warships and U-boats were at Narvik. Despite this news, Wash told his officers, "I'm attacking at dawn."

At midnight it was snowing hard. Another destroyer, the *Hostile,* had joined the four already there. They altered course to turn up Narvik Fjord. The flotilla of five destroyers edged on, through the thickening snow, nearer to Narvik. They met no enemy at that stage. It was 0430 as they glided ghostlike toward Narvik harbor. An unreal silence, sheer mountains, still more snow.

The port was half a mile off. *Hardy* went in alone. With engines stopped, she just floated forward. Suddenly someone said, "There they are." Two enemy destroyers lay alongside each other right in the middle of the harbor with bows turned to the town.

Warburton-Lee at once ordered, "Fire four torpedoes." Then he made twenty knots to take them out of range of retaliation. They saw

*Captain B.A.W. Warburton-Lee
VC, RN. His last words were
"Keep on engaging the enemy."*
Imperial War Museum

more destroyers at the quay. One of the torpedoes hit a merchant ship astern of the destroyers. Then an explosion erupted from the direction of the enemy vessels. It meant that magazines must have been hit. As *Hardy* turned out of the harbor, they fired three more torpedoes in the general direction of the enemy and emerged with only one left.

Hardy kept close to the harbor entrance in case anything tried to leave. She circled in front of the entrance for a second time, firing at enemy flashes when they lit the snow-backed port behind the ships. Heavier gunfire was coming from Narvik now, from the presumed-damaged destroyers. Wash was anxious to find out what damage had, in fact, been inflicted, as they had heard many louder bangs since the first batch earlier. But they could see nothing.

Not only heavy guns aimed at them now. As *Hardy* crossed the entrance, torpedoes tore through the fjord toward her. One actually seemed to go underneath the ship. Lieutenant Stanning counted six torpedoes, but other men saw more and said three went under the vessel. They could be heard from the deck of the *Hardy* as they ran ashore on the beach opposite, whirring weirdly as they tried to scramble up the shore. Each of the five H-class destroyers took a turn at the entrance to the harbor, then finally they all withdrew.

Wash asked the other ships for details of damage or casualties, and how many torpedoes they had left. "No damage, no casualties" came back the signals. The *Hostile* said she still had a full load of torpedoes. Another *Hardy* officer, Mansell, told Wash that they had a small hole in the after-funnel, but everyone was in high spirits. All enemy guns seemed to have ceased fire, so perhaps opposition had been silenced. Perhaps not.

Wash called in his officers. "What do you think about things now?" he wanted to know. "What is it to be—withdraw or go in again?" A chorus of approval greeted his decision to go ahead again. After steaming slowly down-fjord, they were a way from the harbor entrance. They turned around and were soon at the entrance once more. The harbor looked in a chaotic state, but it was difficult to discover the damage from previous attacks.

Then there came a terrible shock.

Wash suddenly sighted three enemy warships heading toward them from the direction of Rombaks Fjord. He took them to be a cruiser and two destroyers. He gave the order, "Engage." The *Hardy* opened fire at the simultaneous second that they did. Wash thought quickly after the first exchange, then ordered the signal to withdraw at thirty knots. Clark, an officer, protested that the *Hardy* was hitting them and wanted to stay. But before another word was possible, two more enemy ships appeared ahead.

They were four miles off and they looked like British cruisers. But Stanning snatched up his glasses and caught sight of hoods on their funnels. "Not ours," he said tersely. Then he thumbed through the pages of the books on the bridge. "Large German destroyers," he added. That clinched it. They were in a tight corner. The two Germans ahead turned sharply to port and opened fire. The *Hardy* engaged them both, leaving the other three to her rear ships. It must have been at this moment, when the *Hardy* was taking on the two ahead, that Warburton-Lee made the last signal of his life:

"Keep on engaging the enemy . . ."

The *Hardy* made a report about the strength of the enemy. She was being hit now and was damaged. Metal was buckling. The firing was uncomfortably accurate. Stanning felt several hits forward, then a tremendous tearing explosion on the bridge. Most of the officers were down there. For a second, he was stunned. He was thrown into the air, then fell on the gyro compass, near the asdic set. Another officer, Cross, had been at his desk, Clark on the starboard side of the bridge forward, Wash by the asdic set, Gordon-Smith behind the gyro compass. Torps was about there, too. Stanning felt as if he had been carrying a tray of china and dropped it.

Stanning came to. Wash was lying on his back, breathing, but with a ghastly gash in the side of his face and another one on his body. The pilot lay on his face; he was kicking. Stanning thought that the bridge had suddenly become very dirty. A strong stench of cordite fumes hung in the air, both compasses were broken, and the chart-table could not be seen. Stanning felt a surge of loneliness; it seemed as if he must be the only one alive in the ship. Yet the vessel was still steaming at speed, making for the southern shore.

"If I don't do something quickly, we'll be on the bricks," he thought.

He hailed the wheelhouse, got no answer, and decided he would have to go down there himself. He must have had his weight on the right foot, for as he put his left foot to the deck he found he could not walk on it. He hopped across the bridge. On the way he rolled the pilot over on his back in the narrow alley by the torpedo control and left him as comfortable as he could.

Stanning slid down to the wheelhouse, which was a shambles. He saw debris of clothes and belongings but no bodies. He wrenched the wheel to starboard to try to stop the ship from being beached. He was surprised to find it working. He looked out to find that the *Hardy* had answered the helm so efficiently that she was swinging fast to starboard and to the enemy. Stanning put some port wheel on and had another look. For a couple of minutes or so, he went on steering the ship down the fjord, when Smale appeared in the doorway. "All right, are you, Smale? Come and take the wheel, so I can get back to the compass platform."

As soon as Stanning reached the platform, he realized that something must be done within the next minute for the ship was nearly abreast of the German destroyers. He saw that both one and two guns were out of action, although some of the after-guns seemed to be firing. The question was whether to try to rush past the Germans or to ram them.

At that second, a whole salvo seemed to strike the engine room and the boilers. A cloud of steam spurted, spluttered. The *Hardy* began to slow down. Stanning assumed the entire engine room must have been obliterated, but actually only one man was wounded by that salvo.

But Stanning did not know that, nor could he believe there were more than a score of survivors aboard. No one could be sent to see what had happened. Another decision had to be made. What should he do with the ship? He decided to put her ashore. It seemed the only thing to do.

Not a second could be lost. The ship was losing speed and Stanning wanted to reach a group of houses a few hundred yards inland. There was the prospect of shelter. As he put the port wheel over, one of the houses was hit by a shell and set on fire. The ship glided to the shallows and grounded gently. People at the back of the bridge began to come to life again. Several signalmen scrambled up as Stanning returned to the bridge.

He knew he must destroy the cyphers and the asdic cabinet and bridge set. He still did not know that almost all the officers were alive. Heppel had defiantly gone off to fire his last torpedo at the enemy. Stanning got up the flag lockers and called some sailors by name to come and help him. Then he sent the chief stoker off to find Mr. McCracken and help throw the safes aft into the oil tank outside the captain's cabin.

"Pope," Stanning shouted to one of the midshipmen, "go and get the cyphers out of the chart-house, shove them into the weighted bag, and chuck them overboard as far aft as you can."

Mansell came up to Stanning. "The asdic cabinet's been blown out of the ship." He confirmed later that the set on the bridge had been destroyed. Up on the bridge, the doctor was attending to the pilot. "The telegraphist in radio control on the bridge was pinned in, but Pope levered the place open and let him out," Mansell told Stanning. "What are we going to do

Enemy ships left derelict after the Battle of Narvik.
Imperial War Museum

now?" he asked, then answered himself, "I want to get the motorboat out."
They both went down on the starboard side, but the after-thread of the
davit was twisted and they could not turn the boat out.

Stanning looked up and saw the pilot coming down from the bridge
alone, seriously wounded but just able to walk. He sat down beside
Stanning and lit a cigarette. Stanning had to go on unreeling. A moment
later the pilot suddenly began choking. Stanning thought he must be
dying, for he lay quite still. The lieutenant got someone to put him in
the narrow cross-passage.

Mansell suggested a Carley float for taking the wounded ashore. The
enemy was shelling the ship and shore. Several shells hit the beach near
those crewmembers who were already ashore and filing up there. The
shelling of the ship intensified. They decided to abandon her at once.
Stanning went aft between the torpedo tubes and took off his oilskins.
A shell burst on the "chief's seat" abaft the after funnel. This must have
been what killed the chief stoker.

Stanning was scared now. He jumped into the sea fully dressed
except for his oilskins. His first urgent concern was to swim clear of the
ship and avoid the shells. The water was icy. He tried to comfort himself that there was not much of him above water to hit. He had blown
up his rubber lifebelt and found he was swimming quite well. Much
sooner than he expected, he touched ground only about fifty yards in
shore from the ship. He could not wade in but had to finish the journey on his stomach.

All the others had got ashore by then. He realized he was being left
behind and could not catch up to them. He shouted to two torpedo men
ahead, and they dropped back to help him. He still had a hundred yards
of foreshore to negotiate, covered with rocks and pools. The pain from
his foot was agonizing. Even with the two men's help he felt he would
never make it and told them to push ahead again. Somehow they got
Stanning to dry land, or snow-clad shore. At the top of the beach, a path
to the road lay waist-deep in snow. They supported Stanning and at last
they reached the road. They trudged along it and then another path deep
in a drift, finally reaching a wooden house.

The three of them groped inside. They saw dozens of men. They
smelt a stench of bodies, the tang of burnt cordite, the dankness of
soaked clothes. The early arrivals had dressed themselves in the clothes
and bedding of the owners, Mrs. Christiansen and her daughter. The

two women were now downstairs tearing the curtains from the windows, ripping up rugs to wrap the shivering men in; they ransacked their larder for food and gave almost everyone a slice of bread and butter.

Stanning and his two sailors merged into the rest of the room. The company stayed like this for some minutes, sorting themselves out, talking things over. The first shock of the ship's loss was over. They were beginning to think what it had meant, who was alive, and who was dead.

Stanning's foot grew more and more painful. Someone cut his boot off, and the foot swelled up like a football. He hobbled over to Dr. Waind. Then he plucked up the courage to ask the question that had been worrying him most:

"What happened to Wash?" He looked straight into Waind's eyes, waiting to tell from them whether hope still survived.

"He was almost dead before he left the ship, old chap, but they got him on to the Carley float. He died on the way."

Stanning was silent for a second. Five words, like his signal: Keep on engaging the enemy. Waind went on: "Guns and Flags must have been killed outright."

"Thanks for telling me," Stanning said. Then he sent a message to Heppel to go back to the ship, fetch the pilot, and make sure all the books in the captain's cabin aft were destroyed.

They were in a peculiar position. Obviously they could not stay long in the crowded house that the Christiansens had now abandoned to them. Yet no one was fit to go far, and many had no boots. They really expected the Germans to send a party ashore to take them prisoner or else get a detachment from Narvik to go by road. But nothing seemed to be happening yet.

Stanning sat outside the house, as it was warmer now. He could speak German, so he thought he could best negotiate with any enemy. At the moment he sat down, he heard an explosion down the fjord. A column of smoke shot high above the mountains. He did not know it then, but *Hostile* was torpedoing Hauenfels. Nor did he or the others discover that the *Hunter* was badly damaged, and a few minutes afterwards the *Hotspur* herself was hit and her steering gear jammed. She was heading for the *Hunter* at the time and rammed the other destroyer fair and square, bowling her over.

The *Hardy* was burning forward, and her small ammunition exploded intermittently, echoing in bursts across the fjord. On the other side of the fjord Stanning could just make out a German destroyer ashore with no sign of life near. Then someone shouted, pointing to the *Hardy:* "Look, there's a man walking about. Must be either Pilot or a missing stoker." Stanning knew the shape of the man. It was the pilot. He was still alive. Stanning hoped Heppel had got back to the ship by now and would bring the pilot ashore.

A lorry and a car drew up outside the house. Stanning was sure they would contain Germans. But a small man in spectacles hurried up the snowy path. He was a doctor. "You ought to put some more clothes on," he told Stanning, who was drying himself and his gear in the spring sun. "I'll get you to hospital. I've got a cottage hospital fifteen miles away at Ballangen. I can take your wounded."

The worst cases were taken out to the lorry, which whisked away. After what seemed ages, they heard it returning. Stanning longed to go to the hospital, as his foot was aching almost unbearably. Heppel was seen on his way ashore with the pilot. A dozen of them got into the lorry—all the wounded that were left—and then the pilot appeared. He was put into the vehicle carefully and, though a terrible sight, once more smoked a cigarette. Even Stanning had never expected to see him again. The pilot lay on the floor of the van, with his feet against the rear door, as they bumped along the snowy road. An hour later they reached a three-story building, which was the hospital. They were told that the worst cases must go on to a better-equipped hospital at Harstad. Stanning looked down at his watch from habit. It registered 7:12—the minute he had jumped from the *Hardy*. Wash must have gone down at about the same time. The pain from his foot seared through him. The doctor did not see him till about four o'clock. Then he had morphine and sank into his first sleep for four nights.

Four days of confusion followed for Stanning under the morphine. Heppel and Torps told him of a plan to get away via Tranoy. Almost as they spoke, a colossal crash heralded the opening of an attack on a German destroyer in Ballangen Bay. The *Warspite* it was, in the fight. That evening Heppel rushed back into Stanning's room with the news that he had been on board the *Ivanhoe,* and that he was taking those who were not wounded aboard that same night. The wounded would follow the next day. So at about 1000 on 14 April Stanning and some of the others were transferred into the lorry, driven down to the little pier, and put into *Ivanhoe*'s boat. Thence to the *Ivanhoe,* to the *Warspite,* and the hospital carrier, the *Isle of Jersey*. It was not until Stanning finally returned to Aberdeen in Scotland that he heard the full facts.

Hardy and the other destroyers caused havoc to supply ships and transports in Narvik harbor and repeatedly hit two enemy destroyers, one of which blew up. In the words of the official Admiralty communiqué: "HMS *Hardy* later engaged three large destroyers. The bridge of the *Hardy* was hit and reduced to a shambles, and Captain Warburton-Lee was mortally wounded." Stanning felt fortunate to have survived.

The Jervis Bay

It was now November 1940. In the air the Battle of Britain had been won. But at sea the Battle of the Atlantic would go on for years yet: Allied convoys protected by warships versus U-boats plus the occasional capital ship. This phase of the battle could be symbolized best by one ship, the *Jervis Bay*, under the command of Fogarty Fegen.

Capt. Edward Fogarty Fegen was not a young man. He had served throughout the previous war and was now in the worst of it once more. He was promoted to captain in March 1940 when he received his command of the *Jervis Bay*. They had survived the ensuing seven months and *Jervis Bay* was again in the Atlantic as part of Convoy HX84, thirty-eight ships that sailed from the New World to the Old with vital supplies for the war—petrol and food.

They sailed in nine columns, with *Jervis Bay* in the center one. The commodore's ship, the *Cornish City*, led this fifth column. The *Jervis Bay* was an eighteen-year-old converted merchant liner. In her charge lay the protection of all the ships, which was no mean task. One of the convoy was already straggling as 5 November dawned. The day was fair and the sea calm for the time of year. Fegen was in his element as he shepherded the ships slowly, certainly, toward Britain like a faithful sheepdog. As he paced the bridge he realized how inadequate the armaments at his disposal were should the ship ever have to call on them. But the convoy came first: he never forgot that.

Nearly a fortnight earlier, on 23 October, the German pocket battleship *Admiral Scheer* had left the port of Gdynia in the Baltic. Now she was at large in the ocean. During that very morning, she had attacked the British ship *Mopan* about 52°N and 31°W and quickly sank her. So sudden was this that no distress message could be signaled. Other shipping sailed on, oblivious to what had happened.

That afternoon, Midshipman Ronnie Butler scanned the seas, his young face lit fleetingly by an early setting sun. Nothing disturbed the scene. A hawser groaned as the *Jervis Bay* rolled slightly. Not much more than a sigh, really. The setting sun shone through. Some of the crew had just finished tea; others were waiting for it. The time: 1650.

"Ship to port, sir, on the horizon," said the midshipman. A simple statement, followed by its bearings. But in a flash Fegen realized the possible situation. He got his glasses on it and saw it all too plainly.

Sound Action Stations. Enemy raider. Tell convoy to scatter and make smoke. Report position to Admiralty and repeat to *Cornish City*. Raider at bearing 328°; twelve miles distance; her course 208°; position 53°N and 32°W.

The continuous clang of the Action Stations quickened men's heartbeats. *Scheer* was veering round, ready for the attack, but did not get any nearer. A few precious minutes passed. The ships in the convoy put on full steam and laid smokescreens. *Cornish City* was shelled but not hit. It was the *Jervis Bay*'s duty to try to shield the convoy. The other ships could think of themselves first, but not the *Jervis Bay*.

The first salvo came from a range of 17,000 yards—nearly ten miles. The convoy scattered rapidly, like smaller animals before a predator. They changed three dozen different directions. The *Scheer* could not catch all of them, obviously, nor did she have the chance to try. Before she had time to fire again, Fegen changed course: straight in the direction of the pocket battleship, not away from her.

The *Jervis Bay* was a ship of 14,164 tons. Her seven 6-inch guns were completely outclassed by *Scheer*'s six 11-inch guns and eight 5.9-inch. But the convoy could escape. Fegen knew that the *Scheer* could not chase the convoy while she was being attacked. *Jervis Bay* closed in, getting between the *Scheer* and the convoy. A shell burst in waters near *Jervis Bay*. She returned the fire but was still out of range. *Scheer* had maneuvered to stay on the fringe of the merchantman's range, so it was a one-sided fight.

Captain E. S. Fogarty Fegen, VC, RN—he went down with the Jervis Bay *to help save a convoy.* Imperial War Museum

The second salvo whined nearer. One shell hit *Jervis Bay*, raking the bridge and hitting the height-finder. The bridge burned and the forward steering gear went out of action. Fegen was himself hit, too—terribly wounded with one arm almost off. But his ship's guns kept firing, and they actually made one hit. Fegen staggered aft to the second bridge, his arm drenched with blood. Lane, at one of the guns, saw him groping his way along. Then Lane's gun got a direct hit. The whole gun and its crew were lifted bodily and hurled into the sea. Lane was the only one to escape.

Jervis Bay was holed below her waterline, and she was blazing from bow to stern. Yet somehow men still managed to keep going and her guns continued to fire. Her engine room was the next to be hit. No water could be gotten to tackle the fire. She began to list slightly, then a little more.

Fegen was on the after-bridge now, trying to control the ship from there. But a shell struck this one, too, and it was shot away. The *Jervis Bay* could now only steam in a straight line. Then a second hit in the engine room stopped her once and forever. Her guns could not be swung round toward the *Scheer*. The forward guns were out of action, and as the ship headed for the *Scheer* her aft guns could not bear on the enemy. An hour had passed; the convoy sailed on. Most danger now came from the *Jervis Bay*'s own shells, likely to explode in the fire encircling her.

Ropes, cordite cases, and cordite itself lay about the deck, directly in the path of the flames. Fresh fires broke out among the debris, and the crew did their best to put them out by stamping on them. They threw burning wood and boxes overboard with their bare hands. *Jervis Bay* listed more. Her decks were awash now and the ship's flag had been blasted away. Someone ran up the rigging amid the showers of shells and nailed a new White Ensign to the mast. Incredible but true.

Fegen somehow clutched a way to the main bridge. He was dying. "Abandon ship," he choked out.

Another officer replied, "Aye, aye, sir," and then hurried over to look at the lifeboats. Only one was left. *Jervis Bay* was settling by the stern. It could not last long.

Capt. Sven Olander, skipper of a Swedish ship in the convoy, had stayed behind the rest to watch the battle. He trained his glasses toward the bridge of the *Jervis Bay*. He saw the ship slowly going down and saw Fegen standing on the shredded remnants of his ship, both arms limp at his sides. Still the shells came from the *Scheer*, pouring at *Jervis Bay*. In clusters they came, five at a time. Only the ribs of the ship remained.

The crew piled into the lifeboat, but before it reached the water it was holed. Middy Ronnie Butler raced round to a man on the fo'c's'le who had not heard the order to abandon ship. He was standing there alone, with earphones over his head, continuing his duty. He laid the phones down calmly and walked to the life-rafts.

The entire superstructure of the *Jervis Bay* was burning. Four life-rafts were still usable. The crew—nearly seventy of them—leapt onto the rafts. Though the ship was sinking fast now, the Germans gave them no mercy. The *Scheer* poured shrapnel at the survivors as they struggled onto the rafts. Practically every one of them was wounded.

The rafts floated clear of the ship. A few of the crew manned the ship's lifeboat, but it could not take many. So sank the *Jervis Bay*, with Fegen aboard her. Five minutes later the *Scheer* went after the convoy.

Captain Olander aboard his Swedish ship mustered all his hands on deck. "Well? Is it to be full steam ahead and escape—or stay to pick up survivors?" They voted to stay. "Good," the skipper said. "They did so well to save us, I wouldn't have liked to leave without trying to save them."

Back on the rectangular rafts, the numbing night was upon the men, the winter wind searing their skin and freezing their faces. Ronnie Butler ripped off part of his clothes to bandage the injured. Two of the crew died on the rafts, but the Swedish ship returned to the scene on a swelling sea and took off the men in the lifeboat.

It was 1700 when the *Scheer* was first sighted; *Jervis Bay* had lasted till nearly eight o'clock. The Swedes manned the lifeboat and rowed over to two of the rafts. Survivors were transferred and then brought back to the ship. When the Swedish sailors could not work the oars any longer, Olander brought his ship alongside the last two rafts and saved the rest.

Sixty-five of the *Jervis Bay*'s crew survived. Two-thirds of them were, in peacetime, members of the Merchant Service and had never been in battle before. Yet they had all stuck to their guns till the barrels no longer fired and the deck was at water-level. Aboard the Swedish ship the wounded had to wait attention, for she carried no doctor of her own, and the *Jervis Bay* surgeon was himself one of the wounded. Someone tended him, then he set about the job of seeing to the wounds.

Although the *Jervis Bay* went down, the sacrifice could be translated into terms of ships and men saved from the *Scheer*. Of the thirty-seven other ships in Convoy HX84, thirty-one reached port. Three of these returned to Canada, where incidentally the *Jervis Bay* survivors were landed.

Nevertheless, five precious vessels perished; the Swedish ship, the *Vingaland*, weathered the *Scheer*'s storm only to be sunk by enemy aircraft three days later. Thus the toll was six ships out of the convoy lost— plus the *Jervis Bay*. Without her heroic fight, many more would have succumbed.

Still the story is incomplete. One of the thirty-one to get across the Atlantic with a load of petrol was the tanker *San Demetrio*. She was set on fire and abandoned. Thirty-six hours after the *Jervis Bay* battle, on the morning of 7 November, one of the boat's crew rowed back to the *San Demetrio*, boarded her, put out the fire, and saved the 11,200 tons of petrol. Then, steering only by wind and wake, the *San Demetrio* sighted the Irish coast six days later. A destroyer escorted her to the Clyde, where she delivered safely her precious cargo. It was an amazing adventure, second only to the *Jervis Bay*.

The *Scheer*'s attack disorganized all Atlantic convoys for twelve days afterwards, till the cycle was regained with HX89 on 17 November. One of his brothers summed up Fogarty Fegen's last action: "It was the end he would have wished."

January—December 1941

Malta Submarines

A handful of submarines helped change the course of the war in North Africa. The setting was Malta and the Mediterranean in 1941 when the island, like Britain, fought on alone. Malta was defended at first by just three old aircraft called *Faith, Hope,* and *Charity.* It was from this vulnerable and isolated island that a pitifully few submarines struck out to stop enemy supplies from reaching North Africa. The whole desert war depended on their success.

By the time the submarines were operating at full strength later on, half of all Axis shipping bound for the African coast was failing to arrive. The submarines sank no fewer than seventy-five enemy vessels. But half of the Royal Navy's submarines failed to return. Ten out of twenty, lost with all hands.

This saga was enacted against the blitzed backdrop of Malta where, by the end of 1941, it was just as hazardous for submarines to be in harbor as at sea. Amid many desperate exploits, one submarine sailed through a maze of mines, became entangled with a cable, and somehow survived. Several others were lost by enemy action at a single stroke. And the climax came when it was the Luftwaffe versus Lazaretto—the base of Malta submarines. The scars are still visible today.

Symbolic of all the hundreds of actions from Malta are a single submarine, her one commander, and just a few of their memorable patrols. The submarine was the *Upholder;* her commander the legendary David Wanklyn, and the dates begin in 1941. What was Wanklyn like? A tall and lean man, with a soft Scottish voice, he had a dark submariner's

*Lt. Cdr. M. D. Wanklyn, VC, DSO, RN (with beard), flanked by
three of his officers of* Upholder. *This most famous of all British
submarines lies alongside at Malta.* Imperial War Museum

beard and large powerful hands. His electric eyes could blaze with an
intensity of purpose. Or they could crinkle softly. For he was a gentle
soul, too—one who hated to think of the consequences of his actions
after a ship had been hit. Returning from patrols, his eyes would be red-
rimmed with too little sleep and too much responsibility.

On her twenty-four successful patrols, *Upholder* sank more than
twenty ships, including a destroyer and a cruiser. Wanklyn's seventh
patrol took them to the southern approaches of the Straits of Messina.
After four days, they attacked a tanker and registered a hit. Then their
asdic listening gear went out of action, so the submarine was deaf to
the outside world. They saw a small enemy convoy. Wanklyn hit a tanker,
which sank by the stern. This was total war. Twenty-six depth-charges

crackled, cracked, and crashed all around them. The submarine shuddered, and so did her crew.

By that time, *Upholder* had been on patrol for about a week. The next evening Wanklyn took a last look around this enemy route starting from Sicily to the Libyan coast. The sun set on 24 May and Wanklyn's watch showed 2020 when the action started.

In a stormy twilit gloom Wanklyn sighted an aircraft patrolling to the north: nothing else. He held on for a few minutes more. The surface swell took *Upholder* with it—to and fro. Depth-keeping was difficult. The sub "pumped" up and down. The horizon seemed shadowy and indistinct to the east but blood-red and clear-cut to the west. One moment the horizon would be startlingly close; the next, while she fell away in a trough, the swell raced by the top window of the periscope—blotting out everything except the darkening water.

Ten minutes passed. 2030. Wanklyn sighted three large two-funnel transports tearing at top speed on a southwesterly course, strongly silhouetted against the afterglow of sunset.

"Ships, Tubby, three of them."

Wanklyn thought in a flash: light failing so periscope useless; listening gear out of order; only two torpedoes left. For some reason these factors did not deter him. He may also have seen the top masts of destroyers, but the swell made sighting more and more difficult each minute. He did not stop to see if the enemy was escorted or not. He was intent to close as fast as he could. But he knew that ships such as these would not be proceeding alone. Light bad, sea bad, time short—and getting worse and shorter.

"They're liners, I should think, getting on for 20,000 tons. One's bigger than the rest."

In fact, they were troop transports, converted liners, sailing in a line of twenty knots for Africa. After *Upholder* followed the troop transports for four minutes, the transports altered course conveniently toward *Upholder*. Seeing that all would be well, or at least that they were coming in his direction, Wanklyn took time for a fleeting spin around with the periscope, although it was practically useless.

"Here they are, Tubby. Four or five destroyers. Didn't see them before. They're screening the convoy. Have to shorten the range. Don't know their speed sufficiently to go ahead yet."

He shortened the attack and brought the submarine around toward the oncoming ships, looming in the last light of the day. He screwed up his eyes to make sure where they were and read off bearings on all of them. He estimated speeds again and checked directions before comparing them to *Upholder*'s. Then he changed course, which marked the start of the assault. He had to hit first time with one of the two torpedoes left. An audacious attack by a "deaf and blind" sub on seven or eight big ships—four or five armed to their topmast and full of the usual fatal ashcans. They practically skated through the destroyer screen.

It was 2037 and dusk, with the periscope eye all but blind. Wanklyn maneuvered *Upholder* into the precise position planned. The mile-off attack was no good and surfacing would be suicidal. So he got the sub right in among the enemy. He peered through the periscope, swiveled it slightly, and saw the first of the transports, then the second. He had no idea where the enemy escorts were. Yet five destroyers roamed at large, and the danger of being rammed remained in his mind.

At 2038 he said, "Fire." The torpedoes slid out of the tubes, their backlash shivering through the sub. And then it happened. As the two torpedoes left, Wanklyn saw a huge black V heading straight for the sub. The bows of a destroyer were thirty seconds off and getting nearer, each one of them.

"Crash dive—deep."

Down, down, went *Upholder*, while Wanklyn counted off the seconds from the time the torpedoes had left. Fifteen, thirty, forty-five. One minute. Seventy-seven seconds—then two mild and inoffensive explosions. The same short interval separated them as the firing of the torpedoes from the tubes. Wanklyn had hit the middle transport twice. They heard the bangs without the aid of "ears."

About 150 seconds passed. Then came the first of the battering bursts of the depth-charges. The lights flickered; shades splintered across the deck; men were caught off balance. The *Upholder* twisted three-dimensionally. Wanklyn could only guess where the destroyers were, which way they headed. It was a lethal game of blind man's bluff on either side, except that the ships knew roughly where the submarine was wriggling.

Down the depth-charges came; nearly two a minute shattered the water around the hull for hectic minutes on end. All the while Wanklyn cocked his ears in the direction of the charges, estimated the positions of the attackers, and steered as far from them as he could contrive. Even so, some ashcans exploded close enough to break the bulbs. The whole area seemed subjected to systematic attack. But miraculously, Wanklyn dodged them all by split-second navigation and course-changing of a high order. *Upholder* continued to trace a crazy zigzag at different depths.

Thirty-three charges came in nineteen minutes. Then they heard the ominous, thunderous beat of propellers as the hunter hurried overhead. Nerve-shattering seconds elapsed which got worse and worse as the throb of the propellers grew louder, till they were racing directly above the submarine. Every man in *Upholder* was sweating now. But the sound at length passed its climax. Then they heard the plop of the charges as they hit the water. The ashcans were dropping. But how near to *Upholder*? On the answer to this depended thirty-three lives. For if you hear propellers by natural ear, it is too late to try and escape—you are right below them.

Four final charges floated downward. Then came the four cracks. Then silence. "Thirty-seven charges in twenty minutes" was what the log entry read.

After half an hour their nerves were challenged again. Even Tubby Crawford felt tense. A series of light tapping noises sounded like a sweep wire passing over the hull. The mystery was never solved, however, and eventually it stopped. The next decision for Wanklyn was to choose between escape and the danger of using his motors at any speed. The engines gave away their position when the attackers came close. So he stopped engines completely for an hour. Not a sound broke the stillness. Thirty-three men sitting silent near the bed of the Mediterranean.

Wanklyn looked tired but happy, having outwitted five destroyers.

"Serve some tea," he whispered, and Cookie pressed his messmates to mugs of hot tea and slices of cake plus the last of the fresh fruit salad.

By the time the meal was over the enemy had evidently given up the hunt. It was 2200. Nothing could be heard. If ever anyone felt cut off from the rest of the world, they did. They were in a static submarine with no listening gear, and it was night-time above. The world might just as well not have existed.

"Periscope depth," Wanklyn decided. He grappled its handles eagerly. He went through the motions of scanning the horizons round 360° but the periscope was practically useless at night.

"Stand by to surface" was the sign for a stifled cheer from the crew. They came up where the transport had gone down. There was nothing to be heard in the darkness as Wanklyn clambered on to the bridge but the breeze blowing across the heaving waters wafted a strong smell of fuel oil. The moon came out from behind a cloud and lit fragments of wood, broken boats, and flotsam—all that remained above water of the 17,800-ton transport liner *Conte Rosso*.

"Strange to think, Tubby," Wanklyn said as they charged batteries on the surface and breathed in the oily night air, "that she is now lying on the bottom just below us. We might have been there, too."

"Thanks for getting us out of it," Crawford said simply.

They set sail for Malta, virtually sure of having sunk the ship. Their view was confirmed a few days later by a lifeboat of a large ship being washed up on the island—bearing the name *Conte Rosso*.

The official communiqué on this patrol ended with the words: "With the greatest courage, coolness and skill, he brought *Upholder* clear of the enemy and back to harbor."

On *Upholder*'s tenth patrol, an escorted supply ship, the 6,000-ton *Laura C*, was sunk. The submarine survived nineteen depth-charges. Eleventh patrol: another supply ship sunk and seventeen depth-charges survived from the escorting destroyer. They probably sank a cruiser, too. Patrol number 12 brought a supply ship, a tanker, and a hit on a 6-inch cruiser. After the tanker exploded in a darkening cloud of belching smoke, an accurate counterattack came from three destroyers. *Upholder* survived her record number of depth-charges—sixty.

Reconnaissance aircraft spotted three large liners at Taranto. *Upholder, Unbeaten, Upright,* and *Ursula* sailed as soon as they could to a preconceived plan. They knew the rough route that these troop transports would take, so three of them assumed a position at an angle across the enemy's expected line. Early on, *Upholder* suffered a setback that would have knocked an officer less gifted than Wanklyn off balance. The sub's gyro compass ceased to function, leaving him to rely on the less-accurate magnetic compass. This put precise steering out of the question and increased the difficulties of any attack.

Unbeaten sighted the convoy at 0320, but they were steaming too fast for her to attack in time. *Unbeaten* made a report to *Upholder* and chased off after the enemy. Wanklyn got the report and had little to do but wait until they hove into sight. The night stayed very dark, ideal for an attack on the surface. They went on waiting for the *Neptunia, Oceania,* and *Vulcania,* escorted by six destroyers.

Wanklyn's first lieutenant was on watch when the enemy was sighted. In a flash the captain was on the bridge. He saw dimly the dark shapes against an also-dark horizon. The sea was choppy. Wanklyn realized that the submarine was some way off the enemy's track. He closed at full throttle.

With torpedo at the ready and his glasses glued to the murky masses on the starboard bow, Wanklyn raced in to try to intercept the three large ships. Penetrating the ring of escorting destroyers with consummate skill, he realized he would have to carry out the attack at a far longer range than desirable, and, more serious still, with the submarine still swaying wildly from side to side. It would have been a waste of torpedoes to fire a salvo of four, for if he was wrong once, through no fault of his own, the vital chance would be gone. He drove on and on, and when he knew he could not get nearer than 5,000 yards, he decided finally to fire from nearly three miles off. *Upholder* still swung from side to side, as the helmsman had to correct the course almost each moment.

"Never get on the line of fire," Wanklyn shouted.

As the sub swung across the target, he made split-second assessments. Through the glasses he saw *Oceania* in the lead, with *Neptunia* overlapping along the line from *Upholder*. The submarine swung across this line, and Wanklyn fired. She swung back again, and he fired again. And a few seconds later, as she came on course for the third time, he fired once more. He was judging entirely by eye. Through three miles of sea they had to travel, on a dark choppy night with aiming almost impossible.

"Ready to dive, sir?" Number One called.

"Not quite. I want to see them hit first."

In the end Number One had to go aloft and persuade him it was high time they were diving. So she dived and moved south. The three torpedoes took over three minutes to reach the target area. Then, as *Upholder* gained depth, Wanklyn's watch became the focus. At the precise second planned, they heard three explosions. One hit on the *Oceania* and two on *Neptunia*. Three out of three. It was an amazing achievement in the adverse circumstances.

The first torpedo tore into *Oceania*'s propellers. She was in no danger of sinking, so two destroyers dashed in to try to get her in tow. But exactly as they did so, the other torpedoes dug deep into *Neptunia* amidships, crippling her. Soon it became certain that she would sink, although she could still crawl along at five knots. The third transport fled at several times that speed.

Obviously it was only a matter of minutes for *Neptunia*. The ship limped and listed to a stop, and then sank. Destroyers clustered around her, collected survivors, and then swung back toward *Oceania*.

But Wanklyn knew nothing of all this at the time. The unaccustomed absence of any counterattack satisfied him that the destroyers were too busy searching for survivors to worry about *Upholder*. So at 0445, he said, "Stand by to surface. I'm going to survey the situation."

Splashing as little as he could, Wanklyn brought the sub up among the enemy destroyers. It was still dark. Yet a ghostly glimmer from the east lit enough for him to see one ship stopped, with a destroyer standing by, and another vessel making to westward. Wanklyn concentrated on the stationary *Oceania*.

He took *Upholder* down again and made off to the eastward while releasing his tubes. The purpose of this maneuver was to get a good position up-sun from which to attack after sunrise. At 0630 the sun edged above the horizon. The sub also edged up to periscope depth and approached the *Oceania* with her attendant destroyers. Both boats lay stopped but drifting slowly. Wanklyn got *Oceania* in his sights, while the periscope slowly picked its way nearer to the transport. He was on the verge of firing when he shouted, "Good God! Forty-five feet."

He had suddenly sighted a second destroyer bows-on only a hundred yards away. Wanklyn took *Upholder* along at forty-five feet and ducked directly underneath the escort! Then he realized that this delay, and the drift of the target, would bring him much too close to fire, so he altered depth.

"Eighty feet."

Upholder went on under the transport, too, so as to come up to windward. Wanklyn looked through his periscope next at an ideal range of 2,000 yards from *Oceania*. Two torpedoes hit her, and the ship sank in eight minutes. Wanklyn, alone and unaided, had sunk two-thirds of a concentrated convoy.

By March 1942 *Upholder* had completed twenty-four successful patrols. Wanklyn was operating with his customary brilliance. He seemed to be invincible. The *Upholder* sailed from Malta on 6 April for patrol in the Gulf of Tripoli. As they slid past Valletta, they saw the blitzed outline of the buildings silhouetted against the sky. On 11 April they were met by the submarine *Unbeaten.* After that rendezvous nothing more was ever heard of *Upholder.* On 14 April *Urge,* which was patrolling in an area nearby, heard prolonged depth-charging. On 18 April the Italians claimed that one of their torpedo boats had sunk a submarine. The assumption was that this boat located *Upholder* on 14 April, while she was stalking an enemy convoy, and sank her. So *Upholder* was lost with all hands— including David Wanklyn. Tubby Crawford had left some time earlier to take a commanding officer's course, so he survived.

The sequel to the story is short. Because of the intense bombing, Malta submarines sailed to Alexandria and operated from there. Then this remnant of the flotilla returned to Malta before the raising of the siege of the island. They were fortified by new submarine arrivals from Britain and continued to wage war on enemy traffic to Africa.

Few of the first band remained to see the enemy driven out of North Africa and the triumphant assault on Europe from the south, culminating in the surrender of the Italian Fleet. But those who were not at Malta in 1943 to witness what they had striven for during the darker years had the satisfaction of reading this classic signal: "FROM: C IN C MEDITER-RANEAN TO: ADMIRALTY. Be pleased to inform Their Lordships that the Italian Battlefleet now lies at anchor under the guns of the fortress of Malta."

Pearl Harbor and After

Sunday, 7 December 1941: Pearl Harbor day. In the words of the U.S. president, Franklin D. Roosevelt: "[A] date which will live in infamy. . . ." Completely unbeknownst to the Americans, a fleet of Japanese warships was sailing some two hundred miles north of Hawaii. At 0610 that morning, enemy dive-bombers, high-altitude bombers, and fighters were launched from aircraft carriers and were headed toward the Hawaiian Islands. By an unlucky coincidence, eighteen American scout bombers took off from their carrier, the USS *Enterprise*, at about the same time, but from exactly the opposite direction—south of Hawaii.

0700: A remote radar station picked up the signal of a large force of aircraft approaching the islands. This was reported but thought to be the U.S. aircraft from the *Enterprise*. No further action was taken.

0720: While an early morning religious service was being held on Oahu, the enemy was launching its second wave of aircraft for Hawaii. A quarter of an hour passed before the first wave crossed the coast. Flying low amidst the mountains on the distant side of Oahu, they went undetected by U.S. radar.

At 0750, the church service was one of the few signs of activity among U.S. military. Elsewhere, all was quiet. Soldiers, Marines, naval personnel, airmen, and servicewomen were all in their quarters—either still in bed, waking up, or having breakfast. A lone member of the U.S. Marine Corps Band carried his clarinet as he walked across a palm-fringed lawn. He was due to play it later, but never did.

Over in the harbor lay the serried rows of U.S. Navy ships, vulnerable to any attack. But none was expected. Few of the men afloat or onshore were on duty yet. Peace prevailed as the sun rose, but only for a few moments more. As the enemy aircraft approached Pearl Harbor, they saw the ships and the base for the first time. Their commander sent the now-notorious message—"Tora! Tora! Tora!"—signifying that they had achieved strategic surprise.

At 0755 that Pacific morning, the attack began on the Americans' main airfields without warning. Japanese dive-bombers descended upon the U.S. Army air base at Hickam Field, screamed over the naval air station on Ford Island, and streamed above the naval air station at Kaneoke Bay. Service personnel looked aghast. What greeted the Americans assailed their senses, and for the first few minutes they actually did not know who was attacking them. Their ears caught the whiz and whine of bullets and the burst of bombs on buildings, planes, and the ground.

Smoke and flames rise over the Naval Air Station in Kaneoke Bay. Imperial War Museum

Their eyes met a succession of oncoming enemy aircraft—often flying at near-ground level so that onlookers could literally see the faces of pilots.

0758: Only three minutes into the attack, horizontal high-level bombers arrived as the first American B-17s throbbed overhead. The enemy bombed the military's installations and civilian locales. Confusion reigned. Although caught completely unaware of the impending attack, ground crews dashed toward the flames that enveloped their planes, now ablaze from incendiaries. Ignoring the pain of burns and a continuous threat of fuel explosions, the crews stripped off any machine guns they could, loaded them hastily, and pointed their muzzles skyward toward their now-retreating attackers. Later, these guns would account for an enemy aircraft that was actually shot down.

In the first few minutes of the raid 150 of the 202 naval aircraft listed on the island of Oahu were destroyed. Seconds after the perfectly timed targeting of the air stations, the enemy's torpedo guns and dive-bombers swung the focus of their attack upon the ships in Pearl Harbor. The actual alarm aboard most ships was sounded at 0755, the same as the ground assault. The minute the ships were alerted, their emergency procedures went into operation. And at 0759, less than four minutes later, the fleet's heavy guns were firing on the dive-bombers as they swooped down. The first enemy plane plunged into the water at exactly 0800.

The torpedoes carried by the bombers were designed to travel through the shallow waters of the harbor. Other torpedo attacks were made by midget submarines that penetrated U.S. defenses. At 0805 the USS *California* received a torpedo hit at about the same minute that the USS *Nevada* opened fire.

0808: Smoke started to envelop the harbor and base. Despite the overwhelming noise, the local radio station continued transmitting early-morning music until they interrupted to tell all U.S. service personnel to report for duty.

At 0808 the first high-level, armor-piercing bomb hit the USS *Arizona*. The ship's boiler exploded, and then at 0810, a bomb passed through the smokestack to the forward magazines, which caught fire and erupted. The *Arizona* sank within ten minutes, with a large loss of life.

0811: The USS *Oklahoma*, due for an official inspection by senior officers later that day, had her portholes open overnight to let in fresh air. It would prove a fatal decision. Ten torpedoes hit the *Oklahoma*, and water surged in through the portholes. Within three or four minutes, the ship capsized and trapped 461 men. How many would survive? That answer would not come until the following day.

On an aircraft carrier moored at the naval air station, fire, started by repeat high-altitude attacks, swept the ship. One of her antiaircraft guns hit a plane, which then tore its way into the decking. At this precise second, the ship's captain chanced to look over the side of the vessel and saw the shadow of a two-man suicide submarine not a dozen yards away. He called to the gunners, but at that instant, a destroyer passed directly over the submarine and sank the craft with one blast from its depth charges. All of this was compressed into a mere thirty seconds.

Within this first half-hour, several ships were going down from the bombs. Men belonging to ships that were put out of action managed to return to the fight. As one vessel capsized, her survivors swam in near scalding oil to clamber up the ladders of other ships and join their gun crews. Survivors of another disabled vessel swam away from the comparative safety of the shoreline, which lay only a few yards off, and instead struck out toward midchannel, where they were hoisted aboard seabound destroyers.

Quick thinking saved lives—and ships. An aviation machinist's mate aboard one ship saw that flames from his huge vessel threatened the repair ship alongside. He did not wait for orders but ran through the blaze and slashed the lines holding the two ships together. Freed, the smaller craft drifted clear to safety.

Only when remaining aboard appeared hopeless would men leave their ships in the final moments. One crew followed around their ship as she capsized, firing their guns first from her side and then from the keel, until they were sinking themselves and had to jump clear. Back on the land, those same men stood and cheered for a more fortunate ship, as she steamed clear of the harbor and after the enemy. Then, taking up their guns, they went on with the fight as more waves of bombers buzzed overhead.

The air was punctuated by the relentless explosions. Ships sank at every imaginable angle—some at their moorings without a stir. Black smoke marked the ships already hit, and rescue became paramount. One ship picked up hundreds of men that had been hurled into the water by the explosions from torpedoes or bombs. Back ashore thirty-eight U.S. fighters took to the air as their pilots braved bullets and bombs. The navy had to rely on antiaircraft fire for its primary weapon. This disastrous condition exposed the Pacific Fleet to continuous air assault. The U.S. gunners were doing all they could to disperse the Japanese bombers, but with U.S. aircraft virtually grounded, the struggle remained one-sided.

Then at 0825 a comparative lull descended upon the scene, although sporadic air activity continued by both dive- and horizontal-bombers. The respite lasted a quarter of an hour.

At 0840 this respite was shattered by bombers from various directions crossing their targets in a devastating raid. Then the dive-bombers reappeared. The enemy pilots put their planes into almost vertical dives and watched as their quarries grew nearer and nearer. Then, just as it seemed they would crash, they pulled out of the dive at the last possible second to roar over the ships—strafing indiscriminately. This wave—numbering seventy-eight dive-bombers, fifty-four high-level bombers, and thirty-six fighters—was hitting onshore military targets, the naval air stations, and more ships. The fighters circled overhead to be sure that they kept control of the skies above Pearl Harbor, while below them, all remained in chaos, with only improvised plans in response. This continued for another hour, until between 0945 and 1000, the last of the enemy aircraft exhausted its weapons and turned for home. American gunfire destroyed approximately twenty-nine planes. Three Japanese submarines went to the bottom.

Throughout the rest of the morning, and indeed that day, the fear of new invasion was uppermost in everyone's minds. But it did not come. The Japanese had planned a last wave of air attack at 1300, but they called it off and withdrew.

The United States began to count its losses at Pearl Harbor. The battleship *Arizona* was gone, with tragically heavy casualties. Only 32 men were saved from the 461 trapped in the capsized *Oklahoma*. In time, she would be repaired. Long-term casualties included the battleships *California, Nevada,* and *West Virginia;* the three destroyers *Shaw, Cassin,* and *Downes;* the line layer *Ogala;* the *Utah,* plus a large floating dock. Three other battleships and three cruisers received less damage, while other minor vessels were also hit. In addition, the Japanese aircraft managed to destroy eighty aircraft and ninety-seven army planes. But, the worst losses were the men and women. Within two hours, 2,117 officers and enlisted personnel of the Navy and Marine Corps were killed, 976 were wounded, and 960 were reported as still missing a year later. By comparison, the Army sustained far fewer losses with 226 killed and 396 wounded.

How had it happened? Many answers have been given. The facts were that the Japanese fleet carrying the aircraft left Hitokappu Bay at the northern extremity of the empire a week earlier, refueled on 3 December, crossed the Date Line far northwest of Pearl Harbor, and then altered course to arrive at a point due north of the Hawaiian Islands by 2130 on 6 December. From there it was a mere step to Pearl.

So the United States was at last in World War II—with a vengeance. Stunned for a moment by the horror of the raid, and then stirred to anger, the nation began slowly to recover. The Japanese, meanwhile, gave the Navy no chance for rest. The American Navy and Marines started to feel further effects of aggression, when air raids were directed next on the advance Marine garrison at Wake Island. Then Midway and Luzon received heavy attacks, and the situation on Guam seemed worse still. By 13 December, less than a week after Pearl Harbor, the Navy Department could not communicate with Guam, the most southerly of the Mariana Islands. Some 400 naval men and 155 Marines were stationed there and reports indicated that bombing raids had been followed up by enemy landings. War was now by land, sea, and air.

The war as a whole was beginning to touch American home soil. Japanese submarines were operating just off their own Pacific coast. The cruel sea was now not only the Atlantic. Allies were in the fight together.

8–22 December 1941: The attacks came against Wake during these fearful two weeks. One man managed to convey as well as anyone the events on that remote island. Maj. W. Bayler was on temporary duty in Wake to help establish the base for Marine Corps aviation unit operations. This unit of a dozen planes arrived shortly before the Japanese attacked. Bayler kept penciled notes on each day:

8 DECEMBER, 0700–1158: Received word bombing Oahu. General quarters station. 24 Jap bombers on a northern course hit airdrome in close column of division Vs from 3,000 feet. 100-pound fragmentation bombs and simultaneous strafing. Casualties 25 dead, 7 wounded, 7 airplanes burned, destroyed.

9 DECEMBER, 1145: 27 Japs bombed hospital, Camp No 2. Killed several patients, 3 dead. Got one Jap plane.

10 DECEMBER, 1045: 27 Jap bombers. No casualties.

11 DECEMBER, 0500: Landing attempted by 12 Jap ships, including light cruisers, destroyers, gunboats, 2 troop or supply ships. Jap casualties: 1 light cruiser, 2 destroyers, 1 gunboat, 2 bombers. Japs closed in to 4,700 yards before 5- and 3-inch guns opened up at pointblank range.

12 DECEMBER: 27 Jap planes bombed Peale and Wake from 2,000 feet. No casualties.

13 DECEMBER: All quiet.

14 DECEMBER: 32 Jap planes hit airdrome. Two killed, 1 plane shot down. 15 December, 1100: Dawn raid by 3 four-engine seaplanes. 27 Jap bombers. Shot down 2 Japs.

16 DECEMBER, 1745: 41 Jap bombers hit Camp 2 and airdrome. Jap four-motor plane raid. One Jap shot down.

USS Helena *(left) torpedoed at her dock.*
Imperial War Museum

17 DECEMBER: 32 Jap bombers at 1317 hit Camp 1, Peale Island, Diesel oil supply, mess hall, and pumps of evaporators, Camp 1.

18 DECEMBER, 1140: One Jap high rec. plane (2 engine).

19 DECEMBER, 1030: Jap bombers hit airport and camp.

20 DECEMBER: All quiet—first day of bad weather. Total casualties: 28 dead, 6 wounded as of 20 December.

The revelation that the Japanese were allowed to close to 4,700 yards in the attempted landing before the defenders' guns opened up showed real courage by the commander.

After these enemy raids, only three U.S. planes at Wake were serviceable. Then the enemy scored a direct hit on one of these before it could get off the ground, while a second one crashed trying to take off too quickly. So then there was one. A lone aircraft against the whole Japanese force being hurled on Wake. Their troops landed on 23 December, and by Christmas Eve the Navy had to admit its capture.

Christmas 1941: So Wake fell, with more losses on both sides. Ships and men went down into the Pacific. The battle continued not only on the islands, but also in the surrounding waters of that large chain. The enemy discovered USS *Heron*, a small seaplane tender, off the Philippines, and attacked her for seven hours. Ten four-engined flying boats and five twin-engine landplane bombers delivered the onslaught, yet the captain and crew were determined she should not go down. The captain handled her with uncanny skill and, although fighting against all odds, he managed to take evasive action so successfully that only one bomb hit the *Heron*, while three very near misses were felt aboard the tender.

The crew counted forty-six 100-pound bombs dropped by enemy planes plus three torpedoes launched against her. The ship's guns shot down a flying boat, damaged at least one other, and generally acquitted themselves well. But the bomb that did hit her ripped the deck badly. Despite this, the *Heron*'s commanding officer, Lt. William Leverette Kabler, navigated her safely out of the holocaust and made port.

January 1942: The U.S. Navy was not long in adopting the offensive. More attacks on convoys in the Makassar Straits accounted for an enemy aircraft carrier believed sunk, while motor torpedo boats (MTBs) continued their particular brand of daring. One got into Subic Bay, through net and boom defenses, but for real daring the laurels went to another MTB which braved Manila Bay itself at night. Speeding in before the full glare of a warship's searchlights and full fire of her guns, the boat launched her two torpedoes and got away.

The offensive ranged far and near. Surface and air units started a surprise attack on the naval and air bases set up by the Japanese south of Wake in the Marshall and Gilbert Islands. Synchronized attacks on four islands resulted in heavy damage to fuel and other stores, aircraft and general installations, while at the anchorage in Kwajalein Island nine ships were sunk, including an aircraft carrier. The officer commanding this operation was Vice Adm. William F. "Bull" Halsey Jr.

20 February: Can one man save an aircraft carrier? The answer is yes if his name is O'Hare. The carrier *Lexington* was with a force of four heavy cruisers and ten destroyers planning to attack Rabaul in New Britain, when they were spotted by enemy flying boats, which wheeled off for some stronger support. Soon they were back and the first heavy bomber approached the *Lexington* and her escorts. Two of the six U.S. fighters keeping constant watch overhead peeled off to attack it, and the plane quickly went down in flames. A second went the same way. The next one copied the course of the original flying boats and went home for reinforcements. When they came, the stage was prepared for one of those "fights to the finish."

Another half-dozen American Navy fighters flew off the deck to join the first six. Nine Japanese bombers in a V formation pointed straight at the carrier. The original fighters were getting short of fuel before the battle began but throttled forward to engage. In a spluttering few minutes, five enemy bombers left trails of flame in the sky as they plunged into the Pacific. This rattled the enemy, who found the next phase too much for them. The U.S. ships loosed all they had at these last four bombers, frightening the pilots so badly that their bombs sank into the sea. They tried to turn and flee back to Rabaul, but the Navy fighters were still airborne and shot down all but one of them.

Something serious was taking shape as the fighters flew in pursuit of these last four planes. The *Lexington* had managed to get fifteen more fighters up to help in the chase, exchanging these for five of the original ones that needed fuel and ammunition. At the exact moment that all the airborne fighters except two were well away from the carrier, dealing with enemy planes, nine more bombers droned dramatically down toward the *Lexington*. As these two U.S. fighters took on this next wave, the machine guns of one of them jammed so he could do nothing but fly clear to safety. This left one lone U.S. fighter flying between the enemy and the ship. Its pilot: Lt. Edward H. (Butch) O'Hare. He took on all nine.

O'Hare raced down on the V formation from the rear and their right. Aboard the *Lexington*, everyone with a moment to spare watched what happened next. O'Hare pressed his gun button just before the fighter reached the enemy right flank. The two end planes of the V collapsed and crashed. Weaving underneath the rest, he then gave another bomber a burst. It limped out of the formation, which was already a ragged arrow. Two more of the group lost bits of their wings and fuselage as they struggled to save the formation. So five of the nine never reached the target to drop their bombs.

The quartet who got through did drop them, but hurriedly and very inaccurately. They were anxious to get away from this daredevil. As the scattered group still sought some order, O'Hare went into them again. One, two, three. All went spiraling into the sea before his guns. In just four minutes he shot down five of the nine and hit three more.

But the brief air battle was not yet over. As the three damaged bombers sputtered homeward, each short of one or more engine, they ran right into the *Lexington*'s main force of fighters flying jubilantly back from wiping out the first bombers. All three Japanese bombers received mortal fire. The last plane ran for it as fast as a bomber could, pursued by Lt. Edward H. Allen in a Navy scout bomber. Both planes flew at about the same speed, but whenever the Americans managed to come in range the recoil from their guns retarded their scout bomber just long enough to allow the enemy to gain ground—or air—again. But the *Lexington* survived. Admiral Brown said that she owed her life to O'Hare alone. So the answer to that question about one man saving an aircraft carrier was yes. He did it.

Off the Marshall Islands on 27 November 1943 O'Hare was flying from the carrier *Enterprise* at night. After a scrap with enemy planes, one lagging Japanese pilot became mixed up with three American Hellcats about to return to the carrier. O'Hare flew in one of them. Somehow his fighter was hit and it took O'Hare with it into the Pacific.

January—May 1942

The Battle of the Channel

12 February 1942: The Battle of the Channel. This is the story as seen through the eyes of Fleet Air Arm pilot Lt. Cdr. Eugene Esmonde. But before it happened, Esmonde had achieved much in his life.

In May 1941 Esmonde was flying from the carrier HMS *Victorious*. Later on in the epic of the German battleship *Bismarck*, he came into the action. The *Victorious* was sent to launch an air attack with the aim of cutting the enemy's speed. The carrier had been commissioned only a short while. Some of the aircrew had hardly any battle experience. She released her nine torpedo-carrying Swordfish aircraft into a biting headwind, raging rain, and low clouds. They were on a 120-mile flight and for two hours they struggled on. Then late in the evening they found the *Bismarck*. Going in under ferocious fire, they somehow scored a direct hit with a torpedo under the bridge.

Now it was night. An Atlantic night, void-black, and still lashed with rain. The squadron had scant experience of deck-landing in daylight. The captain of *Victorious* was very worried about their safe return, always assuming they managed to locate the carrier. The homing beacon aboard had failed. Signal lamps were lit instead, and somehow all nine of the Swordfish staggered back to the carrier.

Esmonde peered into the gloom and saw the pinpricks of light flickering, winking, through the rain: white specks in a black ocean. He lost height. Still no sign of the actual carrier; just the lamps, closer now. How far off? It was hard to tell. They could be bigger lights further off, or smaller ones nearer to him. Life was hit or miss—literally. He guided the Swordfish down to the deck. It bumped. The nose lifted, dropped— and he was down.

First, the *Courageous;* then the *Victorious;* next the *Ark Royal.* The first and third were fated ships. Esmonde joined the *Ark Royal* in August 1941. Mortally hit a few miles from Gibraltar, the famous aircraft carrier limped along in tow for nearly twelve hours. A torpedo had done its work, though, and she began to list badly. But by this time her Swordfish squadron had flown several sorties, carrying members of the crew to the safety of Gibraltar Rock. A destroyer took off the rest of the 1600 ship's company, and before the flight deck tilted too much, the very last Swordfish ever to take off from the carrier winged its way toward Gibraltar. Esmonde took a last look down at the *Ark Royal* as he circled around and headed for safety. The *Courageous* and the *Ark Royal*—what next, he wondered.

February 1942. The German battleships docked in Brest harbor had to find a safer port. The battlecruisers *Scharnhorst* and *Gneisenau,* with the cruiser *Prinz Eugen,* all still needed repairs after the regular hammerings from RAF bombers over the months. Now the need became urgent. The Allies knew this, and Esmonde's squadron, based on the Kent coast at its own request, stood by at the beginning of February for immediate takeoff

Lt. Cdr. Eugene Esmonde, VC, RN, leader of the ill-fated attack by Swordfish aircraft. Imperial War Museum

if any or all of the big three decided to make their run up the coast for home. Esmonde had formed the squadron from *Ark Royal* colleagues.

So finally to Thursday, 12 February 1942, and the Battle of the Channel. The culmination of Esmonde's life. 1100: RAF HQ reported that the three ships had at last broken cover with an escort of destroyers, torpedo boats, E-boats, minesweepers, and a fighter escort described as the biggest ever seen over a naval force.

The Fleet Air Arm did not waste time. Already the enemy ships would be well along the French coast and nearing the Straits of Dover. The aim was to try to intercept this massive force of more than a couple of dozen surface craft and attack before they could reach the sandbanks northeast of Calais—thirty-three craft in all focused on the big three.

So six slow torpedo-carrying Swordfish biplanes battled toward that formidable target. Only a few British motor torpedo boats, the Dover shore batteries, and a handful of fighters were able to support them in their desperate mission. The RAF fighters zigzagged across the course to keep their speed down to the trundling Swordfish, which looked like something more out of World War I. They were about to take on three of the greatest vessels in the world. Although the Swordfish had served the Royal Navy faithfully, by 1942 they were out-of-date with their single gun turrets.

The enemy force had been sailing since fairly early morning. Now it was nearing noon, four hours later. They were actually through the Straits of Dover and some ten miles north of Calais when Esmonde first spotted them. The other five crews had heard his orders earlier and were intent on carrying them out:

"The *Scharnhorst, Gneisenau,* and *Prinz Eugen* have had the cheek to put their noses into the Channel. We're going to deal with them. Fly at 50 feet, close line astern. Individual attacks. Find your own way home."

So the Swordfish sighted the enemy: first, the white wake of the destroyer screen all around. The Swordfish were six sitting targets for a hundred and more guns. Into the Channel of death . . . they flew in, arranged as two subflights of three aircraft each, flying in echelon. The first subflight, headed by Esmonde in his aircraft, W 5984/825, met a brutal barrage of fire as it covered the air only seventeen yards above the wintry waters. This fire came only from the smaller ships. A shell actually ricocheted off the water and hit the belly of Esmonde's aircraft, scarring those numbers. At the same time, the gunner of the following plane was killed. But both aircraft, and the third one in this first half of the assault, struggled on toward the targets as ordered.

Then the accompanying enemy fighters came into action as Messerschmitt 109s and Focke-Wulf 190s swooped down toward the trio of Swordfish. Some of the Luftwaffe managed to zip through the RAF fighter screen and attack Esmonde and his pair of following Swordfish. The enemy fighters lowered their flaps and undercarriages to keep them down to the speed of the sluggishly slow, torpedo-laden Swordfish. Esmonde lost contact with all his fighters after that.

Then almost at once, a Focke-Wulf picked out Esmonde's plane, loosed a stream of fire from its guns, and completely destroyed the upper main plane of the Swordfish. Esmonde and his crew spun into the sea, never to be seen again.

Now it became merely a matter of time before the others were hit, too. Carrying on at housetop or mast height, the next two received a raking from sea and air so devastating that it seemed superhuman to expect them to stay in the air. Hit after hit fireworked into the cumbersome, vulnerable biplanes. But still they flew on, and they managed to deliver their attacks before plunging into the sea close to the enemy armada. Five men of the two crews were later rescued. These wet and wounded survivors said that they had seen one of their torpedoes traveling well and thought it had scored a strike. They were all decorated.

So much for the fate of the first flight. The second one followed. Shattering salvos spat across the air toward them. An inferno of fire now focused on this pitiful little flight. Shells, fragments, tracer—all converged around them as they went into the attack close line astern. The last that any of the survivors saw of these three planes was when they had to take violent evasive action over the thickest part of the German destroyer screen. None were ever seen again.

So the price exacted was all six Swordfish and thirteen men. Eugene Esmonde's aim was to do what the fortunes of war had assigned to him to the fullest extent of his ability. It was not his fault that half a dozen Swordfish could never hope to sink what seemed to be nearly half of the German navy. He had done his duty. Whether the whole operation was worth undertaking in the first place remains open to serious question.

The Atlantic and the Pacific

The United States was rapidly getting used to the idea that this was going to be a world war. At sea this meant the Atlantic as well as the Pacific. And the U.S. Navy had to accept the inevitable truth that with every victory came a defeat. Not always from the enemy—sometimes from the weather.

In the Atlantic the old U.S. destroyer *Truxton* and the cargo ship *Pollux* both ran aground in an angry sea off the Newfoundland coast. Men made heroic efforts to swim lines ashore, but it was impossible to handle the ropes once oil from the stricken ships soaked the hemp. At last a breeches buoy was rigged to a ledge at sea level and the crew of one of the vessels began to swing ashore only a few feet above a raging sea and rocky beach.

The *Truxton* broke up almost as soon as she grounded, and the *Pollux* lasted little longer. Meanwhile, many of the men who did manage to reach the rocky ledge were swept cruelly into the sea again before help could come to them and get them up the cliff. So the life of a sailor at sea at war meant facing the elements as well as the enemy.

Another time it was a combination of enemy and weather. On the last day of February 1942, just before dawn, the World War I destroyer *Jacob Jones* was steaming off Cape May, New Jersey, and most of her crew slept soundly in their bunks. Outside, the wind lashed the sea into a swirling mass. Suddenly an enemy submarine surfaced in the predawn and fired a first torpedo toward the destroyer. It met the bow of the ship and exploded. Every man sleeping in the forward living compartment was killed outright, many without ever knowing they'd been hit. All those on duty on the bridge died as well. Chaos prevailed as the ship slowed, halted, and lowered in the water. The submarine circled ominously ahead of her and fired a second torpedo, which struck the stern and set off all the depth-charges. The destruction could hardly have been more complete. Everyone at both ends of the ship was dead as the *Jacob Jones* began to sink. Miraculously, though, eleven men still lived. They were all amidships and they struggled to get a ship's boat or a life-raft away before the ship sank and sucked them down. The submarine made off. The eleven men got clear and were picked up soon after dawn.

Across in the Pacific the Japanese threat extended from the eastern limits of Seattle and San Francisco to Sumatra and Java in the west. The enemy was preparing for a two-sided encirclement of Java. As the Japanese convoy assembled, all that the hard-pressed Dutch Admiral Doorman could do was gather his outnumbered and crippled fleet together and try to connect with only one convoy at a time. For five days he cruised with all the ships he had: the American cruiser *Houston*, without her after-turret; the old British heavy cruiser *Exeter;* the Australian light cruiser *Perth;* two Dutch cruisers; and ten destroyers, four American.

27 February: In the afternoon, this Allied fleet was at sea north of Surabaya when reconnaissance reported a major convoy halfway across the Java Sea. Doorman had just sent a signal by radio: Exhaustion point far exceeded. His men had been at their stations for nearly two days nonstop. But he veered round toward the nearing enemy.

1600: As the Allies approached, they found that the estimate of two enemy cruisers and four destroyers was hopelessly wrong. Eight or nine cruisers hove into sight, plus a dozen destroyers. The crippled Allied fleet formed into battle lines and at 1614 the action began. Fourteen miles away the Japanese fleet also lined up for battle. Four salvos skimmed across the sullen Java Sea at a range of 25,000 yards. *Houston* and *Exeter* were the only Allied ships able to engage at such a range, and they exchanged fire with the superior force of heavy warships. Doorman quickly realized that the enemy held an advantage at this distance, so he made a quarter-circle turn and reduced the range to 20,000 yards. Leaping into full fury, the opposing lines fired shell after shell while the echoes throbbed through the intervening air. Shells swapped in great

USCG cutter firing a depth-charge. Imperial War Museum

arcs. Black billowing smoke spread as a Japanese destroyer lay, hit and helpless.

1700: After three-quarters of an hour, the tempo quickened and the noise grew more deafening, as if someone had turned up the volume control. Suddenly, from the last ship in the enemy line, eight of the destroyers pounded through the sea, spoiling for a large-scale torpedo attack. Laying a smokescreen to cover their charge forward, the destroyers forged ahead, as HMS *Electra* and HMS *Jupiter* rushed right into the screen to meet the threat. *Electra* was never seen again. An underwater explosion of some sort disabled *Jupiter*, which sank four hours later near the Javanese coastline. A U.S. submarine sped in to rescue some of the fifty-three survivors.

Back at the battle scene, the Allied cruisers, including the *Houston*, took up the challenge. Closing the range still further, they hit one of the enemy's heavy cruisers, which was seen flaming. The *Perth* and the Dutch cruiser *Java* turned to try to stop the destroyers as they continued their headlong rush. An enemy cruiser fired her last gun as she staggered out of line after an Allied hit and scored a freak shot directly into the *Exeter*'s boiler room, bursting her main steam line. Now it was *Exeter*'s turn to leave the fighting line, and several small escorts went with her as protection. Defense was the key. A Dutch destroyer broke in half and sank with a grinding, grating roar.

The Allies withdrew; the Japanese did not follow. A bright tropic moon rose to silhouette the remaining ships. *Exeter* and the American destroyer headed for Surabaya to refuel after their long days of steaming. The rest aimed for a rendezvous off eastern Java. But around midnight successive sudden explosions reached them. Presumably hit by mines or submarines, the two Dutch cruisers never reached the appointed rendezvous, and were never heard of again. That was the harsh way of the Far East war at sea. Both the *Perth* and the *Houston* sustained some damage but made port by 0700 next morning. It had been a harrowing twelve hours or so.

28 February: After dark, the *Perth* and *Houston* steamed on through the Sunda Straits. Just before midnight the *Perth* signaled that they had come into contact with a force of enemy ships. There was no further word from either ship. So an Australian and an American cruiser were lost. On this same sad day, the destroyers *Exeter*, *Encounter*, and USS *Pope* were all presumed lost after trying to sneak out of Surabaya to safety. The

last signal came when the *Exeter* sent word that she had sighted three enemy cruisers steering straight toward them.

Only a destroyer squadron managed to get away to safety, leaving Java to the Japanese. Rapidly the enemy sped south through the Spice Islands, taking them as simply as they would pick the ripe fruit that abounded there. Ahead of them lay Australia—luring them on like a precious pearl.

Bomb Disposal
on a Submarine

In 1942 Lt. Peter Roberts was second-in-command of the British submarine *Thrasher*. After various adventures in the Mediterranean, she sailed to the waters off Crete and on 16 February followed several ships into Suda Bay. She fired torpedoes at a heavily escorted supply ship, which was almost certainly sunk. Then she spotted an enemy aircraft as she was at periscope depth and just diving.

About forty feet down, the crew heard two loud clonks. But they forgot these as the first of thirty-three depth-charges fizzed down in surrounding water and rocked the sub to its very bolts. At length the counterattack ended.

Thrasher remained submerged till night, then surfaced—still close to the enemy-held coast and in waters where antisubmarine patrols were active day and night. The crew always knew that the sub might have to crash-dive at any second while she was taking in fresh air and recharging her batteries. As she came up to the surface, *Thrasher* began to roll.

"What do you think it is?" Roberts asked the captain, Lt. H. S. Mackenzie.

But before an answer was forthcoming, the two senior officers heard a loud clang and a grating noise as of metal rubbing against metal.

"Sounds as if there's something up on deck causing it."

The conning tower was opened, and a rating reported a dark object rolling about on the deck casing.

"Someone will have to go and take a look. The only thing it can be, I suppose, is a bomb from that aircraft," Mackenzie said. The inevitable surge forward followed. All the crew within range rushed to volunteer.

"I'm the obvious one for this," Roberts said quickly. "You can't go," he added to Mackenzie.

"I'll go with you, sir," Petty Officer Thomas Gould piped up.

"Very well, you two," Mackenzie decided. "See what you can do, will you, but do be careful."

Gould was second coxswain in charge of the seamen on the upper deck, so he knew the shape of the submarine on the outside better than most of the others. He would need to because the night was fairly black and they could not risk torches. He was also quite an old hand in submarines, having joined them five years previously. A comparative veteran.

Mackenzie tapped his fingers on the periscope. He knew that, apart from the hazards to the crew of a bomb exploding, the effect on Roberts and Gould would certainly be fatal. More than this, if he had to crash-dive due to enemy action, he would have no alternative but to slam the conning tower shut and leave the two men on top to drown. Every single second counted in a crash-dive. Both Roberts and Gould knew that they would be between the casing and the hull, trapped as the

Removing a live bomb from HM Submarine Thrasher.

submarine dived, buried beneath an ever-growing volume of water pouring in through the perforations of the casing.

Roberts got up on deck first. Gould followed. It was cold. They accustomed their eyes to the dark but did not dare waste too much time. Every minute was a danger not only to themselves, but to the rest of the crew.

Roberts saw the bomb. Then he saw a second one.

"Two of them to tackle, P.O. Better get a couple of empty sacks and a rope." Gould reappeared shortly with them.

The first bomb lay fairly accessible on the perforated metal platform that was the casing. They crouched low over it. Just then the sub gave a lurch under the weight of the weapons. The bomb rolled from the port side of the casing over to starboard, where a rail stopped it. Between them, the two men slipped the sacks underneath the bomb and girdled it with the rope. Roberts eased past the weapon, then motioned the petty officer to do likewise. Roberts held the rope and handed a length of it to Gould. Together they dragged the bomb along the casing. Even on the sacks, it still seemed to grate and rub against the metal surface.

"How are you getting on?" Mackenzie called. "Tell me when you've got it to the stern and I'll send her full speed ahead."

The lieutenant and the petty officer pulled 200 pounds of high explosive to the stern of the submarine.

"Steady. I'll shout 'Now' when we're about to ditch it. Now."

Mackenzie sounded full speed ahead. The engines whined to life. A final heave and the bomb plopped into the water. No report. The sub had steamed clear just in case, though. That was the end of the first bomb. The second one was a different proposition.

"Not going to be so easy," Roberts summed up after peering down at it. The danger in dealing with it was going to be greater. It had penetrated the perforated casing and lay among the maze of pipes and torpedo tubes between the pressure hull and the casing. To reach it, Roberts and Gould had to wriggle their way through the hole that the bomb had made in the metal grating. The torn metal edges scratched their clothes as they eased themselves through on their stomachs. Now they were really in cramped quarters: trapped beneath the mesh of metal that was the platform, with a live bomb for company. Luckily, as both were submariners they did not suffer from claustrophobia.

Roberts did not recognize the type of bomb, so he slipped his hand in his pocket and managed to get out a notebook and pencil. Gould shone a dimmed-out torch on the fuses of the bomb while Roberts wrote their details down shakily.

"Right. Let's get on with shifting it." He stuffed the book back in his pocket. His elbow hit the deck. Still on their stomachs, they set about removing the bomb. Gould worked his way around to the after-side and pushed at it. Roberts pulled it from the forward-side.

The gap it had torn through the casing was not really enough to let them get it out that way. The nearest exit was a grating some twenty feet from the bomb's present position. Between this spot and the grating lay various projections that could not have been better designed as obstacles. Very slowly, Roberts pulled it. Suddenly it emitted a loud twang. They both gasped. A sound like a broken spring trying to make a contact of some sort. This could have been the reason why the bomb had not gone off, and why at any moment it might.

Gould pushed it gently, Roberts pulled again. Over a pipe it bumped. Once more the twang sounded loud in the middle-of-the-night air. Up top a seaman peered anxiously down and reported progress back to the commanding officer. Another effort and the bomb moved another foot. For half an hour now they had been working, yet there still lay seventeen feet to go to the grating, and still the bomb twanged regularly. It was a bomb with big tail-fins, and it measured some three and a half feet. Like its companion, it weighed about a couple of hundred pounds.

They could not use a rope on this one: just their bare hands, which slipped every so often around the smooth sides of the black metal bomb. Roberts gripped the hull with his knees as he pulled it along. Gould got it almost lovingly in his hands. And all the while the water washed against the side of the submarine. Still no moon shone; only the faintest glimmer of ghost light, and that even dulled by the casing above them.

"Not much further," Roberts whispered.

Three-quarters of an hour had elapsed since *Thrasher* surfaced. They got past the last obstacle.

"Right. Let's lift it now."

The seaman also lent a hand from aloft, and in a minute they appeared through the grating, groping with the bomb. Soon it was up on the casing. Roberts lifted himself up by his arms. Gould followed. The rest was fairly easy. They rolled the bomb gently along the same way as the first had gone. At the stern they gave the signal. The engines turned, the submarine shot ahead, the bomb dropped astern. They were safe. Roberts and Gould clanged their way back amidships, down the conning tower, and into control. A slap on the back from Mackenzie for both of them.

"Come and have a drink, you two. You deserve a double."

Thrasher eventually got back to base. Peter Roberts went on a commanding officer's qualifying course. But the course did not go well. He had chalked up only two and a half years in submarines, scarcely sufficient for a commanding officer. He failed the course and was out of submarines—a bitter blow at the time, especially to a man who had thought that what he and Gould did off Crete "wasn't very difficult." But the war was being waged and there was no time for second chances. Still, Roberts and Gould have gone down in naval history for their incredible bomb disposal on a submarine.

Enter the Rescue Ships

The rescue ships symbolized the Battle of the Atlantic. And not only Atlantic convoys, but Mediterranean and Russian convoys, too. They sailed with 797 convoys and saved 4,194 lives. Out of twenty-eight rescue ships, seven were sunk. One in four. These were the odds of survival at sea. Take a typical convoy from Canada in the middle year of the war. The rescue ship attached to this convoy was the *Melrose Abbey*. She was one of the lucky ones; she was not lost. And this was a typical March night. One night of one ship of one convoy of 800 convoys.

The usual winter weather had set in, with snow squalls gusting over the great waves. Soon after entering the dangerous mid-Atlantic area, the escort spotted a U-boat, but no attack developed until the next day. *Melrose Abbey* suddenly intercepted several signals, all saying, "Torpedoes passing convoy vessels."

It began at 1728 on 9 March, when *Melrose Abbey* spotted white distress rockets off the dark starboard bow. A radio message said tersely, "Ship no. 102 has been torpedoed." Capt. R. Good, the rescue ship's master, instinctively ordered speed to be reduced so that he could pass astern of the starboard columns of the convoy. The wind raked them strongly from the west, the sea ran high and was breaking angrily. In the spasmodic snow squalls, the early night seemed especially void, the convoy vulnerable.

The stricken ship was the American SS *Melantic*. The *Melrose Abbey* steered toward watery-white lights winking Morse-like on the surface. As she came close to them, the crew could see that the lights shone from empty rafts. Across the darkness sounded thin cries and then the first survivors were hoisted out of the sea. Then a light fireworked over the scene, giving the initial clue to the existence and position of a boat from the sunken ship. The *Melrose Abbey* drifted down toward it, but the survivors did not realize she was a rescue ship, and friendly, and so they frantically tried to row away. A poignant moment. One of countless others in the war at sea.

The *Melrose Abbey* hailed over the sea wastes: "Stand by to take a line," and then the boat was eventually brought alongside. Eleven men in the craft, including the captain who had been badly injured during abandoning ship. They helped him out of the lifeboat first and nine others followed, climbing up the rescue net with the crew's assistance.

While these ten men were being taken on board, the eleventh man attended to the line securing the boat. When it came to his turn to be saved, he felt too weak to manage. As soon as he got on the net, the violent lurching of the lifeboat and the rescue ship knocked him off again, and he was trapped between the two. Before anyone could grab him, his strength failed and he was swept away by the sea. The man was the second cook on the American vessel and this had been his very first voyage.

All the time that this rescue went on, more messages were pouring in. Ship no. 74 had been torpedoed. The weather was worsening, too, with sleet and snow freezing the scene into a nightmarish immobility. The survivors told the master that a second lifeboat had been launched from the *Melantic* and was thought to be badly waterlogged. At first it could not be located, but then came clues of occasionally flashing torchlight. Closing again, the crew glimpsed the familiar markers of red lifejacket lights, blinking, bobbing, dipping. These meant men. The *Melrose Abbey* circled around to windward and a boat loomed upon the starboard side, but before they could catch it, the sea swept it past them. All they could see was an outline, a shape, entirely waterlogged and scarcely floating at all, with men clutching, clinging inside and out.

When this first attempt failed, some of the men left the lifeboat, hoping to be rescued separately. The second time the boat came alongside, those nearest the rescue ship fingered at the life-link of the net. The half-sunk boat turned over completely and some of the pitiful figures were trapped underneath and lost. But some survived. It was impossible to retrieve them with lines in the frothing, foaming gloom, so

Survivors from a torpedoed vessel climbing scrambling nets to a rescue ship. Imperial War Museum

as a last resort the master ordered the rescue squad to open the gangway door in the forward well-deck. As the sea swept and scooped up the men, the crew grasped, grabbed, and held them from being washed away again. Ten men got aboard. Others were lost. Someone saw an arm fall from sight into the ocean. It seemed to symbolize this whole bloody struggle. The cruel sea at its cruelest.

From the survivors, the crew learned that the only way they had known whether or not the lifeboat was still there at all was by holding on to its grablines all the time. The rescuers had been fortunate to save even ten men with the seas streaming though the well-deck door at every roll. So the total tally was twenty-one saved out of a complement of forty-six. The American second officer confirmed that this lifeboat had contained the whole balance of his crew, so as soon as the nets were secured on the rail and the gangway shut to the sea, they sped from the spot in search of the next casualty: No. 74. Meanwhile, they heard that three more of the convoy had been hit.

2300: The same endless night. After *Melrose Abbey* steamed on the course of the convoy for some time, the screen escort signaled: "You have missed two boats. Turn and follow me. Can you make ten knots?"

In the heavy head seas, the 1,908-ton rescue ship could only just manage half that speed. Her top rate was thirteen knots in the ideal conditions of coastal waters for which she had been designed. Not March in the mid-Atlantic. The escort told them to steer north toward two lights. When they got there, one appeared to be attached to a derelict ship and the other one was a drifting lifebuoy lamp. Nothing else. No human beings. The time was then 0100 on 10 March.

0251: The rescue ship was on course again along convoy track when from the direction of the starboard bow came voices quite close. Disembodied. Then the escort signaled: "There is boat with survivors. Stop and pick them up."

Melrose Abbey turned to starboard and in so doing shipped a vast violent sea overall. The master brought her up into the wind to try to locate survivors. His only aid: an infrequent flash of light. Edging alongside, they found four men clinging to an upturned lifeboat. The guiding light came from a hand-held torch, clutched desperately by one of the men and showing only intermittently when the boat crested the waves. With the rescue lines, all the men were taken aboard and found in good condition, considering the ordeal of some hours since their ship had gone down. The time of man's survival in this sea was measurable more in minutes than in hours.

The rescue crew spotted a second small red lifejacket light, which slowly shaped itself into another lifeboat with one sole survivor. This boat also contained four bodies lying under water in the bottom of it. Both these boats came from the convoy ship no. 81, the Norwegian *Bonnieville*. This had been torpedoed at 2215 and carried the commodore and staff of the convoy. None of them were among the survivors.

At 0335 an R/T message from the local escort warned: "Do not leave the area. There are more boats in the vicinity." A corvette also searched the area, but no others could be found.

0530: A signal received from the screen escort said simply: "Rejoin convoy at utmost speed on course 094 degrees." The fresh gale blew snowflakes into numbing squalls and the seas into torrents. The engines raced and heaved, as if in protest. About 0615, they were steaming with the corvette and screen escort when yet another signal reached them: "Men sighted on rafts."

Captain Good spotted the raft from his bridge and, lowering his glasses, he ordered a turn to starboard. The crew passed noosed lines to the two occupants of the raft. One man was in reasonable shape, but the other was far gone through exposure and could not manage to clear the line. It had caught in his life-waistcoat light when he had groped to pass it over his second arm. The wild sea threw the raft at extreme angles, and during one of these the man was jerked backwards over the end of the raft and he caught one foot in its wooden framework. He lay with his head underwater, unable to move or to be helped until the next sea washed him clear.

The ropes from the rescue ship had slipped off by then, and so the Third Officer, Mr. Maclagan, tried to reach him by going overside on the net. Unhappily the man was swept away. As the ship rolled and the raft rose on a wave, the second man made a jump for the rail and the crew got him. They learned that the raft came from the British SS *Nailsea Court*, torpedoed eight hours earlier.

As the survivors were brought on board, the uninjured were rubbed down, given a stimulant, and soon settled comfortably. Those with injuries or exposure were treated and then put to bed in the sickbay. One of these was Captain Lane, of the SS *Melantic*, who had broken ribs.

The chief engineer of the *Melrose Abbey*, A. D. Low, said later,

> For 12 ½ hours, with mountainous seas running, Captain Good handled his ship in a manner which won the admiration of the entire ship's company. It is one of the wonders of the world when a Master gets praise from a chief engineer, but I, like the rest of the crew, feel his deeds should not pass unrecorded.

It took *Melrose Abbey* a further twenty-two hours to regain the convoy. During that time, one U-boat was rammed and sunk by the escort, while the rescue ship picked up many U-boat bearings. In the whole homeward voyage, *Melrose Abbey* secured 167 bearings of submarines.

That same winter, the rescue ship *Perth* left on her voyage no. 17 at 2005, with the Clyde section of a convoy. She slid past the friendly facade of Gourock boardinghouses on one side of the Clyde, with Helensburgh on the other. The air blitz had flattened a lot of the Clydeside towns of Greenock, Gourock, and others, all near Glasgow in Scotland. Then in no time the Clyde faded, but for how long? Would they ever see the gentle green slopes flanking its northern shoreline?

The *Perth* and the convoy had been shadowed for several days by a pack of U-boats and at about 2000 one night the Germans made the first attack. The very first salvo of torpedoes made contact with two ships simultaneously with the all-too-familiar sickening sound that was always worse at night. The *Perth* hurried to the Greek SS *Mount Taurus* first, as the vessel had gone down almost in seconds after the strike. Despite the suddenness, the *Perth* located two boats with a total of thirty-eight men at 2025. The time read 2145 before they had all been rescued. The master of the *Perth*, Ambrose Williamson, asked if all the Greek crew had been saved and was told that two still remained missing. He continued to search till 2300 without luck, so then sped after the convoy. It was not safe to be left behind for too long.

At 0230 the U-boats struck for a second time, sinking the SS *Parismina* and the SS *President Sergeant,* the commodore ship of the convoy. The survivors of the *Parismina* struck out with the instinct of men whose lives are at stake. They swam clear of the ship and then paddled about singly or in small groups. Some clawed their way into a lifeboat. All were almost at once smothered in oil fuel that coated them and dragged at them. The zero cold of the night sea hastened exposure and most of them could not do more than keep afloat or lie in the boat. When rescue came, their helplessness and greasy state made it all the harder to accomplish.

It took a whole hour to pick up one man on a small raft. He had no light and only the enfeebled note of his emergency whistle helped them pinpoint him. But somehow they saved him. Most of the fifty-four survivors had been in the water for some time. The crew of the *Perth* was upset to see that one man seemed dead on arrival aboard and all their efforts to revive him failed. They counted failures more than successes. Each single man meant something to them. Perhaps that was a difference between the Allies and the enemy.

When the SS *President Sergeant* was first hit at 0307 one of the crew—a Chinese man—dived from the deck on the order to abandon ship. He landed headfirst in the bottom of one of the lifeboats. Immediately he sustained a severe compound and depressed fracture of the skull, apart from a broken wrist and left-side paralysis. After searching among life-rafts and wreckage until 0545, the *Perth* then steamed for two boats showing flares. One of the men rescued from these boats was the Chinese man with the split skull.

Meanwhile, at 0700 the master sent in his motorboat to pick up ten men in the wreck of the French vessel, which was still afloat four hours after being hit. Among those saved was the commodore, J. N. Brooke, DSO, and the master of the ship, Capt. P. Dove. For the latter officer, it was his first trip since release from the infamous German prison ship *Altmark*.

Back on board the *Perth*, the ship's doctor, Surgeon Lt. J. F. Kelly, decided that he would have to operate at once to remove a piece of bone pressing on the Chinese man's brain, if he were to have a chance of saving the man. Amid all the confusion, Kelly asked Captain Williamson, "Can you try to nurse the ship as much as possible? I've got to go ahead with this operation."

All the sick-berth attendants were fully occupied with other survivors. The radio officer knew this and so he volunteered to help the doctor with the operation. Kelly went on with the preliminaries and then started the actual surgery. The *Perth* was steaming at a moderate pace, with consequent vibration of the engines through the deck of the operating room. Added to this was the interminable motion of the ship in a wintry ocean. By 1127 the operation had just reached its most critical point when the lookout gave the alarm: "Two periscopes to starboard." They were all too visible five points abaft the starboard beam at a range of about 200 yards. The order was almost automatic: "Open fire."

Every gun that could bear on that direction flared into life and the *Perth* pressed to full speed. The captain took masterly evasive action and, despite it being broad daylight, he managed to serpentine and elude both the U-boats. No one can know how Kelly went on with his delicate operation. Through the vibration, the routine rolling, and the frantic zigzag course forced on the ship, the brain surgery proceeded. None of the inevitable jolts proved fatal and the operation was concluded successfully.

The *Perth* then had on board 136 survivors and the master felt very vulnerable, as he was still some distance from the bulk of the convoy, with U-boats between him and it. Later that afternoon, they saw yet more U-boats, but so successfully did the corvette *Rose* screen her that the enemy could not close in to attack range. The *Perth* rejoined the rest of the convoy in the early hours of the next day, after an absence of twenty-four hours. The time was then 0245.

At 1100 they committed to the deep with due if simple religious ceremony, the body of George Campbell, engineer of the SS *President Sergeant*. The Chinese man was landed safely at Halifax, Nova Scotia, with every chance of complete recovery, thanks to the remarkable skill of Surgeon Lieutenant Kelly, later mentioned in dispatches. They had sailed from Scotland to New Scotland, Nova Scotia.

A week or so in Canada, and then the crew of the *Perth* found themselves at 2200 one night sailing with the Halifax section to join the main return convoy of over 100 ships. These Britain-bound cargoes were crucial to the country's survival. One week out of port, Ship no. 101 was torpedoed at 2325. *Empire Spencer* had been laden with a full cargo of aviation spirit for the war effort. The torpedo tore into her metal hull and hit the number one hold. By the time the *Perth* had raced to her, the midnight sky was illuminated by a floating inferno, literally from stem to stern. The crew of the *Perth* looked at her in awed silence.

Williamson said, "No one can be alive on board her."

But the *Perth* continued to close her, which was just as well. For the entire crew of the petrol tanker, minus only one man, was clinging to nets on the windward side of the ship. The *Perth* could not finally close until she had turned head on to the wind at about 0050, due to a sea simmering with burning oil. Then they rescued the whole crew, who were well, taking everything into account. Two men had severe burns, while another pair had leg injuries. The commodore of the convoy refused to believe at first that so many men could have been saved from such a situation—in the middle of a fire, in the middle of the night, in the middle of an ocean.

Soon after, the *Charles L.D.* received a direct hit and capsized. The men below decks had no chance of escape. Racing to the rescue the *Perth* searched the fragments of flotsam and sighted one man on a raft and another in a lifeboat. They then saw random blobs of men struggling.

The master at once decided, "We'll have to leave those two for the moment and get the others out of the water." They trawled up ten men, plucking them from an imminent grave. Then the *Perth* swung round to help the first two men. Though only minutes later, the pair were now utterly numbed. Even when a lifeline actually hit one, he made no move to try and catch hold of it. So the crew had to get on the raft and the lifeboat in turn and transfer the men. The one on the raft was the master of the *Charles L.D.* When he came round later after rest and treatment, he told the surgeon that he had not the vaguest recollection of being rescued. He recalled the *Perth* passing by them and heading for the men in the water. At that stage, he gave himself up for lost and drifted into unconsciousness. "Death from exposure seemed quite a pleasant one at the time," he said later.

This was just one two-way convoy voyage by the *Perth*. She sailed on sixty altogether and saved 455 lives during her four years, four months on active war service. Quite a record.

Submarine Attack
in Corfu Harbor

Tony Miers was one of the four greatest British submariners of World War II and he became a commander, RN, at the age of only thirty-five. By the end of 1941 he had taken part in sinking eleven enemy ships in the Mediterranean. Miers was in command of HM Submarine *Torbay* and on 31 December 1941 he became a full commander.

The familiar pattern of patrols and attacks on supply ships went on and on. Many times Miers admitted to feeling frightened while ominous explosions got nearer and louder to the *Torbay*. Yet he never betrayed any emotion, nor did his crew, who reacted to each attack with depth-charges by keeping the score of the number dropped on a board constructed for the purpose.

It was the third day of the third month of 1942. Patrolling at depth, Miers suddenly spotted a large convoy on the horizon escorted by three Italian destroyers.

"All out of range," he announced to Lt. Hugh Kidd. "But I'm going to trail 'em. May take some time, but it might be worthwhile."

The day drew on. Miers took *Torbay* along well behind the convoy. Hours dragged by.

"Land ahead," he said. "Looks like a harbor. Must be Corfu."

The convoy changed course slightly as the leading ship in the line reached the approach to the harbor. "They're going in. We'll follow later. Can't catch them otherwise, and we're not coming all this way for nothing. Don't you agree, Kidd?" The two-ringer nodded from the depths of the electrical equipment.

The long convoy wound its tortuous way into port, the destroyers bringing up the rear, tucking the supply ships in safely, as it were. Miers took the *Torbay* toward the harbor entrance. He saw further warships at anchor inside the harbor. "Not going to be easy," he concluded.

He observed the route the ships took, noticing that the only way in was through a single narrow channel. If he went off course, he risked grounding the sub or else striking a mine. With infinite care Miers steered his craft in slowly, along the channel. Through his periscope he could see the enemy ships getting steadily nearer. They were still a long way off, however, much too far to chance a torpedo with any high hope of recording a hit. No one spoke much in the sub as she crept gradually into the heart of the harbor.

Then they were in, surrounded on three and a half sides by enemy territory and enemy vessels. There were probably half a dozen destroyers, all within gun range.

Delicately, so as not to disturb the surface of the water more than necessary, he glided the periscope up and scanned the scene. The sun had set, and the outlines of the ships were already becoming hazy in the March evening air. He would have to wait for the next morning to make an attack, for the trip up-harbor had taken most of the afternoon and conditions were against a successful assault. Miers pulled the periscope down again and then took a walk beyond the control room to the messes. He ran into Engine Room Artificer Pinch.

"Hello, Pinch. Bit of an awkward spot to spend the night, under the water in some strange port? How long is it since you joined *Torbay*? You've got about the longest service in her, haven't you?"

"Two years ago this week, sir. March 1940, I first saw her, and we've been a few miles in her since then, sir."

"We certainly have," Miers agreed. "And there's many a patrol to be done after this one, so don't worry—we'll get back to base."

Miers wandered as far as he could, watching the ratings at rest and on watch. One was reading a book. Another was writing a letter home. Miers wondered where he would post it. A third sailor smiled at him as he passed the bunk. The night wore off in quietness; the engines had never turned above slow since the sub was its harbor, and they had been stopped for hours. Kidd came up to Miers. "Some bad news, sir. We'll have to recharge batteries. Never make it out of here tomorrow unless we do."

Miers could try to take the *Torbay* out of Corfu Harbor now, of course, and surface in safety, clear of the coast. But he preferred to stay.

"Right. Nothing for it, I suppose, but to take her up. I'll just take a look aloft first."

Miers screwed up his eyes to get them used to the darkness that he expected to see through the periscope. What he did see gave him a shock. It was almost as light as day. A brilliant full moon shone over the water, streaking the harbor with quicksilver shafts.

"It's as bright as broad daylight up there," he said, and then added, "Stand by to surface."

In slowest motion, the sub broke surface, the bows and conning tower parting the wavelets in two places. She slid to a full stop and a duty rating eased the two hatches open to take in some fresh air. There, on the surface, well within the foreign harbor, the submarine lay silhouetted for all to see, black as jet against the silver-grey sea.

"No talking. Nothing above a whisper," went the order.

Minutes ticked off. The batteries gained new life. Men sat around, still. The brass clock turned one revolution, then a second. Two hours *Torbay* had to stay surfaced. If just one lookout spotted her, she could not escape destruction, but no one did. The spring moon moved behind a cloud after the first hour, then came out again and the light seemed more vivid than ever. They heard in the distance some sailors changing watch at the dead of night.

"How much longer?" Miers asked.

"Batteries charged," came back the welcome assurance.

"Well, let's get below again as quick as we can."

The hatches were closed carefully, quietly. The engines turned over scarcely above a murmur; the men breathed more freely and with better air; and the long metallic craft vanished underwater as mysteriously as she had risen a couple of hours earlier. Morning came.

"Periscope depth."

Miers grabbed the instrument eagerly and swung it round to get a look at the shipping in full daylight.

"Convoy all gone," he told Kidd. "But there are a couple of supply ships left over there—and one of the destroyers. The others seem to have flitted. Must have been after we submerged. Right. Stand by to attack."

The engines moved at a more urgent pace. The sub swung forward. Miers pressed her home fairly close to the anchorages and, on a swinging turn, smacked a torpedo at each of the three ships in ultra-rapid succession. Her periscope traced an arc of foam in the glassy-calm harbor water. As the *Torbay* completed her turn, or even earlier, both supply ships exploded amidships with a shatter.

Miers took the sub down deep and she almost touched bottom. She lay there for half an hour. At that stage, he did not know that he had sunk the two supply ships and missed the destroyer. He brought them up to periscope depth again and ran right among some small boats all searching frantically for *Torbay*. He crash-dived deep as depth-charges volleyed down after the sub. The crew kept count. Ten, twenty, forty. Miers made for the nearest exit from the harbor, in a straight line and very fast, at periscope depth to guide them through.

"Nearly at the end of the channel." Then: "Crash dive."

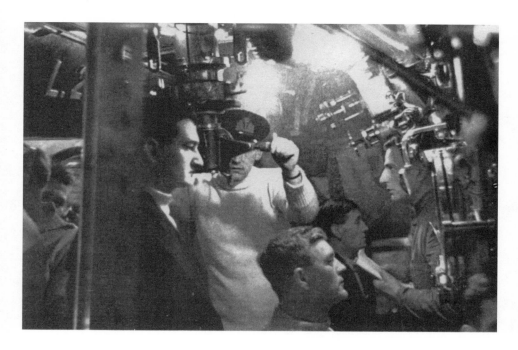

At the periscope, the captain prepares to attack. The team is grouped around him, plotting relative positions of submarine and quarry. Imperial War Museum

Into the periscope at the shortest possible range headed a patrol vessel, only yards from the sub's bow. For the second time, the crash-dive came off. He had thwarted the antisub craft hovering all along the long exit channel and the air patrol overhead. It was mid-morning when Miers reached open water once more, seventeen hours after he had led the *Torbay* into the enemy enclosure.

The Battle of the Coral Sea

Back to the Pacific. Another day and another battle. This time it was the Battle of the Coral Sea, fought among the reefs off the northeast coast of Australia. The war was getting close to that country. By March 1942 the Japanese had concentrated transport and combatant ships in New Guinea ports, apparently preparing to attack Port Moresby on the south side of that island.

10 March: An Allied Pacific fleet task force blasted the two New Guinea ports of Salamaua and Lae, sinking or damaging more than twenty enemy ships gathered there. This interruption of their plans proved so successful that it delayed any attempt to advance south by sea for two months. During April U.S. Army planes spotted Japanese transports gathering again for a projected advance into the Solomon and Louisiade Islands. In early May these moves were actually made, bases seized, and the whole north of the Coral Sea opened to enemy aircraft reconnaissance.

3 May: A task force, including the massive carriers *Yorktown* and *Lexington*, patrolled in the Coral Sea. Reconnaissance planes from the force suddenly spotted part of the Japanese invasion group at anchor around the harbor of Tulagi in the Solomons. But between the carrier force and the enemy lay a slight obstacle—the island of Guadalcanal, which extended seventy miles by fifty miles with peaks of 6,000 feet.

It was thought that the enemy would scarcely be contemplating an air attack right over the top of the island, so a strategy was developed: In one night, the *Lexington* could run close to the rear of Guadalcanal and then at dawn send its planes down over Tulagi. *Yorktown* would protect the rear and supply reinforcements. No time was wasted and the plan was accepted. *Lexington* steamed as silently as possible through the night, and before dawn on 4 May the floating airfield turned into the wind to launch its planes for the 120-mile flight to Tulagi.

0615: "Battle Stations."

The terse order sounded through every deck of the great ship. A shiver of suppressed excitement ran among the men. No one quite knew what might happen. The Navy fliers were right in the forefront of the Pacific war. The first waves of bombers and torpedo planes hurtled off the flight deck. They dipped imperceptibly at the end of the carrier before gaining power and climbing away. Scout planes followed them, scouring to see that there were no Japanese carriers on this side of Guadalcanal. As the bombers thundered over the wild jungle territory of the island, the scout planes were back by their side again. Up over the lower mountains now, and at the increased altitude, the silver of the aircraft glinted for a moment in the rising sun while the earth below still lay in shadow.

Once they were beyond the peaks, the torpedo planes pushed their noses down in a dive to water level for the final miles to the harbor and the unsuspecting transports. The raid was well synchronized. As the torpedo planes arrived, the bombers began their dive from high above. A 20,000-ton troopship sank. Big bombs plunged and plowed into the decks of a cruiser. Two destroyers turned over on their sides and sank. A seaplane tender somehow sneaked out of harbor. Although hit, it got away, leaving a trail of oil on the water. Three more ships down now. The pilots headed for home and another load of bombs or torpedoes. Returning to Tulagi they found some surviving ships trying to escape. They fanned out overhead and chased several, hitting or sinking them.

Bombers alone made the third raid. This time they sank an already damaged destroyer and dive-bombed the rest of the enemy still afloat within the harbor. Only fifty feet above the waterline, they flew back and forth, actually unable to find targets for their last bombs. So they veered off to sea again, where they located a limping destroyer. The Navy planes came down low, systematically shot her up, and left her with steam and smoke pouring out of her hatches and oil bleeding from ragged holes in her hull. A reply to Pearl.

Back aboard the *Lexington,* the duty officer counted the aircraft in and made notes. They were three planes short, but two of the crews had been picked up safely. So the human loss was one crew. The air attack had sunk or damaged fourteen out of the fifteen main Japanese ships found at Tulagi. It could have almost been called annihilation.

That night, the *Lexington* was far from Guadalcanal, refueling with the rest of the force. Next morning, the ships pushed into the Coral Sea, where Army bombers had found an enemy fleet in the Louisiade Archipelago. Scouts reported a large enemy force heading south by east. The carriers turned and sped through the night. At dawn they found the main body of this enemy naval force: a carrier, three cruisers, six destroyers. A major group.

Flying low enough to get a good degree of accuracy, despite ceaseless fire from ack-ack guns, the aircraft recorded fifteen bomb hits on the new Japanese carrier *Ryukaku.* Coming in lower still, with enemy guns trained almost horizontally at them, other planes pressed home torpedo thrusts on the same carrier.

From every side the weapons embedded themselves into the hull of the doomed carrier. She was just turning into the wind to launch her fighters as the blasts of twenty-five bomb and torpedo explosions finished her off. With water cascading through ten torpedo holes, and her deck ripped by bombs, she sank in a few minutes, dragging most of her planes down with her and hundreds of Japanese sailors.

The same afternoon enemy aircraft spotted two American ships alone in the Coral Sea: the destroyer *Sims* and tanker *Neosho.* They sank the *Sims* and caused such damage to the *Neosho* that she sank several days later. The next day, 8 May, the enemy secured their one major success in the Battle of the Coral Sea: the destruction of the famous aircraft carrier *Lexington.*

One of the two largest carriers in the world, *Lexington* normally carried 1,899 officers and men and had room for ninety aircraft. She never saw the carriers that launched the planes that were to attack her. While American aircraft were away still attacking the enemy the Japanese found the *Lexington.* Most of her planes were missing. The commander of the *Lexington* takes up the story:

At dawn 8 May our escorting forces went out and finally located two Japanese aircraft carriers and several other enemy ships, hidden in a rain squall about 200 miles away.

It was evident to us our forces and the enemy had contacted each other at about the same time, however, so we prepared for attack as we sent two raiding squadrons out.

We found one of the Japs, the *Sho Kaku,* about 1100, and pounded it with heavy 1,000-pound bombs and hit it with five torpedoes. Our planes left her settling fast, with flames and smoke rising nearly 1,000 feet in the air.

Thirteen minutes later they came at each of our carriers with 54 planes. We shot down 40 of their 108 planes, but not before they had dropped bombs and torpedoes. We counted 11 torpedo wakes in our direction. We avoided all but two. The Jap dive bombers got us with three bombs, one of heavy caliber. There were a lot of close misses, and many men on the flight deck were killed by fragments.

The colossal carrier was being handled with superb skill to have been hit by only two torpedoes, but they might yet be enough to sink her. Noon now, and a hot tropic sun shone down on the scene. Yeoman Third Class Charles Dorton continues the chronicle of these hours:

The pilots of the torpedo planes were nervous. You could see them as they swept in toward the ship through our machine-gun fire. They're lousy shots. Things were happening fast. Anti-aircraft racket was awful. The sky was filled with lead. One Jap torpedo plane was hit by our machine-gun when it was about 200 yards away and only about 60 feet above the water. The Jap didn't have a chance to launch his fish, but turned into a slow barrel-roll and kept coming right at us. He crashed into the ship near the port forward gun battery. Our boys quickly shoved the wreck off into the water before it could catch fire and explode the torpedo.

The rest of the enemy aircraft veered off and vanished into the sun. But their work was not finished. On the *Lexington* they left men grim and grimy, and the carrier with flames leaping through the mess decks. Now came the next fight, against the fires. Every available crewmember played water over them. Meanwhile, the carrier was on a six-degree list. The damage-control squads worked feverishly to get the upper hand, and after half an hour their officer reported that three of the four fires were being extinguished. The fourth one still smoldered. The limited list was righted, and things looked more hopeful to the captain. The *Lexington* could increase speed, which had been reduced to minimize the risk of the fires spreading further. She was once more on an even keel.

Five minutes later she accelerated steadily to 20 knots, when the entire vessel shuddered under a blast. A major internal explosion wrecked much of the below-deck area. Fires broke out in fresh places and spread toward the flight deck. And the ship's entire communication system broke down.

The fire mains, carrying the water pressure, were severed, and it became difficult to fight the conflagration. Flames licked through the hangar deck and reached a store of ammunition forward. This went off with dreadful regularity every few minutes through the afternoon. The next stage came when the captain had to order the hangar deck to be abandoned. Despite intense heat blistering the bulkhead paint, the crew below decks stuck gamely to their posts, fighting a losing battle.

"Come up on deck."

The order was delayed as long as possible, but eventually the fire made it inevitable. And as soon as they trooped up, ashen-faced and sweating, the telephone system failed, too. Another minute or two and the engineers would never have come out at all.

It was five hours now since the fury of that eruption in the bowels of the *Lexington*. Most of the firefighting gear was gone; all her communications were out of action; the steering gear had been smashed; and the fires were beyond control. Fortunately, the *Lexington* was not on her own. Destroyers waited alongside. Nothing more could be done except to transfer the wounded from the burning carrier to the safety of the smaller ships. As the sun set, all the carrier's machinery was out of use, but the crew never panicked. From the nearby vessels, none of the midships of the carrier could be seen at all. Only a grey-black haze of smoke, and men staggering away from it toward bow or stern.

The destroyers were waiting to pick up the crew, but the men did not want to go. Some of them had served for years on the *Lexington* and she meant home to them—a feeling that cannot be conveyed, only felt.

Last stage in the destruction of the Lexington.
*All hands have abandoned ship. Not one man
was lost.* Imperial War Museum

"Abandon ship," the captain ordered reluctantly.

The men took the order in stride. Some tossed coins to see who would go first. Others swapped stories. Two gobs curled up and went to sleep while waiting orders to leave. Ice cream was distributed from the ship's stores. Some men filled their hats with it when they went over the side.

Some men slid down lines to waiting boats. Others crawled aboard life-rafts and rubber boats, calmly arranging their shoes in a neat row on the deck before abandoning ship. And still others jumped into the warm sea, as sailors from the adjacent ships took pictures of the hundreds of men dotted on the ropes or in the water.

Over a hundred men had already been lost in the earlier action. But during the actual abandoning not one man lost his life. True to tradition, Capt. F. C. Sherman was the last to leave the *Lexington,* yet even now the final act had not been seen. As Sherman prepared to slide down his rope, the torpedo warhead locker exploded. Debris flew high into the air, but the captain ducked under the edge of the deck and went hand over hand down the rope. Despite the loss of the *Lexington,* Coral Sea added up to a victory. The Midway battle still lay ahead.

June — December 1942

Convoy PQ17

Atlantic convoys brought supplies from North America to Britain. Russian convoys meant shipping supplies from Britain to Russia. PQ17 was one of the most vital of all. So important was its scope and so vast its scale that three rescue ships were assigned instead of the usual one or two: *Rathlin, Zamalek,* and *Zaafaran.* One of these did not survive. Each had a distinguished rescue record, the *Rathlin* sailing on a total of sixty convoys and saving 634 survivors.

The starting date of this historic convoy was 24 June 1942. *Zamalek* and *Rathlin* cleared the boom defense at Cloch Point by 0700, and three days later to the hour they were in Iceland, where bunkers were topped up, ready for the rest of the voyage. PQ17 sailed at noon on 29 June with their destination Archangel. Nothing lay between them but hundreds of miles of ice-ridden water, laced with the hazards of enemy vessels, both surface and submarine. As the last day of the month dawned, icy fog laid waste to the seascape, broken only by an occasional clearer patch. By 1350 the *Zamalek* had taken up her station, no. 95, in Convoy PQ17. To her master, Capt. Owen C. Morris, the letters and number meant nothing. They soon would.

For a while on 1 July, visibility eased to half a mile, allowing a twin-engine Focke-Wulf to fly over the convoy. So they had been spotted. It was an eerie sensation to hear the faint aircraft drone unseen amid intermittent banks of fog. By 2000 that evening the fog had closed in again: good as protection but bad for navigation in those desolate seas. At this time, night virtually did not exist, and when a squadron of German bombers flew overhead at 2120 the light was still quite strong.

"Action Stations." Crews heard the order for the first time.

2 July, 1200: Clearance of the weather coincided with the appearance of enemy aircraft. Two hours later a trio of aircraft circled the convoy, trying to edge nearer, but accurate gunfire, coupled with the rapid hoisting of barrage balloons at 500 feet, kept them away.

1645: Six torpedo-carrying and bombing Heinkels pressed in low. Nothing hit the *Zamalek,* which had been singled out, but the crew felt the effect of machine guns spraying the ship. Three gunners were wounded, one on the Bofors gun and two on midship gunpit. All recovered, but one lost an eye.

The *Zaafaran* crew spotted four Heinkel 115s approaching soon after 1700 and within half an hour they began to attack. They flew toward the convoy, two from each quarter port and starboard. One was angling for a thrust on a Russian tanker, plodding vulnerably along, but just before he seemed right and ripe to drop his torpedoes, the four-inch gun of the rescue ship scored a direct hit. They saw their shell explode under his engine and force the machine upwards against the nature of gravity. It rose, stopped, started to fall, careered, and then crashed into the sea on the far side of the convoy. A British destroyer at once altered course to try to rescue the crew of the enemy aircraft, but before they could reach it another Heinkel 115 made a smart landing on the surface, picked up the German aviators, and flew off.

By 1800 another attack had begun, but once more the enemy sustained the loss of an aircraft. A shell shot the floats off and it wobbled erratically into the sea. The escorts also sank a U-boat. So PQ17 had to face danger from three sources: sea level with its ice and fog; aircraft above them; and U-boats below them. During the night of 2–3 July, the fog shrouded all 100-odd ships but it soon lifted. At 1006 the shadowing enemy aircraft came into the binoculars of Capt. C. K. McGowan, master of the *Zaafaran.* They circled the convoy like vultures, watching, waiting, just out of gun range. And, like birds of prey, they flew on awaiting a kill.

At 1700 the *Zaafaran* passed a four-engine flying boat, probably a Sunderland, static on the sea, covered with ice, and frozen into immobility. They never solved the mystery of this aircraft. Then they had the welcome company of a Walrus scout aircraft, but the attacks went on, parried only by powerful convoy outbursts from the guns. As well as frequent fog patches, they now had to contend with icebergs.

At 0259 on 4 July, American Independence Day began with a bang, but not of celebration. Only in these latitudes could a torpedo-bomber operate at such an apparently impossible hour. The *Zamalek* spotted enemy aircraft in and out of low white clouds and actually saw torpedoes drop into the sea off the starboard bow. The vessels ahead of her took violent avoiding action, but one of the torpedoes struck Ship no. 81 and lit up the gloom. *Zamalek* steamed to her aid. The order to abandon ship was given at once and the U.S. cargo boat, the *Christopher Newport*, started to sink. The sea had already streamed into her engine room; her steering had utterly gone; and three men in the engine room were trapped and drowned by the insurgence. *Zamalek* picked up forty-

Anglo-American cooperation: American cruiser Wichita *and* HMS London *formed covering force for Convoy PQ17, together with* USS Tuscaloosa *and* HMS Norfolk. *Imperial War Museum*

seven survivors from her lifeboats and rejoined the rest of the convoy at 0450. The summer sky was lightening by the minute.

Noon: Several aircraft still circled the convoy and their numbers gradually grew into a sizable flock. By afternoon between twenty and twenty-five Heinkels growled and throbbed nearer. Livid gunfire spat around the sky like so many tongues of snakes. Two dozen aircraft, each carrying three torpedoes. Every single weapon was dropped. The sea seemed alive with torpedoes all around them. Seventy or more monsters switchbacked in the general direction of various vessels of the convoy.

Meanwhile, at 1820 the *Zaafaran* first met the air attack. Twenty-five Heinkels, again each with three torpedoes, joined the aircraft already on the spot and they all put their noses down and snorted into the onslaught. The leader of the formation flew a mile or more ahead of the rest. They came in at an amazing altitude of thirty feet above the Arctic surface.

The second that the leader took shape in the gunsights of the ship, the Oerlikon gun crew on the *Zaafaran* opened fire and shot him straight into the sea. The rest watched aghast as their leader was lost and then climbed rapidly to 150–200 feet before releasing their torpedoes. Captain McGowan made a mental note of eighty-seven torpedoes dropped. Many fell half a mile from the starboard quarter, while others were released up to three miles distant.

Captain Morris on the *Zamalek* swung the helm hard over and raised engine speed in a frantic effort to evade their lethal tracery. The rescue ship's guns registered hits. As the attack developed the *Rathlin* had a good view from the rear of the convoy. At times enemy bombers flew in low, mere cables' lengths away from the vessel. It was not a pleasant sensation seeing the enemy aiming straight for them almost at eye level. Being in the thick of the convoy's own barrage, the *Rathlin* ran the risk of a hit from the shells of her fellow ships, but luckily their aim remained good.

The visual and aural intensity of the barrage forced most of the aircraft to veer off, but not before they dropped their torpedoes. Some exploded prematurely on striking the water, while a few went in the wrong direction altogether. Capt. A. Banning of the *Rathlin* said he saw some sixty of them in the water at the same instant. Two whirred close to the ship, but he managed to anticipate their course in time. However, they hit two ships on her port quarter instead.

The *Rathlin* rushed in to rescue the crews from these ships, the American SS *William Hooper* and the British SS *Navarino. Rathlin* stopped in a position that could scarcely have been more dangerous but completed the humanitarian operation without being hit.

At least three aircraft were shot down and three ships had been hit. The third was the Russian tanker *Azeboidsan,* struck by bombs. Later on she was able to proceed and rejoin the convoy, but in the heat of the moment some of her crew had already left her. Some had jumped overboard, others been blown there by the blast. The *Zaafaran* swept in to save them.

1930: The *Zamalek* took on board ten survivors from a raft, while its motorboat snatched one man from the sea. He was still alive, fortunate in these extreme latitudes. That night all three rescue ships received orders to scatter, as it was known that the German battleship *Tirpitz* was probably heading for the convoy.

2050: *Zamalek* rejoined the convoy to receive a similar signal: "Scatter and proceed to port of destination independently." She pushed up engines and with *Zaafaran* started to put as many nautical miles as clockable between their present position and the immediate future. But the respite was short-lived.

5 July, 0400: *Zamalek* sighted five merchant ships on the horizon. Even at that hour visibility was incredibly clear. None of them seemed likely to remain undetected for long, as the light, luminous in its quality, strengthened hourly. The *Zamalek* encountered the British sloop *J86,* which invited her to join the fleet oiler SS *Aldersdale* and the *Ocean Freedom.* They felt fractionally more secure as a quartet.

1100: Six Junkers attacked the *Zaafaran.* The nearest friendly ships were some twelve miles off, so no help could be expected. The Junkers droned in from 3,000 feet or so, dropping bombs. Visibility had stayed very good and the sea looked like gently beaten silver, hammered only by the lightest of airs. Down through this air screeched the bombs, in a terrifying trailer of what was to come. Some bombs churned up the calm waters as close as 100 yards from the rescue ship. So they survived—for a while, anyway.

1530: *Zamalek* came under a pulverizingly powerful attack from more Junkers dive-bombers. They hit *Aldersdale* and scored several near-misses on both *Zamalek* and *Ocean Freedom.* The bombers made their familiar spine-shivering noise as they dived. *Zamalek* saw a ship nine miles away disintegrate. The rescue ship turned to help her, but she left the horizon long before they could cover the distance. The time was 1540 and her bows piled high in death-throes before settling and vanishing forever. PQ17 was still not at its nadir.

The *Zaafaran's* position was charted as 75°03,N, 42°34,E: deep in the icy fastnesses of the Barents Sea and by a coincidence exactly due north of their destination of Archangel. An enemy aircraft stole in from starboard to port bow and dropped a trio of bombs. This was typical of what happened all the way along the track toward their goal. No crew really knew what was going on elsewhere, or what would happen to themselves from one minute to the next. For days and nights on end they went virtually without sleep.

The first of this stick of bombs fell fifty feet from the *Zaafaran*. The second struck the starboard side below the waterline in the after-end of the engine room, piercing the bulkhead. The third one landed ten feet off the port side. The second bomb did the damage, like a fatal bullet wound in a human body. The *Zaafaran* took a list to starboard while the effects of the bomb were carrying away the after-bulkhead. She started to settle by the stern. The engine room, stokehold, and after-hold were all flooded and Captain McGowan expected the ship to make a fatal move at any moment. He had to take decisions at a rate of one per second, as the water weighted the vessel increasingly all the time.

"No. 3 lifeboat blown away, sir," someone shouted to him. No. 4 lifeboat, too, was useless, having been blown ten or more feet inboard and smashed with the ease of a boy breaking a wooden toy boat.

McGowan was left with the prospect of saving ninety-eight souls with one small lifeboat, a motor lifeboat, and a number of rafts. They could not expect a rescue ship to come to *their* aid. They put three injured men and the survivors from the *Navarino* into the power boat and three of the *Zaafaran* crew into the lifeboat. The other crew then took to the rafts. The bomb had doomed her at 1530. Everyone was clear of the ship at 1537. She sank at 1538. She went down very quickly, very quietly, without any suction, so at least no one was lost in an undertow.

The *Zaafaran* was seen to sink by the *Atlantic*. Perhaps rescue might be on hand after all. At 1600 *Zamalek* signaled to the antiaircraft ship HMS *Palomares* requesting protection while she plowed forward to pick

up survivors. *Palomares* covered her as far as she could, with the air attacks still persisting nonstop. *Zamalek* had to beat off with bullets and
shells any stray aircraft that got through.

By 1630 she had come alongside the boats and rafts. It was only then
that the rescuers realized that the crew below were off her sister rescue
ship. By 1703 she had transferred all survivors safely aboard, a total of
ninety-seven men including one casualty: thirty-eight of these were the
survivors collected by *Zaafaran* from the previous sinkings. Every man
on board the *Zaafaran* was saved except for a single rating who had
been killed by wreckage when the ship went down. One of the survivors was a galley boy from another sunken ship who had just been cel-
ebrating his sixteenth birthday. This boy had also been on a vessel torpedoed only a month or two earlier in Convoy PQ15. At 1705 the
Zamalek steamed from the spot with escorts and *Ocean Freedom.*

After PQ17 Captain McGowan of the sunken *Zaafaran* took command of another rescue ship, *St. Sunnivia,* and was lost on her first voyage with all her ship's company.

6 July: In company with four escorts and a cargo ship on a course of
120 degrees, the *Zamalek*'s milk-white bow-wave churned for Matokhin
at thirteen knots. By 0900 they saw land ahead. It was not a mirage and
they entered the straits, dropping anchor in time for lunch. Other merchantmen and escorts came in during the rest of the day, but it was no more
than a respite to consider their next move.

Meanwhile, the *Rathlin* found herself with one antiaircraft ship and
a couple of corvettes, but as soon as booming notes of gunfire and aircraft rumbled across the air they had to leave her. The *Rathlin* arrowed
on north until she was right among the icefields and icebergs. Here she
met an American vessel, the SS *Bellingham,* and they paired up to head
for the White Sea. The U.S. ship was suddenly struck by a torpedo. They
could not tell whether it came from an aircraft or a U-boat. But by one
of those fortunate flukes that made war far beyond fiction, the weapon
failed to go off. It only made a dome-shaped dent near the ship's engine room and she was able to proceed. Later that day, the *Rathlin* transferred a sick man from the *Bellingham* for treatment in the hospital.

In the evening, a single FW aircraft caught sight of the two ships.
Its high screeching sound warned the crews that the enemy had started
to dive down on the Americans. But the *Rathlin* happened to be well
placed to put up an accurate shell-spray to umbrella the merchantman.

The concentration of fire forced the enemy to swerve in mid-dive and the two bombs intended for the *Bellingham* just missed the mark.

In the very mistaken belief that the little *Rathlin*, just 1,599 tons gross, would be easy meat, the FW had the temerity to fly over quite low toward her. A brief burst from the ship's guns caused the bomber to be blown out of the Arctic air. True to her tradition of saving lives wherever possible—no matter whose—the *Rathlin* turned to investigate the wreck of the aircraft, still floating on the surface. But they found all five occupants dead. The *Rathlin* and *Bellingham* chased on for Archangel. For them the worst was over.

But not for the *Zamalek*.

7 July, 1100: After a hurried conference on the commodore's ship, the convoy re-formed with six merchantmen and eleven escorts. A trawler was appointed as a rescue ship, since by this time *Zamalek* had 154 survivors on board. Out at sea fog descended densely, five miles from the jagged northern coastline. Cover for the convoy but dangerous for its navigation. With ice-packs thrown in just as a bonus.

8 July: Amid eye-watering white fog prevailing all day, they met a heavy ice-pack. The master gave the order: "Full astern."

1500: Large ice floes hemmed them on all sides as they tried to extricate themselves. They got clear of that pack by 1540. But they were

Destroyer USS Wainwright *successfully broke up an air attack on PQ17 on 4 July 1942.* Imperial War Museum

still separate amid fog and ice. Whistles from other ships warned them of relative positions.

2130: They set a course of 240 degrees.

2145: They sighted a heavy ice-pack.

"Engines full astern." That rare order again.

2147: They struck the pack end-on. The damage was only slight and five minutes later they wriggled the stern clear of the ice. But the situation was nasty, with the danger of becoming immobile and a tempting target.

2200: They signaled to the corvette *La Malaouin,* who collected another ship and led them to the escort commodore. The weather and the ice eased and within an hour they joined up, setting a fresh course to skirt the ice-field. But they were all still a mere fifteen degrees or less from the North Pole, not a nice region for waging war on the scale of the totality of PQ17. 9 July now. The *Rathlin* berthed in the bleak surroundings of Archangel, yet her crew breathed an almost audible sigh of relief for this landfall. She was the very first ship of the historic convoy to arrive in North Russia.

Throughout that day, the *Zamalek* was still very much at sea, amid ice and fog. Then, at 1845, the curtains parted, the weather lifted, revealing an enemy U-boat dead astern about six miles. Aircraft were in sight as well. And again the sickening frequency-changing note of the dive-bombers, followed by the nerve-baring noise of the bursts themselves. Exploding on water or superstructure. The *Zamalek* saw several drop only yards away. That cauldron in the sea could have meant death if it had hit the ship. *El Capitan* got a near-miss, and at 2210 *Housier* had to be abandoned. This meant more work for *Zamalek.* Rescue was hazardous enough with only the sea to fight. Now they had to fend off dive-bombers, returning like flies despite being swatted away repeatedly. Attacks were either starting, happening, or ending. A seamless cycle.

The *Zamalek*'s guns kept on firing to keep the enemy flying high. Once they broke through to a low-level bomb run, the ship might well be finished. The captain tried to anticipate them with masterly evasive action, the bow curving great arcs in the Arctic as the course changed crazily. And above them, the aircraft actually regrouped, weaving to counteract this evasion. It became like giant three-dimensional chess. One near-hit fell twenty feet from the stern. As the bomb erupted a huge spray of water swamped everyone. Those on the bridge could easily have drowned. The standard compass on the monkey island was unshipped. Down in the engine room, the keeps of the propeller shafts were broken and practically all the electric lights smashed.

Yet the twelve-pounder guns under the charge of Third Officer J. Black fired and fired, his men gritting teeth, while Sgt. F. Leach and his Bofors gun crew hit several planes. At about this time, a few of the survivors on board panicked and launched one of the large life-rafts, certain that the ship must have only minutes to live. The crew prevented them from jumping overboard to get on it. Added to all this, the master and crew knew too well that the *Zamalek* had on board fifty tons of phosphorous bombs destined for Russia. They were very aware that a hit on the ship would be doubly disastrous.

Into another day or night now—they seemed to merge. 10 July, 0045. And another near-miss, as bombs fell barely twenty feet off the starboard side. The engines were jolted to a grinding pause and the dynamo bedplate broke. Lights were out yet again, but although the engine room remained in oblivion, the chief engineer somehow managed to get the pistons moving in ten minutes. The oil pipe to the settling tank had been severed by the blast. The commodore of the convoy peered through the twilight from his own ship and frequently thought that the *Zamalek* had gone. Again and again bomb splashes fountained up, engulfing and hiding her, but every time she nosed through it all with her guns still on the boil. Enemy aircraft still encircled the convoy—now five escorts plus the *Zamalek*.

0200: A friendly aircraft got through to them and then the air attacks ended. Gaunt, grey-faced men blinked at the outline of Iokanka anchorage. They were safe. Not really. An hour later they hove up and put to sea once more. Three more hours and this time dive-bombers made their fittingly final raid. There were no more hits.

11 July, 1605: The *Zamalek* berthed alongside Archangel, landing her eighty survivors. The crew of seventy-four stayed on board, shattered into silence by the experiences endured for a week and more. Losses had been severe on PQ17, yet most of the ships had gotten through to this forsaken spot with supplies for Russia. For those who lived, perhaps the name of Archangel was their salvation. Yet even then there was no peace for the crews. Coal and food both ran critically short and the enemy bombed the port. In one raid the British naval stores were struck.

Nine weeks later and the return convoy set sail, including both the *Zamalek* and *Rathlin*. So they had to face it all again. It seemed too much to expect men to endure. "Cot" cases—survivors from the outward convoy—were put on board the *Rathlin* for transport and treatment; forty-four other survivors also sailed with them, including three Russian women. The voyage began on 13 September. This time, though, they had the boon of six hours' darkness, compared with the near-total daylight on the summer outward passage.

One week later, the minesweeper HMS *Leda* was torpedoed and the *Rathlin* rescued thirty-two survivors. That same evening U-boats again got through the screen and the ship next to the *Rathlin* was hit twice. At once the *Rathlin* went to the rescue and this time got fifty-five survivors plus a dog. The *Zamalek* accounted for the remaining five of the crew. HMS *Somali* was hit, too, and lost her funnels. She was taken in tow but sank later.

Many of the survivors on the *Rathlin* were badly injured either by explosives or exposure. The medical officer did his duty tirelessly. One man was a mass of blood and died. Yet up to the very moment of being brought aboard, he had been helping others get away from their stricken ship.

After a lull on 21 September, three ships were sunk at once on the following morning. *Rathlin* attended to the doomed Royal Fleet Auxiliary *Gray Ranger*, saving thirty-three of her crew. Then they had a call to hurry over to her old companion, the SS *Bellingham*, struck by two torpedoes amidships. A stricken ship was always like a dying animal, proud, poignant. The crew had just 120 seconds to be saved, and between the *Rathlin* and *Zamalek* they managed it.

Throughout attacks on a scale similar to the outward leg, the medical officer of the *Rathlin* performed no fewer than six major operations. One of the patients put on board at Archangel was suffering from two gangrenous feet from the outward voyage. He had spent too long immersed in the icy sea after being torpedoed. Early on this trip, he had to be given a blood transfusion to keep him alive. The donor was one of the other survivors. Later on, the patient became rapidly worse. The medical officer was in the middle of an operation to remove gangrenous bones when the man collapsed. "Respiration ceased," an assistant told him.

With the pulse not perceptible, the medical officer looked anxious. For twenty minutes they sweated. They administered a series of injections and applied artificial respiration. Oxygen was pumped into him.

Just when hope seemed gone, the man showed a faint flicker of life. An hour later he had recovered sufficiently to be removed to the ship's hospital, where he went on progressing.

The *Rathlin* then had on board 210 survivors and also passengers, plus her crew of seventy-one. Permission was granted for her and *Zamalek* to proceed to Iceland for urgent food and other stores, as by then they had practically none left. The crew tasted their first decent meal since leaving Britain.

The tailpiece to the immortal convoy PQ17 is the strange story of an officer saved three separate times by this same ship. On his way to Russia he had been torpedoed and was rescued by another ship, which was also torpedoed. The *Rathlin* picked him up. Then on the return voyage, this time as a passenger on a naval minesweeper, the same thing happened again. He was torpedoed, rescued, and retorpedoed. Once more the *Rathlin* rescued him. So four times sunk and twice rescued by the *Rathlin*. Back in Britain, he joined a tanker shortly afterwards, which was torpedoed on a westbound Atlantic convoy. Altogether he had been sunk five times in as many months. He spent the familiar few hours in a lifeboat before being rescued by the *Rathlin*.

On Sunday, 13 September 1942, the same day as the start of PQ17's return voyage, U-boats began another onslaught on the next convoy, PQ18, six days out of Iceland and bound for Archangel. Rescue ship *Copeland* met the challenge. Torpedoes tore through the water and embedded themselves into the SS *Empire Beaumont*. The *Copeland* charged in to the rescue. By the following day she had 205 survivors on board from several ships, all saved from certain death. And so it went on . . .

Midway

After the Japanese defeat in the Battle of the Coral Sea, the American shore-based reconnaissance aircraft and submarines reported a general withdrawal of enemy ships from the southwest toward Japan, first to lick their wounds and then to prepare for further thrusts in some other less-defended sea. Acting on estimates of the locality of these next attacks—in an ocean where 1,000 miles is a mere hop from one island to another—strong U.S. naval surface forces were deployed in the area between Midway and the Aleutian Islands, far away to the north.

Midway was well named as being halfway between American and Asiatic continents and only comparatively few miles east of the International Date Line. It lies a little over 1,000 miles westward of Pearl Harbor. That infamous raid was still less than six months earlier.

3 June 1942: U.S. Navy patrol planes spotted a major enemy fleet some 700 miles off Midway, proceeding eastward. Nine Flying Fortresses from Midway intercepted this massive force and hit a cruiser and a transport.

4 June, dawn: Army and Marine Corps bombers and torpedo planes also took off from Midway. Four Army torpedo planes swept down from the clear summer skies to release their fish. As they did so, they met a screen of Japanese fighters and ships' fire. They managed a hit on an aircraft carrier, but half of this small bomber force failed to make Midway again. Six Marine Corps torpedo planes fared even worse. Only one of these recrossed the Date Line to see the familiar outline of Midway again. Equally tragic was the loss of eight out of sixteen dive-bombers.

0635: Soon after the Marine Corps planes took off on their missions, the island itself was subjected to a mass air assault by carrier-based enemy planes. The Japanese pilots were already showing their suicidal tendencies and forty machines were shot to pieces or fell screeching.

At sea, too, the American air attacks caused the enemy to change their course. But some U.S. naval forces remained unaware of the Japanese change of plans. One group of carrier-based fighters and dive-bombers searched along the track on which the enemy were reported, failing to find them. Most had to abandon the search, but some were too far from their carriers to get back and were forced to go down into the drink as their planes ran out of fuel. Frantic radio signals located most of the pilots and luckily the sea was calm. Nevertheless, a few were lost.

Nothing was now given or expected in this war. Next in the air-to-sea battle came retaliation from the Japanese. Mere numbers cannot convey the attack on the U.S. carrier *Yorktown:* one group of eighteen bombers sent their noses toward *Yorktown.* Naval fighters picked off eleven before they could drop their bombloads. Seven pierced the fighter protection. Then came the antiaircraft barrage. Number one disintegrated into fragments, gleaming in the sun. Number two dropped its load into the sea and plunged after them into eternity. Number three was literally smashed to shreds by a machine gun that kept the plane in its sights the whole time it approached. The other four bombers escaped after scoring three direct hits. No more action during the morning.

4 June, afternoon: More blows on the *Yorktown.* A dozen enemy torpedo planes thundered down parallel to the carrier. Fighters and ships' guns accounted for seven of them on the run-in, but the remaining five launched their torpedoes and turned in a vain attempt to escape. None did. So the dozen planes and pilots all perished.

Those torpedoes that had hit the *Yorktown* added to the bomb damage already besetting her. A heavy and increasing list gave good warning of what was to come. As the crew abandoned her, to be picked up safely, tugs hurried to take her in tow, while a special salvage party boarded her.

6 June, morning: *Yorktown's* list grew less and the chance to save the flattop rose. The destroyer USS *Hammann* went alongside to assist. Its crew was having lunch when an enemy submarine stole into range and aimed two torpedoes at each warship. All four weapons hit home, and the *Hammann* sank suddenly. With a great gaping hole amidships, *Yorktown* was really in a critical condition by now and had not long to float.

7 June, morning: The *Yorktown* capsized and plowed into the depths of the Pacific, six miles down at its deepest.

The *Yorktown* and the *Hammann* were the only American naval losses at Midway. On the same afternoon that the *Yorktown* was hit, an American submarine finished off an enemy carrier. The *Soryu* was already damaged when three torpedo strikes started fresh flames that forced the crew to leave her. Then, as the sun set, the submarine heard heavy explosions and saw telltale black billowing smoke. The carrier went down in the night. Other enemy ships had received damaging bombs, too, during that day of 4 June.

The American planes flew back to their carriers and the whole task force set course for harbor. The seventy-two hours or so of Midway meant a lot in terms of enemy ships and personnel. The Americans did the following: sank four aircraft carriers; hit three battleships; sank two cruisers; hit four cruisers; sank three destroyers; hit three transports; destroyed 275 aircraft; killed 4,000 Japanese. After the battle and the bloodshed the U.S. fleet sailed serenely eastward, threading through the still sea. The silvery wakes trailed off and merged into the blue. And all was once again pacific.

Examining the damage aboard the doomed
Yorktown. *Imperial War Museum*

While the battle off Midway was reaching its height, far away in the north another enemy thrust aimed at those U.S. outposts of the Aleutian Islands. For nearly six months the soldiers manning these islands had been performing K.P. with no more excitement than their buddies back home. Then they got their first taste of the war.

3 June, 0600: Fog enfolds the Aleutians for much of the year. As it lifted, there came the drone of planes with the Rising Sun on their fuselage. The raid was aimed against Dutch Harbor and Fort Mears. But this was not to be another Pearl Harbor. The defenses were well prepared here and the ack-ack crews had already reached their battle stations as five waves of three planes each approached them. Unlike Pearl Harbor, too, the shore batteries opened up a full five minutes before the first bomb fell. The few vessels in harbor at once got up steam and started to maneuver with the dual purpose of taking evasive action and getting better placed for offensive fire. Bombs whined down on Dutch Harbor, but from their cockpits the Japanese witnessed the frustrating sight of bombs burrowing deep into waters where a vessel had been only a few seconds earlier. Not a single ship was hit. The next day U.S. planes located and attacked carriers that had launched these aircraft.

Onlookers from the hills overhanging Dutch Harbor saw the scene of the raid almost as a painting. Against a background of white-painted houses and equally white snow rose black plumes of smoke from bombs and fires vertical in the windless air.

The threat at the Aleutians looked like an invasion threat. The Catalinas that took off to try to intercept these planes were cumbersome and slow flying boats, but they flew through a fury of flak to do their job. They gave and got a beating. Many never came home. An enemy Zero swooped on one, forcing the Catalina to float on the water, where it machine-gunned the flying boat. Another Catalina ran right into a group of Zeros. In fact, for two days they flew on till they were either shot down or ran out of fuel.

Neither at Midway nor in the Aleutians were the Americans caught napping, with their planes drawn up for destruction, as they had been at Pearl Harbor. They had learned a lesson the hard way.

A Girl Called Johnnie

Johnnie Ferguson was a passenger aboard the liner *Avila Star*. This attractive girl was on her way from Buenos Aires to Britain to join the Wrens. She was tall, slightly freckled, with auburn hair—and although she had been christened Maria Elizabeth they called her Johnnie. Her epic story is the record of a journey to the far frontiers of human endurance.

The Canary Islands and Madeira were already behind them. The liner was almost level with the Azores. Towards dusk on 5 July 1942 the blackout drill came into operation as usual; all on board had to wear their life-jackets or have them on hand. The ship's surgeon, Dr. Crawford, kept all his emergency equipment ready. He settled down in his cabin to bring his medical reports up to date. Chief Officer Eric Pearce was also in his own cabin.

Johnnie was not in hers. She was chatting with Jim Perry, the assistant purser, in his office. The name of the purser was Mr. Weston. The captain was on duty on the bridge. Engineer Officer Ralph Ginn lay on his bunk in vest, pants, shorts, and socks. Some of the crew lads were having a sing-song. Inside their mess someone said, "Let's hear the other side," and the man with a record in his hands turned it over.

Suddenly the needle slid right across the record. The music stopped. The ship lurched, throwing them about the crowded mess. A torpedo had torn into the starboard side at fifteen feet depth. It struck the oil-fuel settling tank, between engine room and boiler room.

The lights flickered and went out as the ship took a list to starboard. Crawford pulled the cord of his emergency lighting. He was already halfway out of the door. Eric Pearce could smell the explosion. He found his two torches in the darkness and then hurried on deck. Pearce gave Fisher one of the torches. Fisher was giving orders for the boats to be lowered. The klaxons sounded Abandon Ship. Crawford was going straight to the boat station, according to orders. His place was in number 7 lifeboat.

After the initial shock of the explosion, Johnnie groped about in the sudden dark. She had left her life-jacket outside the office door and could not find it. She followed the boat drill and floundered onto the deck. The most vivid things to her were the smell, the tilt, and some fitful lights. The list made the most impression. The deck where she had played quoits was now tilted sharply.

Arthur Brown picked up the getaway bag he always kept ready packed. Ralph Ginn and Turner had adjacent cabins. The torpedo struck the chef's cabin alongside them. It killed the chef and blew the cabin to smithereens. Ginn and Turner found a ladder escape hatch to get on deck. All this took them less than five minutes, and they reached the boat in time to be lowered. They were fortunate. The firemen and stokers on watch in the boiler room were all trapped and lost.

Jim Perry helped to swing out his lifeboat and lower it. He made sure that everyone who should be there was present. The poor donkey-man had been badly burned and lay in agony. Crawford put on his life-jacket and slung on his precious haversack. Then the stern of 5 lifeboat crashed down, spilling out most of the men into the sea.

By the time Johnnie got to her lifeboat station, things were getting confused. A man said suddenly, "Haven't you got a life-jacket? Here, take mine." And he thrust it on her, forcing her to accept it. She never knew if he survived or not. She returned to her own boat station. By then they were starting to lower 7 lifeboat. To Crawford the images of this alarming experience were being imprinted on him like a series of film shots. Not real life at all. He was near 7 boat. A voice called to him, "Jump in, we're lowering." Crawford did as he was told and landed safely in its stern. About the same time, too, Johnnie reached the boat and jumped aboard. They started to descend rapidly, jerkily. The liner was now listing very badly. Crawford spotted the purser in the boat.

"That you, Weston? All right?"

Johnnie Ferguson, having recovered from her twenty-one days adrift in an open boat.

"Yes, Doc. All aboard, I think," the purser replied.

Those were the last words the purser ever spoke.

The journey down to water-level was short but slow. Johnnie just sat and waited. Then they were afloat in the swell, which swept up to reach them. They were still too close to the hull of the liner and the only whole lifeboat not yet away.

Then the second torpedo struck. The sea streamed into the ship anew, cascading down the companionways. The torpedo hit right under 7 lifeboat. It blew the boat right into the air. Johnnie flew fifteen feet up, cracking her head on a big block. Only a glancing blow, but enough to scar her. The blow knocked her out for a moment, but the shock of the water on her face quickly brought her around. Her arms and legs reacted.

She realized that she was afloat, and her limbs took over and did the rest. As she surfaced she struck out for the nearest object she could see. It was what remained of 7 boat, with no bottom in it. Johnnie was covered in fuel oil, and as she swam she was almost sick. She swallowed some, but not enough to do lasting harm. Her only idea was to get out of the oil and the water. She knew that even an hour in the water could be fatal—but she had health and youth on her side.

Survival was her primary thought, so she speeded up her strokes toward the derelict 7 boat. Someone must have hauled her inboard, because she could hardly have done it alone. She simply knew she was there. Emergency arc-lights pierced and probed at small groups of survivors. Johnnie saw heads and arms thrashing about. Others swam up to this wreck of a lifeboat and they were all helped on. Johnnie fished a couple of men out, though she was quivering with cold and shock.

She was sitting on the sternpost of the boat, with her feet on the sodden seats. Two men lay propped against her, one supported by each of her knees. They were blackened by the penetrating, cloying, head-to-toe oil. Johnnie could not do any more for them at the moment, nor for two others whom she helped that night. The first pair had both hurt their ribs. They were in pain, so she comforted them as best she could. This had to be on a basic scale—in a bottomless boat. "Just hang on," she said. "We'll be all right."

Rowing was hard work, as the boat dragged with water. All its occupants were wet as well as oily. They rowed feverishly now, with the

mast of the liner leaning lower each minute. Johnnie was so busy count-
ing the strokes that she did not see the U-boat on the surface quite near.
The enemy did not machine gun them anyway. The liner sank.

Johnnie was sick as a result of the oil she had swallowed, and again
later. She passed the night icy cold and cramped with nursing the four
invalids. They were the bathroom steward with a broken leg, another
steward with broken ribs, an elderly man who died later on the motorboat, and a fourth man who was terribly scalded and also died later. She
attended to these four all night without worrying about herself at all.
The sharp, clear night dragged on.

Reluctant grey dawn. Shadows slowly turned into human forms.
Monday morning. No naval patrols would be scouting for them. Nor was
this blank bit of ocean covered by Allied air patrols. Nor were they on
a regular sea route. Nor did they know if anyone had heard their SOS.
The outlook seemed bleak.

As 2 boat closed with Johnnie's sinking 7, someone flung a rope over
as a guide for Johnnie, but she spurned it, tipped herself over into the
sea, and swam for the other boat. A quick tug on the line and she was
aboard. She had amazed the men on 7 boat by her spirit. Arthur Brown
in 2 boat did not recognize her as she struggled over the gunwale. The
reason was simple: she looked utterly black. Throughout the rest of the
day, the five surviving boats steered eastward under sail, though they
had difficulty in keeping good contact.

Everyone in 2 boat went on strict rations for food and water. These
would be high among factors deciding survival. Other things came in,
too, such as health and weather. Johnnie got her first taste of the rations:
food she grew to loathe later on. The biscuit was hard to bite. The
malted-milk tablets dry and sweet. And pemmican she disliked most of
all. This was khaki-colored meat paste. The specially made lifeboat
chocolate was reinforced, bitter, sustaining, and the ration started at two
squares each. Water was allotted on a ratio of 4½ ounces per person
per day. Johnnie managed the biscuits for the first day or two. She did
not feel thirst acutely yet, at least for a few days. This water ration
amounted to about a quarter of a pint.

Johnnie's usual place to sleep was half on the rudder, with the post
rigid down her spine. She managed to stretch across the boat but had
various heads using her legs as pillows. Anson, Clarke, Ginn, and oth-

ers kept continual watch near her. They daren't let a single chance of rescue pass unnoticed. Evans and Brown issued the food and water; this took quite a time for thirty-eight people.

Tuesday, 7 July, dawn: "God rest your soul" someone said, as a man was dropped gently over the side. Boats 2 and 6 were outsailing the rest.

Thursday, 9 July: Johnnie was keeping a calm and philosophic outlook on their plight, even managing to appear outwardly bright. The weather worsened, with rain squalls. Not a good prospect on the fifth day of total exposure. The injured men seemed a little worse.

Friday, 10 July, and still the same story. Aboard 2 boat, the interminable night of 10–11 July rolled and roared on. Around dawn, however, the weather let up a little and they proceeded in company with 6 boat. Then the wind and sea got up again, with waves ten feet at times. Even Johnnie, usually cheerful and phlegmatic, found the ceaseless pounding nerve-wracking. Tons of water were flung at them, buffeting the boat and drenching all its occupants.

Boats 2 and 6 parted, never to sight each other again. The northeast trades were beginning to hit them. Nurse Botham and six other women were lost in 6 boat. It did not bear thinking about. From then on 2 boat was on its own. And at that time no one was looking for it. The outlook, like the weather, was worsening.

Johnnie watched as the waves towered twice, three times, the height of a man. She tried to get reconciled to it, if the worst should come. But she couldn't.

Monday, 13 July: A man jumped overboard and died. As the last light drained from the sky, Johnnie felt a great loneliness. None of them had an iota of power to alter anything. They were in the hands of God. She began to get her own life into perspective. The vast darkening sky and the cruel sea both conveyed to her the minuteness of her life and yet its precious quality, the value of something appreciated only when it becomes endangered. This was the worst night so far.

0400: They hove up the sea anchor and proceeded. The sea was rough, the swell long, the sky overcast. The elements could last longer than they could. Three times a day they had two malted-milk tablets, a teaspoon of pemmican, and a bit of chocolate. Plus a few gulps of water.

Now they were into their second week and thirsts grew worse. Not yet desperate, but bad. Their first emergency beaker of water had lasted eight days, but the second one would do for only five days. And there was only one more beaker after that. Throats felt like cotton-wool, choked, parched.

They were near the halfway point in their ordeal. Some would survive. The combination of spiritual stamina and physical strength would tell in the end.

Wednesday, 15 July, 0400. They hove up the sea anchor and went on again. There was no choice. Lack of sleep, lack of food, less than half a pint of water a day, plus appalling conditions. Their health suffered. Just as everyone was at an ebb lower than they had imagined possible, the weather relented a fraction.

Friday, 17 July: The sick had little appetite. It was a very vicious circle. They needed food but could not take it, so they became weaker still. The water ration was cut from 7 ounces to the original 4½ ounces. Half a glass. The barest for survival.

Five Portuguese naval aircraft started to search for survivors on 17 July. Someone was making an effort at last. The odds still seemed slim: spotting a lifeboat in an area roughly 300 miles square.

The weather worsened again cruelly. The sick grew worse, especially one man supported by Johnnie, who soothed him through endless hours. The next day Johnnie found that he was dead in her arms. The vigil was over.

20 July: The first two beakers of water were finished. They tried to catch rain in the tarpaulin but could not. It was pitiful. Johnnie was finding that she had to concentrate on her own survival, after thinking so much of others. "It's not my time to die yet," she said to herself. She repeated it several times under her breath.

Johnnie simply sucked a button to keep the saliva going, to encourage a minute amount of moisture. Her mouth and throat felt terrible. And still the search for the two boats went on. Her father was in Buenos Aires; her mother was in London.

On their port side they suddenly saw a great wall of water rearing over them. They were swamped. The next few minutes were touch and go. The crisis had an enlivening effect, though, with everyone bailing furiously. It was life or death. That night passed appallingly, with men moaning.

The morning of 21 July: Johnnie herself felt slightly hazy. Three men died that day.

22 July, dawn: Another of the crew had died unseen in the darkness of that eighteenth night. Briefly, but with dignity still, they disposed of him. The weather actually became fine. Sea birds circled and cried aloft in a pellucid turquoise dawn. The birds had been their only living companions through the weeks past.

"What's that noise?"

"A plane. It's a plane."

An explosive surge of tension tore out of them. Weak cries came from dry throats.

"Will they see us? Oh, God, are they going to see us?"

Frantically they soaked rags in the remaining petrol and started to send up flares. Tired and worn as she was, Johnnie was trying to light the flares quickly. But she could not hold them firmly enough the first time and they kept dropping. Then they got one or two more burning and sent them soaring upwards. The faint engine noise reverberated in their brains. Getting nearer.

"There they are—two of them." And out of the western sky were two Portuguese naval aircraft. Men wrung their hands, shook each other's, embraced, wept. Johnnie was pretty weak, but she managed to prop her body up straight. No doubt about it now. The aircraft had seen the boat. So salvation was on its way. They dropped two canisters with a map and a message: "Good luck and courage. Help will come soon. Portuguese Naval Authority."

The planes only had to radio the nearest ship and it would be over soon. That was the general verdict. They were wrong.

High hopes ran the length of the sturdy little lifeboat. Brown had to restrain men croaking for still more water. Darkness fell for the nineteenth time and gloom returned to some of them, too. Not so much active despair as passive weakness. There was a limit, and they had reached it, gone beyond it. They were at the far frontiers of human endurance. Some had passed it and were no longer aboard. The rest felt fairly sure that rescue must come on the next day, Thursday, 23 July.

23 July: "Deaths continue amongst crew," read the log. They had lost nine men. Ralph Ginn did not despair—he went on praying.

Friday, 24 July 1942: They really felt they could not stand any more. The tenth loss of life. Johnnie felt it badly, too. There were no words for the following twenty-four hours. Nothing adequate to describe the feelings. Now it was nearly three days since the planes had spotted them. They felt the despair of the lost. The water would not last long.

Up in the bows, the faithful Robinson was once more in the look-out at 1000 hours that morning. At sea level, visibility was not very far. Clarke and Brown were up by the tiller. Then Robinson said evenly, "There's smoke over there." In the silence that followed, he added, "Ship's mast, sir."

They all looked out, almost too afraid to allow hope. Three or four miles off, they could see the wonderful spectacle of a mast looking like a matchstick on the horizon. Then came the next fear. Would the ship see them? Johnnie helped several of the men to get the flares going. The terrible anxiety about the ship remained for a few minutes. Then the mast took the dim form of a warship. But was she really heading for them? *Yes.*

At that moment, when they felt sure that she must have seen them, they hauled down the begrimed sail and got out the oars in a pitiful final effort to row. It was sad to see men going through the motions of

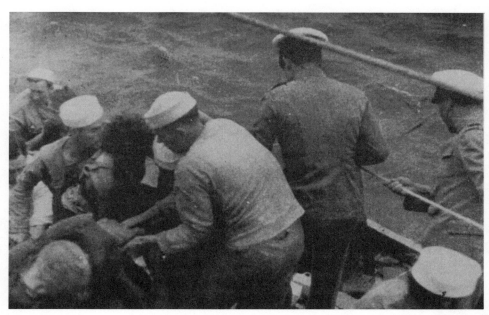

The moment of rescue: Johnnie (below) is being helped by Portuguese sailors. Several men died even after rescue.

trying to row and not being able to. They all knew in their souls that here was their last hope on earth. Men had died of despair after the planes had gone. Johnnie would have lived only two more days.

Johnnie had the honor and thrill of becoming the first woman passenger ever to be awarded the Lloyd's Medal for bravery at sea. Later she applied for the Wrens, specifying boat crew. She was summoned to a Wrens center. They had all the details of her experience to date. A woman interviewing officer looked solemnly through these particulars, then at Johnnie, and asked her in all seriousness:

"But have you had any boating experience?"

"Yes," said Johnnie simply.

Invasion of the Solomons

August 1942: Enter the U.S. Marines. Their goal: the Solomons. A great convoy set sail and for three peaceful days it plowed uneventfully through the South Pacific. Then smoke on the horizon told them that a naval force was approaching. Soon they saw the whole panoply of carriers, cruisers, and massive transports. Excitement intensified, although all the Marines could do was to wait and pass the time cleaning rifles and polishing bayonets. Both would be needed in the forthcoming days.

Their one question was: "Where are we going?" Scuttlebutt ranged from Yokohama to the Admiral Byrd Mountains of Little America. But in their hearts they knew what they would be up against—and they were glad it had come. Waiting and training were always the worst.

Two more days and the blue skies turned grey. Strange, solid cloud banks drifted down to water level, blacking out everything, making it all the more unreal. Were they really going to attack the Japanese somewhere ashore? At least the enemy could not spot them through this cloud and fog. All the Marines glimpsed on 4 and 5 August were the faint fringes of friendly islands. How many thousands of isles were there in this endless ocean? One looked like another.

6 August: The unit commanders broke the news: "We're heading straight for the Solomons, men."

The Solomon Islands flank the Coral Sea and marked the most southerly limit of the Japanese conquest to date. The enemy wanted to develop them into a base to attack ships bound between the United

States and Australasia. That night the clouds cleared and the ships slipped through the offshore waters.

7 August, 0200: All hands turned out. A final check and then below for a breakfast of steak, scrambled eggs, fried potatoes, toast, jam, and coffee. This would be their last galley meal for days. For a few, their last meal.

"Good chow," a young Marine said nervously to relieve his tension. Up on deck again, they saw the Southern Cross still shining brilliantly. The black outline of an island crept by them to starboard. It was Guadalcanal. Another one, to port this time. Florida. So far from the American playground of the same name. No greater contrast could be conceived than these two Floridas before dawn on 7 August 1942.

The element of surprise, which would mean literally life or death to some men, had to be preserved. So the giant ships stole slowly and silently between the islands. Now they were a mere fifteen miles from Tulagi harbor, the heart of the Solomons. They heard nothing yet from either shore.

0525: Battle stations.

0605: Stand by to lower boats.

0617: The boom of the big guns from the cruisers heralded a barrage startling in its scale. The Pacific dawn lay shattered. There was no return now. The barrage continued as Navy bombers and smaller dive-bombers timed attacks on shore targets to the very second. They hit anything that looked as if it might be military. Then they strafed the whole area just to make sure. Utter surprise was achieved, especially in Tulagi harbor itself. Nine Zeros equipped with floats, five big patrol seaplanes, and a bomber were all sunk in seconds before they could get off the water. That left the enemy with not one plane left to fly.

The combined sea and air assault all along the fifteen-mile stretch of water brought havoc to the garrison. Bombardment was so accurate that no shore battery replied to the landings. Only a few half-hearted machine-gun bursts came from the Japs.

So now the Marines' moment came at last. Boats swung out on davits and were lowered away as combat groups prepared to strike for shore. Here was the biggest amphibious landing of the war so far. Around the hefty transports swarmed dozens of landing craft: barges, tank lighters, and even amphibious tanks and tractors.

H-hour, about 0800: The first company of Marines to land, under Capt. E. J. Crane, set foot on a promontory on Florida Island actually overlooking Tulagi harbor. No Japanese appeared. Next ashore came a battalion under Col. Merritt Edson, on Tulagi itself this time. Still not a shot fired. An amber flare from the shore of Guadalcanal announced a third landing under Lt. Col. L. P. Hunt. After the ferocity of the air and sea bombardment the quiet seemed strange, especially to men keyed up to the chance of death on those shores. In fact, the enemy had been surprised and scared by the withering preinvasion attack and had fled to the hills where they proceeded to dig in among a network of caverns and caves. This tactic would be used frequently later on in the Pacific war.

Over on Tulagi the day went differently. After landing, the Marines had to scale steep cliffs. With heavy packs on their backs, they also had to drag machine guns up behind them. Splitting into two groups, they headed cautiously for the town of Tulagi. But it was a hilly, heavily wooded area. Then they ran into their first opposition: a series of machine-gun nests completely concealed in limestone caves dug into the hillside. The only way to deal with these nests was for Marines to crawl up the face of the hill under fire and then slip down a cliff face to hurl grenades into the mouths of the caves. This gave the Americans the first sign of the powerful opposition that they would be facing.

Then the Marines met even more formidable foes: a ravine and, on the other side, an incline literally studded with pillboxes and dugouts. Fire focused on the Marines from all of these, the enemy's main line of defense on the whole island. Capt. Harold T. A. Richmond, commanding this party, saw that he could do no more than hold on, so he defended while waiting for reinforcements.

Over to the two small islands of Gavutu and Tanambogo, connected by a concrete causeway: The seaplane base on the former, devastated by the bombing, was assaulted at noon by the Marines under Maj. Robert H. Williams. Landing under fire on the wharf, Williams was at once hit, stumbled, and fell badly wounded. Capt. George Stallings took over.

Gavutu was the best fortified island of the group. Rising to a height of 148 feet in the center, it was honeycombed with scores of spacious limestone caves. Tunnels linked many of these chambers, some of which even had radio communications. Ideal for defense, the enemy made maximum use of them. But they overlooked the fact that a castle can also become a prison, or even a tomb.

As soon as the Marines felt the leaden rain of fire from these caves, they realized that the only way to clear the enemy from the Solomons was to force them literally to "cave in." Capt. Harry L. Torgeson led the way up Gavutu. He crept slowly up the hill, covered by the fire of just four men. When he had gotten as close as he dared, he hurled charges of TNT, tied to boards with short fuses, into the mouth of the first cave. A second or two of silence ensued, then a blast. The whole hillside seemed as if it might collapse. The Japanese inside were either blown up or buried. Torgeson proceeded to call on other caves for hours, picking his way with care and determination. He used up twenty cases of TNT. Once he ran out of matches to light the fuses and had to call hoarsely for another box. Then his wristwatch was smashed. Finally his pants were blasted off him. But he blew up fifty caves and an unknown number of enemy troops. There was no time for regrets.

The fighting got grimmer and closer. Cpl. Ralph W. Fordice mopped up seven dugouts; from one alone he dragged eight dead men. Cpl. George F. Brady shot two enemy with his machine gun; as another Japanese came at him, the gun jammed. Brady swung the butt around and killed the man. Two more emerged from the cave. Brady knifed them both. It was kill or be killed. As basic as that.

Afternoon: The Marines planted the Stars and Stripes on the Gavutu hilltop, the buglers blew, and for a moment the Marines stopped fighting to cheer. But the rival Rising Sun was still fluttering above Tanambogo only 500 yards away. Marine sharpshooters ripped it away by their fire, but the battle was not yet over.

Evening: The first attack on Tanambogo began. Enemy fire covered the connecting causeway, so an advance across it would have been suicidal. The answer was another landing. U.S. destroyers synchronized a barrage as boats brought Marines in to land. The success of the barrage proved a mixed blessing, however, for the very last shell fell on a fuel dump. The resulting explosion lit up the landing dock so vividly that the Marines were thrown into full relief before the enemy gunners. The attack had to be suddenly stopped and called off for that night.

8 August, morning: Two amphibians went over to Tanambogo in advance of the main landing party. The first chugged through the water and 100 feet up the beach when the desperate Japanese troops came out of hiding and started to swarm all over it. They thrust iron rods into its treads, poured gasoline over the chassis, and set fire to it. A terrible moment for the tank crew, knowing that they were on fire and outside

waited a horde of the enemy. At that instant, the Marine lieutenant operating the tank opened the turret top through the smoke and swung his gun on the Japanese—killing twenty-three before being knifed to death himself. Within an hour, his life had been avenged when the Marines had eliminated the enemy on Tanambogo.

Now the Marines held all of Gavutu, most of Tulagi, and had toeholds on Florida and Guadalcanal. After taking Tanambogo, their next orders came to clear out the dangerous Tulagi ravines. With reinforcements, the Marines covered the gully by fire from three sides, and with utter thoroughness they killed everyone in the caves by afternoon.

The Japanese fought with fanatical courage. No dugout was silenced until every one of them inside had died. As one machine-gunner dropped his weapon, another would push him away and take his place. One lone gunner held out in a cave for two days surrounded by the corpses of eight fellow soldiers. He, too, finally died. In another cave three Japanese fought on until they had just three bullets left. One of them shot his two colleagues and then used the third bullet on himself.

On Guadalcanal the Marines moved inland to capture an 85 percent completed airfield with a 1,400-foot runway. Later on they ran into the enemy, but here the Japanese offered no such fanaticism as on Tulagi and operated mostly from isolated machine-gun nests.

Even here, however, the occasional raw situation occurred. Platoon Sgt. Frank L. Few, a part–American Indian from Arizona, came in close contact with three of the enemy. Too close for his rifle, he took them on, hand-to-hand, killing all three. Almost exhausted by this struggle, Few then had to return to the safety of his unit, which meant a four-and-a-half-mile swim across the channel.

As the Marines surged forward to overrun enemy billets and positions, it became more and more obvious that the Japanese had been overwhelmed by the sudden surprise of the invasion. They left breakfast tables strewn with bowls of half-eaten rice. Chopsticks lay nearby at crazy angles, as if thrown down in frenzy. Their trousers hung on wash lines in one field, and the Americans stumbled on an outdoor bath still filled with water. Its occupants had clearly left in a hurry.

Among the supplies left behind by the enemy in their haste were large stores of beer, soda pop, soap, clothing—even champagne. Of more use from the military angle were ammunition dumps, fuel, a radio, trucks, cars, refrigerators, even an electric-light plant. And the gear for finishing the airfield, complete with a roller, was all there waiting for the Marines.

Noon: Although assault forces were ferreting out all the remaining enemy troops, the Japanese still had a trick or two left. Forty torpedo planes aimed their loads on the ships in harbor, hitting an empty transport and a destroyer; a dozen of this suicidal wing screamed down into the sea before accurate fire. One spun madly away overland to crash with a burst of amber in the green hillside. Their losses were forty-seven planes. Later this figure rose to 100.

9 August, noon: By now it could be claimed that all major resistance on five islands had been overcome and the Solomons were virtually in U.S. hands. The Americans could only guess how many Japanese were buried alive or killed among the hills, but on Tulagi alone there must have been at least 600 Japanese—and not one surrendered. On Gavutu the number was twice this, and they all died. Several hundred more were on both Tanambogo and Guadalcanal. The only ones captured during the first two days' fighting amounted to seven men from a labor battalion and three suffering from malaria who had been left behind in their camps when their comrades took to the hills.

After it was all over, the Americans held a service for their dead in the Gavutu fighting. The Marines stood bareheaded in the sun remembering colleagues they had known. And perhaps thinking that they were lucky to be alive—at least for another day.

Loss of the Leedstown

Now the war was eleven months old for the Americans and their theaters of operations began to span the world. Ships were being sunk in the Pacific, Atlantic, and now the Mediterranean. Early in 1942, while the U.S. forces were occupying North Africa, the troopship USS *Leedstown* was sunk off Algiers, as were several other U.S. vessels.

The *Leedstown* was christened *Santa Lucia* when she was launched as a luxury liner to sail between North and South America. Now, as the *Leedstown*, she was carrying U.S. troops to North Africa. Embarking from the eastern seaboard of the United States, she accompanied the American invasion of Algeria with her cabins and hold crammed full of soldiers and sailors. One of those hundreds was eighteen-year-old Walter S. Jones Jr., who vividly recalled her last hours.

8 November: The *Leedstown* reached the African coast on a pitch-black night, which added to the element of surprise necessary to the whole Allied operation. Landing boats were lowered and gathered in a wide circle; big black shapes blurred in the night. Landing nets were let over the side, while a portable blinker signaled the boats to come alongside. 2200: The first boatload of men was ready for the run ashore. The unloading and loading operations went on all night. Immediately after the landings were over, the ship started its next role. The *Leedstown* began loading wounded for transportation out of the battle area. So men were landed, wounded, and returned to the *Leedstown*.

Seaman Walter Jones was in a landing craft alongside, helping to get a wounded private and a lieutenant aboard, when the first air attack hit the ship. Enemy planes machine-gunned the *Leedstown,* but the bullets spattered harmlessly. Jones said:

> I worked all day on the landing nets, helping repair some boats that had been damaged by the rocks and surf. It was at dusk that the next air attack arrived. You always get them at dusk and dawn, because in that light the planes are hard to spot. They used an old gag this time to distract our attention. One plane came in close to draw the fire of our gunners. While this was going on, another plane came with an aerial torpedo.
>
> The soldiers on the sun-deck winged the first plane but they didn't stop it. But as it swung past the fantail, the boys got it with a three-pounder set with a two-second fuse. The plane burst into flames and crashed into the rocks on the shore. While we'd been working on that plane, the other one managed to put a torpedo into our fantail, which put our steering gear out of commission.
>
> All during this attack, there was an operation going on in the sick bay, where the doctor was operating on a lieutenant with a fractured skull.

9 November: The convoy moved into Algiers, leaving the *Leedstown* behind with one British corvette. All she could do was wait while the corvette prowled around for possible torpedoes. About 1000 the corvette heard a U-boat somewhere and dropped a depth-charge. Lunchtime now, and at 1330 two enemy bombers flew over and aimed wildly with their loads. Some Spitfires appeared out of nowhere to chase them off. All quiet again.

Suddenly two torpedoes sizzled toward the *Leedstown.* They hit amidships with a terrible tearing nose. Most of the men in the boiler room were killed, although those in the engine room somehow scrambled up the metal ladders and out of the inferno of rushing water and spreading fire. Jones said:

> I don't know for sure whether the torpedoes started a fire or not, but there was a lot of smoke coming from amidships. I guess the captain decided with what we were carrying he couldn't take any chances, so he ordered "abandon ship." About a hundred of the crew had regular stations for "abandon ship" and I was one of them.

We had to carry out the patients and put them in the one boat we had left. The motor was so clogged with sand it couldn't run. But we figured it would drift to shore, and it was a lot better than the rafts.

We started to dump the rafts overboard. They are supposed to be fixed on slides so that you can just cut the lines and let them drop into the water. Somehow ours were all fouled up, so we had to throw them over. Some of the guys were in too much of a hurry to wait for the rafts and jumped into the water. A lot of them got hit by the rafts. Some who couldn't swim jumped over without life-belts. One soldier dived off the bridge with his helmet on and broke his neck.

The crew as a whole was pretty calm. A few jumped off who should have stayed at battle stations. Many more, however, who were supposed to leave the ship stayed to help. Forty minutes after the captain gave the order, the ship was finally abandoned. Then it really was every man for himself. Those in the water who could swim went after the rafts as fast as possible, their arms thrashing through the Mediterranean. Jones struggled to swim to one raft that had eleven other men on or half on it. The canoe paddles were nowhere to be found. They could only hope that the raft would drift toward the shore, which luckily it did.

It was not plain sailing, though, for the surf began to get rough. To make things worse, the raft started drifting straight toward a stretch of rugged rocks between the two beaches where the landings had been made the previous night. It was really rough by now, pounding against those rocks. Jones and his mates grabbed a piece of flooring that floated by them and hauled it aboard to try to use it for a sail. It worked. Others were not so fortunate. Raft after raft dashed against the rocks, killing some of the men, who could do nothing but hang on, waiting for their fate. A cruel end.

When they hit the surf, Jones did not see what happened to the others because he was knocked out. When he recovered, he was on the Algerian beach with two Frenchmen who were trying to pour some cognac into him. He had been hauled out of the vicious surf. Meanwhile, the *Leedstown* was lost—but the Algerian landings had gone according to plan.

Guadalcanal and Tassafaronga

One of the fiercest fifty minutes in naval history—this was the next Pacific battle. And to make it worse, it happened at night, so there was only darkness, sea, and warfare. Over in the Solomons air reconnaissance noticed heavy concentrations of enemy transports, cargo vessels, and combatant ships. It did not take much imagination to deduce that this indicated a future enemy attempt to recapture the American positions in Guadalcanal and Tulagi.

10 November: Enemy naval units approached the southeast Solomons, while their transports throbbed toward Guadalcanal. General MacArthur's Army aircraft came to the aid of the Navy at this stage by bombing the Japanese at Rabaul and Buin. As in so many other Pacific actions, this one would involve land, sea and air forces—the land troops being Japanese.

The spearhead of the enemy attack comprised a force of two battleships, half a dozen cruisers, and about ten destroyers. They reached the Guadalcanal area soon after midnight on the morning of 13 November. They intended to bombard U.S. shore positions prior to a large-scale landing. Exactly forty-eight hours later, the battle broke. Look at it first through the eyes of one man aboard a U.S. battleship.

15 November, 0015: A crash, then a rolling explosion and the rattle of metal fragments as they clattered into cables, guns, and superstructure. The ship shrugged, shuddered, as a volley of shells raked through the sky control tower.

At ease in their ready room on the carrier Hornet.
Imperial War Museum

Hogden Othello Patrick, yeoman first class, talker on the sky patrol where the ship took this initial hit, geared himself for battle. From his high perch, he saw the enemy vessels come up. He also saw that first salvo leave the flagship—got a good view of it.

The next thing Patrick remembered was being hurled against a bulkhead and finding an arm—without a body—across his face. A weight across his chest pinned him down. I'm dead, he thought. Here I am, dead. This is what it's like to be dead. He was certainly as close to it as anyone could be. But the feel of shrapnel in his knee and hip convinced him that he was alive. He looked around him, up there in the exposed lookout post. It was a scene of tattered devastation. He was not alone up there. The two officers lay dead. Definitely. Seven enlisted men were quite still. Four wounded looked at Patrick, wondering what to do next.

Quickly, Rufus Mathewson, yeoman second class, called sky control on the battle phone: "Patrick, you there?"

Hogden Othello managed to get over to it and answered, "Here, but our officers are dead, and all of us are hurt."

Mathewson knew Patrick well and asked for permission to go and relieve him. His request was rightly refused by his senior. Fires were burning below sky control, and Mathewson could not help thinking of Patrick up there injured. But he had to stay in the conning tower.

Patrick pressed the button on his headset: "Sickbay—send help."

The fury of firing reverberated from the ship's guns. It was hardly surprising that no help came.

Patrick ordered the two least-wounded men to go below, and then he put tourniquets on the other two, using their own belts for the job. He treated his own leg in the same way above the knee. It was bleeding from shrapnel. Then he had to remember to loosen all three every quarter of an hour throughout the night. It was utter darkness now, broken only by the glare of the shells. Patrick hunted a long time for the morphine that he knew was up there somewhere. At last he found it and shared the drug with the others. Just as he was going to take his share, he noticed that several of the other men he had thought dead seemed to be stirring. Without hesitation, he gave them some of his share. He did not feel heroic about it. He did not even think about it at all.

Soon afterwards, the ship was pummeled and pounded by the guns of three hard-hitting warships. Shells ripped through the top of her superstructure where Patrick was still at his post. Then they swept into her secondary gun positions. Shellfire peppered the bridge with more steel fragments. Shrapnel could not really pierce the bridge's armor, but the men inside heard one shell smash through the gun director just aft of the bridge and then explode against the charthouse. Course-and-bearing instructions stopped abruptly after that. Over the amplifier from the charthouse came, "My God, this man's bleeding to death. Send help. Hurry. Please hurry."

During one ten-minute spell of nonstop punishment, one of the lookouts standing by a slot kept repeating in a low voice, "Lord, I'm scared. Nobody has any idea how scared I am. How could anyone be this scared? My God, I'm scared." He said that over and over. Nobody thought it strange.

Men began crawling to their feet to find the decks spattered with shrapnel, fire in the tattered superstructure, and broken bits of wreckage everywhere. A shambles. The men asked each other who was hurt, where the ship was damaged, how high were the flames. They swapped brief opinions of their chances of getting out of it alive.

So the fierce fifty minutes continued. John Hagenbuch was a nozzle man on a hose party of damage control. As he directed the stream on a fire in the shadow of no. 3 turret, Chief Turret Captain Bowman came out from inside and passed the word for the group to move along. He was ready to fire a salvo and the concussion would be tremendous.

Everyone except Hagenbuch evacuated the area. Standing at the head of the line, he had been forgotten when the word was passed. The guns went off with a fearful flash right over his head. Thrown to the deck with their force, he slowly staggered to his feet, temporarily blind and deaf. As he groped his way back and forth, the guns emitted another violent roar, which again threw him to the deck. One of his hosemen rushed out, lifted him to his feet, and dragged him away from the turret as a third salvo broke. Half an hour later, Hagenbuch was back on his feet, volunteering to climb to the top of a smokestack to put out a fire up there.

John P. Buck was a chaplain's yeoman, but at general quarters he became after-battery lookout. Buck smelled the scent of the gardenias from shore as midnight approached. He leaned against the open door to the compartment, savoring the silence of the tropic night. Then the 16-inch barrels exploded and he was literally thrown inside and blinded for fifteen minutes. After a short lull a 14-inch shell screamed out of the muzzle of a gun on a Japanese battleship. Buck actually saw it while it was still about two miles away from him—looming larger and larger. He knew it must hit and he knelt down.

The shell came through at deck level. Tearing a slight coaming where the deck joined the hull, it made two neat holes through a rim around a hatch leading below. Then the shell met the barbette of the after-turret. A roar, and a rain of shrapnel. Buck mentally marked turret no. 3 off his list. But it still went on firing.

Looking over the starboard rail, he saw an enemy ship racing up in the gloom. The secondary guns started to fire at it. Then the after-turret turned toward this approaching ship, and the elevation on the barrels was almost nil. The enemy was hit pointblank by all three shells in the salvo. A flashpoint where the ship had been and, afterwards, just simmering, bubbling water. Buck saw one of the enemy ship's turrets fly into the air before the inevitable sinking.

Next Buck went down to help in the sickbay. It was a ghastly sight. Men were stretched out on every available table, with doctors and pharmacist's mates working over them while standing in a deep mixture of blood and water.

On a tour with a doctor to try to help the wounded not yet in sickbay, Buck found a man lying on one of the upper levels with a leg shot off. He took out his knife and walked over to a dangling electrical wire, cut it loose, and wrapped it around the injured man's leg. Buck wrenched off the rung of a ladder and used it to twist through the wire, making a tourniquet. Wherever he turned, there was work for him to do.

Meanwhile, in the engine-control room below decks, Chief Yeoman Cheek had been reading a magazine. The huge panel of gauges in front of him was functioning perfectly. The engine was at top speed, the boilers maintained a magnificent head of steam, and the blowers were keeping the room quite cool and comfortable. When a command came through, Cheek carried it out as usual and returned to his reading. There was nothing else to do. The noise of the battle seemed remote from him and his colleagues. Around him, men stood talking quietly or merely looking at the gauges. In a vague sort of way they all worried about the 600 pounds of steam coursing through the pipes. But they had faith in the armor, the engine, and each other. So Cheek sat comfortably, lazily turning pages. And what was happening up there off Savo Island?

Despite all the battering she got, the ship kept right on rolling. Her main battery stayed trained on the enemy. Her secondaries chattered away all the time, too; tongues of fire licked the skies from every main ship in range around the island. The battleship and other U.S. ships ran completely around Savo and in the pulverizing fifty minutes wiped out an enemy fleet. Less than an hour, though at times the men swore it seemed like all night. And at the end of that time, they knew their ship had won.

Through it all, through the fire and the fear, Patrick stayed at his sky patrol post. After doling out morphine, he found he could get onto his feet and actually report better while standing. So he stood. The knee was agony but he stood. At the end of the battle, he fell exhausted but never stopped giving his regular reports from his high, hot spot until he was relieved the next morning. When the doctor finally reached the position, in the early hours, all the other wounded were down below being treated. Only Patrick remained up there—with the dead. The doctor gave him a shot and later someone was sent up in his place. Patrick had the honor of being the only enlisted man of the crew recommended for the Navy Cross. Everyone agreed that he deserved it.

In the communiqué on this battle, Rear Adm. W. A. Lee Jr. commended the U.S. task force and reported an enemy battleship, three cruisers, and one destroyer sunk, with others damaged. During all the naval engagements of 13–15 November, about twenty Japanese ships went to the bottom. American losses were two light cruisers and seven destroyers, but the Battle of Guadalcanal was regarded as a victory.

30 November: The next struggle at sea had close connections with Guadalcanal. This is the saga of a single ship, the cruiser USS *Minneapolis*—the ship that wouldn't sink—in the Battle of Tassafaronga. The *"Minnie,"* with Capt. Charles E. Rosendahl, was making twenty-seven knots off the north coast of Guadalcanal as evening approached. She was accompanied by ten other ships all acting on Adm. William F. Halsey's orders to find and destroy the enemy ships that were getting ready to try to reinforce their fighting forces on the island. The Americans found this transport train in the darkness, and at 2318 the enemy destroyers were within range. Rear Adm. Carleton H. Wright, Task Force Commander, South Pacific Fleet, told the cruisers to open fire as well, and the *Minnie* went into action.

The American force soon sank or hit two troop transports and three other vessels. But they could not know at the time that the enemy escorts had split into two; before they did know it, the remaining Japanese

Scoreboard of successes on the Hornet. *Imperial War Museum*

hammered home an attack on the cruisers. The *Minnie* was the first of four struck within seconds of each other. Torpedoes tore into the *Minnie* around midnight. In the darkness, water and oil cascaded in a sinister stream. Lights failed, compartments collapsed, and the water went on gushing into her.

Water Tender Second Class F. I. Coppage was standing by in a compartment when he and two shipmates were hurled to the deck by the explosions. He suffered a broken leg. The water rose quickly. Coppage could have gotten out, but the other two men were knocked out and would have drowned. So somehow he began pushing them out of the compartment. Bones actually protruded out of his leg, but he kept on till he had got the men through the door and closed it.

As soon as the first shock was over, all the drill to meet an emergency like this went smoothly into action. But not much can be done in engine rooms or fire rooms of a ship struck by torpedoes. The water engulfed the entire forward fire rooms and only one man of the thirty-seven working there escaped, Water Tender Second Class Bob Collins. He saw a wall of oil and water swirling across the room at him. The liquid must have lifted him up the ladder, because he could not remember how he had gotten into the airlock. But he did somehow stagger into it just below the armored deck.

Collins partly closed the door behind him and started to try to loosen the eight dogs on the door above with a hammer. He got three of them free when he dropped the hammer and had to dive down into the rising tide. He could not find it, so he had to wait and hope, while the water came higher. They opened the hatch from overhead and pulled him out just in time. One man out of thirty-seven.

No. 1 engine room filled with steam and forced everyone out of it. But Machinist's Mate First Class William Robert Anderson volunteered to try to locate the leaking steam pipe and close the valve. He went into the withering heat three times before he found the valve and closed it. The exposed parts of his body were burned in the process. Despite his heroism, the steam still continued to come out, so they could not go back there. In no. 4 fire room, the men and engines kept going. Fresh water for the tanks gave out, so they had to go ahead on saltwater.

Now the fight was on to save the ship. Eighty feet of twisted bow dragged her downward, water frothed into a great gap amidships, and her screws scarcely turned at all. Yet she started to fire on the enemy again.

Soon after the torpedo hits, Admiral Wright thought the *Minnie* must sink but between him and Captain Rosendahl they decided to try to make for Lunga Point, where if necessary they could beach the stricken ship in friendly surroundings. The situation seemed almost hopeless, since the *Minnie* was surrounded by enemy warships. The bow of a Japanese destroyer or cruiser actually almost fouled her. Throughout the rest of the night, the *Minnie* edged at three grinding knots, using improvised gear.

This was far from the end of the story. She did not sink, but she was a floating wreck. Somehow they got her into the shallows at Tulagi. Next came the job of camouflaging her from enemy aircraft. The Marines provided nets, and the crew cut branches and palms to drape over the armaments and other prominent parts. The ship was plastered with oil and other filth. They had to begin the dreary job of cleaning her with water. While this went on, the damage to the electric supply received attention. And all the time, the enemy never seemed to discover her presence. The *Minnie* could hardly have been more vulnerable.

By 5 December they had made her watertight, when a minor eruption undid all their efforts and the ship started to sink: seven feet in a minute or two. So the shoring and repairing started all over again. The bulkheads were really too thin to take the force of the ocean, so they brought four dollars' worth of logs from the natives, floated them out to the ship, hoisted them aboard, and lashed them across the bow.

At last the *Minnie* was ready to risk a run to a safer berth. Through submarine-straddled seas, she steamed slowly, surviving two sub contacts. Then on 16 December the *Minneapolis* moved in a crablike limp toward her harbor berth, to the sound of music and cheers from other vessels there.

After three weeks' reconditioning, with a stub bow of steel plates in place of the natives' logs, she was ready on 7 January 1943 to set sail for Pearl Harbor. But 185 miles out, in company with other ships, her damaged boiler tubes gave out and she had to be towed back. They had gone through too much to give up now. Another month's hard labor and the *Minneapolis* set out again. This time she reached Pearl on 2 March. The Navy yard had blow plates ready to be set in place. So at last she reached home—only to sail out under the Golden Gate once more after repairs to rejoin the Pacific fleet.

Rescue Ships in Trouble

Rescue ships could not always avoid disaster to themselves. It was bound to happen. The *Stockport* served for one year, two months, yet in that brief period she saved 413 survivors, more lives in proportion than any other vessel of the same service.

Her epic voyage no. 7 started on 27 October. Four days out of Halifax, Nova Scotia, on Convoy SC107, the first signs of trouble were detected. The time read 0005 on 1 November when an attack began which went on for a complete night and day. Time lost all normal meaning and men lived from moment to moment. It seemed just a succession of ships being sunk, followed by a stream of survivors gratefully grabbing their way on board and back to life—for the time being, anyway. The crew of the *Stockport*, hardened as they were, witnessed heartbreaking sights: two steamers blown to shreds in front of their eyes. No survivors emerged from either of them. This was how it all began.

0005: The *Stockport* saved the total complement of fifty-one men from the first ship they could reach, the British SS *Empire Sunrise*. Three hours later, still in the desolation of darkness, torpedoes found the *Dalcroy*; the *Stockport* sped in to whisk all forty-nine of her crew to safety.

The next to be hit was the Greek steamer *Rinos*. While the *Stockport* put on full steam to survivors spotted from this vessels, she nearly collided with the wreck of the *Rinos*, by then floating bottom up. In this rescue, the chief officer, Mr. Earnshaw, used a holed and waterlogged lifeboat from the sunken ship to save some sailors from a raft. One of the men from this raft had become so demented that he would not stop blowing his rescue whistle long after he had been saved. Despite the dark, they saved twenty-six from the ship, which lost five men. The *Stockport*'s saga had barely begun.

Torpedo trails skimming almost in parallel came to their desired goal in two more British ships of this huge convoy: *Empire Antelope* and *Empire Leopard*. All fifty crew were saved from the former, but only four men survived the explosion aboard the latter, and one of these died later.

Meanwhile, the day continued to take its tragic course. At 1650 torpedoes doomed another Greek ship, the *Parthenon*. While the *Stockport* churned full astern to her aid, the propeller of the rescue ship struck an abandoned steel lifeboat and her engines stopped. Luckily the interruption was only temporary.

Most of the *Parthenon*'s crew were plucked up and then the ship saved fifty-three out of the crew of fifty-six of the American SS *Hahira*. A total of 233 survivors were saved in twenty-four hours. This record was never equaled in the annals of the rescue ships. With a total complement of thirty-two on board, the *Stockport* was permitted to proceed to Iceland, reached safely under the hand of her master, Capt. T. E. Fea.

The sequel came on the very next voyage. No. 8 commenced on 11 February. By 24 February the *Stockport* had already rescued ninety-one from more torpedoed ships. On that day she received an SOS from some stragglers well astern of the convoy. In spite of atrocious weather, the distance, and the danger, the *Stockport* turned back at once. Neither the *Stockport* nor the stragglers were ever heard of again . . .

It can only be assumed that a U-boat was waiting near the stricken ships and that it sank the *Stockport* while she was stopped and picking up survivors. This was the Battle of the Atlantic at the full height (or depth) of its horror. The crew of sixty-four and ninety-one survivors on board were all lost. So ended the distinguished life of this rescue ship.

What was it really like to be torpedoed? Some survived to tell, such as the men from the rescue ship *Pinto*, when it became a case of the rescuers needing rescue.

In the convoy comprising ninety-seven vessels, the *Pinto* was no. 58, rear ship of the fifth column. Under the master, Capt. L. S. Boggs, they slipped out of Halifax on 27 August. Nothing much happened until 0510 on 8 September, when they were almost home. Then they got the message that one of the convoy had been hit. When they reached the spot, nothing was left visible of the SS *Empire Heritage*, except evidence of life-jacket lights strewn over the water. When they started rescue operations, the *Pinto* was actually only eight miles northwest of Inistrahull in Ireland. They lowered the motorboat, dropped nets and booms, and brought two survivors on board. Suddenly someone on the bridge shouted, "Periscope—starboard bow."

Some six feet of the telltale eye could be seen for a few minutes as the U-boat crossed their bow from starboard to port. It slunk close ahead through wreckage and rafts only six yards from the *Pinto*. The crew of the twelve-pounder was closed up, ready for action.

"Shall we open fire?"

"No. There are men over there in the water."

It was a decision needing rapid thought and sense of proportion. The master's training to save lives really made it inevitable that he could not attack the U-boat. The escort trawler *Northern Wave* was standing by on *Pinto*'s port quarter and the enemy probably saw her. They crash-dived, and their wireless aerial actually fouled the British escort as the craft submerged to escape. Then it happened almost at once. The second officer and two ABs in the rescue boat some two ships' length astern shouted a warning across the to the *Pinto:* "Torpedo track approaching from starboard."

The torpedo struck the starboard side right under the bridge. The chief officer, Mr. Thomson, did not see how it could have been fired from the same U-boat unless the weapon circled.

The bulkhead between the engine room and no. 2 collapsed and both compartments flooded in seconds. When the explosion occurred, they were lowering a rescue basket over the side with a greaser in it to assist survivors to get on board. He was never seen again. The force of the torpedo threw Thomson high into the air and he had to hang on to the fore-rigging as a huge column of water cascaded surf-like over the starboard side.

Surgeon Lieutenant Holmes was near the coal locker, which lay up against the operating theater, when he heard a rushing sound blended into a "tremendous explosive crash." The deck seemed to leap up and the ship shudder as if in a death agony—which indeed she was.

At the instant of impact, the master was on the bridge. The man at the wheel found him lying on his back.

"I'm all right," he told the man. "You look after yourself." Then the master staggered to the port side of the boat deck. He met one of the radio officers and told him to get over the side quickly.

*Survivor poignantly symbolizing the humane
work of the rescue ships.* Imperial War Museum

Smoke, water, and coal mixed and misted all around Holmes. The force of the eruption had flung him against the rails. He was dazed by debris, including galley coal, which landed on his head and back. Much of the superstructure of the ship seemed to be toppling down. The mainmast collapsed over to starboard, and the vessel took a severe list that way, too. Holmes tried to trace the sick-berth attendant and a few moments later he heard the man's voice from somewhere outside. Water was rushing, gushing, along the alleyway and the *Pinto* began to sink by the stern. Holmes went to make sure that the hospital was clear of men and then ran to report to the captain, whom he found standing against the rails opposite the port entrance to his cabin shouting to his men, "Get over the side—she's going down."

All the crew had been at their rescue stations when the torpedo scored its fatal shot. Thomson collected several of them and cut the falls of no. 5 lifeboat, which they swung outboard. Then they released the jolly boat. Thomson rapidly released the gripes of no. 6 lifeboat on skids on the fore deck. Holmes went down the ladder to have a last look around, and about three seconds after he spoke to the master the *Pinto* seemed to make a sudden drop. Holmes was standing on the deck, up to his waist in water, when he last saw the master.

Thomson noticed that the bottom of no. 6 boat was damaged. They released the raft in the forward rigging and four other rafts floated clear, too, as the ship sank. The deluge of water hurled up by the explosion washed the twelve-pounder gun crew overboard. Only P/O Stephens was seen in the water.

Holmes was carried down a long way as the *Pinto* plunged. He became jammed against the rigging, possibly one of the ship's stays. When he got free, he began to rise. As he bobbed to the broken surface, the ship had already gone. She sank one and a half minutes after being hit. Holmes clung to wreckage awaiting rescue.

The weather worsened as morning wore on, with a fresh westerly wind plus sleet and rain squalls. Visibility was variable. Survivors from both the *Empire Heritage* and the *Pinto* clung desperately to desultory debris or swam about with the support of their life-jackets. The rafts were tied together by then, and some of the men clambered aboard. Thomson got on one after half an hour in the water. In two or three hours, the *Northern Wave* took on the rescue role and picked up all the survivors. Holmes was saved. They hurried to Londonberry, where the survivors were landed at 2000 that same night. The trawler landed forty-one men from the *Pinto*.

The fourth engineer, Mr. Galbraith, said that he really owed his life to Ordinary Seaman Skelton, aged seventeen. Skelton was on a raft with two or three others when he saw Galbraith struggling. Skelton stripped off his life-jacket and swam over to the officer's assistance. Galbraith weighed fourteen stone, but in spite of the youth's light build he towed the engineer officer to the raft and helped him on it.

Surgeon Lieutenant Holmes had been badly shaken as a result of being trapped under the shrouds, but as soon as he was saved he insisted on attending to the wounded on board the *Northern Wave* for three hours—without stopping to change into dry clothes. Neither the master, Captain Boggs, nor the occupants of a dinghy were seen again.

January—December 1943

Americans in the Atlantic

On 7 December 1942 the war was a year old for the Yanks. They were happy to learn that out of the nineteen naval vessels originally listed as sunk or damaged at Pearl Harbor, only the battleship *Arizona* was permanently and totally lost. Preparations to right the capsized *Oklahoma* were in progress. The main and auxiliary engine machinery of the *Cassin* and *Downes* was saved. And the other fifteen vessels had been or would be salvaged and repaired. Eight vessels returned to the fleet within months of Pearl Harbor. Others were in full service as well, but the rest needed further work.

By the beginning of 1943 the war under the sea steadily grew more merciless. Lt. Richard E. Schreder was keeping his usual rigid control of a Catalina patrol bomber over the Atlantic one day when his radioman reported seeing a large submarine basking on the surface. Schreder changed course and in a few moments prepared his plan of attack. With meticulous piloting precision, he kept the sun behind him to blind the lookouts on the submarine. The heavy plane responded well as he put its nose into a sharp dive.

The bomber roared down, right between the raider and the sun, and a depth charge exploded just under the sub's stern. They made a frantic attempt to crash-dive, and then a second depth-charge was released, which zoomed downward and struck squarely on the U-boat's deck, exploding in full view of the bomber's crew as they climbed into a patch of clouds. Wreckage hurtled over the ocean and the plane headed for home.

So it went on. Sometimes results were spectacular, like the time a U-boat in the South Atlantic was blown in two by depth-charges from a Catalina while the crew appeared to be taking sun baths on the deck. After the explosion the American fliers saw it break up. The submarine's stern rose vertically ten feet out of the water, bobbed up and down a bit, and then plunged down in a rough sea.

Another Catalina flying boat featured an especially skillful piece of piloting by Lt. John Dryden Jr. Patrolling among the West Indies islands, Dryden came on an enemy submarine eight miles distant. These large craft had substantial surface armament, so an air attack was by no means assured of success. Dryden brought his Catalina down from 4,500 to 1,200 feet on the run-in and then, a mere quarter of a mile off, he pushed the great flying boat into a 45-degree dive. It shuddered slightly, as if in protest, but took them down safely to 300 yards from the enemy.

The 200-foot submarine still moved serenely on at a little under ten knots, ignorant of the aircraft. Two Germans were basking on deck, enjoying fresh air after the stale substitute they had to endure when submerged. A 100-round of machine-gun fire from the flying boat killed them both.

As the plane pulled out of its dive, Dryden and Lt. Stetson Beal, the copilot, jerked the switches, releasing four depth-charges in salvo from an altitude of less than a hundred feet. The two port charges left their racks and hit the water ten to fifteen feet starboard of the U-boat and just aft of the conning tower. A few seconds later the whole submarine lifted and broke in two amidships. The center went under first, then the bow and stern rose in the air before submerging. Finally the familiar explosion of debris, smoke, and water went forty feet into the air.

Two hundred feet had been the length of the U-boat. This was also the extent of the large patch of frothing foam that stayed on the surface for four or five minutes. Then in its place appeared a green oil slick. This expanded until it was three-quarters of a mile long and a quarter of a mile wide.

The Catalina could only wait, circling around overhead. Then, emerging from the wreckage below, the Americans saw eleven of the submarine's crew clinging for life to debris. Dryden did not hesitate. He cruised low over the struggling men while the crew of the Catalina dropped life-rafts along with emergency rations tied to life-jackets. The

Germans waved frantically for the flying boat to land, but the rough sea put any rescue out of the question.

The Americans looked out of the Catalina again, down into the rolling sea, and saw six of the Germans gradually lose their grasp on fragments of wreckage. Covered from head to waist with the thick green liquid, they slipped beneath the oily waters. The five others heaved themselves onto one of the rafts. But although the Catalina cruised the area for nearly two hours waiting for the weather to calm, a dwindling fuel supply forced it to give up and return to base.

"That's it, then. They've had it—poor devils."

The war at sea.

USCG Spencer *sank U-boat in the Atlantic.*
Cdr. Harold Berdine talks over action with
Capt. Paul Heineman. Imperial War Museum

January 1943: Far colder than the Caribbean, the North Atlantic was stormswept by some of the worst winter weather in its history. Yet in this setting, where to survive the elements was achievement enough, small ships had to take on German submarines as well.

The U.S. Coast Guard cutter *Campbell* was one of many on ocean escort duty in such seas and this was just one of their experiences during early 1943. The precise date: 21 February. Only when the *Campbell* got safely into port could her crew tell how she took on six U-boats in a twelve-hour running fight. Twelve times in one day and one night the men heard that staccato signal to battle stations.

The cutter had left Convoy ON166 when ordered to look for U-boats and had scanned the surrounding sea for twenty-five miles. No contact. It seemed pointless to proceed further afield and that night she circled around to rejoin the convoy.

"General quarters." The order came quietly enough. For as she was furrowing through a swirling sea, officers on the bridge suddenly saw a U-boat surfaced in the distance. The men moved to their battle stations as the 2,000-ton ship cut across toward the submarine. But the Germans were not to be caught, and long before the cutter could approach near enough to train her guns on the U-boat the enemy submerged. The *Campbell* continued her course to the spot where the sub had last been spotted, but all she could do was to drop depth-charges over the area. Time was precious if the cutter was to rejoin the convoy according to plan, so she could not waste it by waiting to see the result of their efforts. The vessel sped away and the crew looked vainly for signs of wreckage.

But other opportunities were to come on this dark, depressing winter day. Soon after this, the radio operator on the *Campbell* picked up a call for help from one of the Canadian corvettes, which had engaged another submarine. At battle stations again, the crew tautened as the cutter careered to the area. But another anticlimax. The sub slid down long before she got within range.

The next morning the *Campbell* was steaming on course. Their lookout saw a periscope peering ahead of them, but it disappeared so fast that they could only imagine the shock the U-boat commander must have had as the cutter came into his sights. Once more they raced to the position and thundered down a pattern of depth-charges. But still no signs of hitting anything. Three subs were enough evidence, however, to show that a whole pack of wolves were baying after the convoy.

The *Campbell* plodded on toward the convoy. The sextant took the noon sight; watch was carried out from every section of the ship; sailors arranged ropes tidily; and they waited, while all the other routine work went on. Yet somehow they knew that things might not be routine for much longer. As night fell, they caught a first glimpse of the nearest ships in the convoy, with their multicolored, patterned flags flying in the evening breeze.

Across the gloom-grey waters, the *Campbell*'s light blinked a signal to the leading escort. And a submarine dived desperately to get away from her. The cutter had only a short way to race to reach the spot. More depth-charges and then the muffled, echoing effects. A churning chaos of water. No confirmation of a hit.

Almost before the ship could get back to normal and the noise had died down, it was general quarters yet again. A fifth U-boat. Its conning tower was starting to submerge and so all they could do was repeat the dose. More depth-charges—with shells as well this time. Still in a hurry, the *Campbell* could not stop to search for evidence, but her crew claimed some success since they saw an oil slick.

The darkness now of a friendless, fearful Atlantic night, with the unseen enemy below. The chances of living at night were slim if they were hit. The *Campbell*'s crew talked and argued among themselves about the frustrations of the day.

Then someone saw it.

The sub was surfaced when the *Campbell* surprised her. Men moved on deck. She slid through the icy waters off the cutter's prow—very near now. Things started to happen simultaneously on the sub and the ship. The sub began frantic maneuvers. The cutter's crew heard wild guttural voices across the watery yards between them. A *Campbell* officer called, "Right full rudder."

The cutter swung, steering her collision course to try to ram the raider. Never had the men moved more quickly to battle stations. It seemed that forward guns fired only seconds after the alarm. The thin beam from the cutter's searchlight rested on the sub for an instant. The enemy still on deck stood transfixed. All this was happening in seconds.

Still trying to get out of the way, the sub crossed the *Campbell*'s bow and scurried off starboard, churning the water in a kind of choking panic. The *Campbell* kept to her collision course, her forward deck guns and armament all blazing and the entire crew yelling. A few more seconds and the sub was so close beneath the bows that the forward guns could not be lowered enough to go on firing.

Because the sub had moved so fast, the *Campbell* struck her a glancing blow instead of full on. But even above their own yells, the crew could hear the sharp sound as the bows knifed through the thin metal of the U-boat. A grinding as the two vessels slid past each other, and the sub drifted away with a great gash in its side. Through the dark, the *Campbell* crew saw the conning tower and heavy guns of the stricken enemy craft. Now the sub was within range of the rear guns of the cutter. This was it, and at pointblank distance. Their tracer bullets bedded into the hull and superstructure of the U-boat; they peppered the deck and blew as many holes in her as they possibly could.

Firing furiously from all rear guns, the *Campbell* eased away. The sub could not reply. She started to go down slowly by her tail. Still the guns fired, until the whole bulk began to slip down and eventually settled into the depths of the Atlantic. She took most of her crew with her. So there existed one less of Hitler's U-boats to roam among our convoys. That was the end of *U-606*. That was the war in the bitter Battle of the Atlantic.

Yanks on Their Way Back

On 21 February 1943 the Yanks were on their way back, up the string of Solomon Islands. First step on the northwesterly route was the Russell Islands, only thirty miles from the bitter battle that had been fought ashore for Guadalcanal. Dawn in a blinding rainstorm—this was the time and setting for the Russell operation.

June: The New Georgia group was invaded. The campaign went well on land, but an air assault against the Navy escorts left its inevitable imprint. Twenty-four new Mitsubishi torpedo bombers, skimming level with the waterline, suddenly materialized along with Zero fighters. Flying at 300 MPH, they aimed first for the *McCawley,* the nearest transport, and other vessels. The one to be hit first was the destroyer *Farenholt.* Two torpedoes plowed past harmlessly, but the third thudded right into her. Then the worst did not happen—the torpedo never exploded.

The *McCalla,* meanwhile, was cutting a pretty pattern in the water and by brilliant navigation avoided three torpedoes by a few feet. The *McCawley's* captain saw another one whirring at them with no time to put her parallel to the track. The bang wrecked much of the amidships and put the rudder and engines out of action. Every single one of the Japanese aircraft was shot down. But that did not really help the *McCawley.* Dive-bombers tried to finish her off, but gun crews kept them off their fast-fading ship. Now she lay almost at water level and had to be evacuated. Even after dark she was still floating, however, and it took three final torpedoes actually from the *McCalla* to sink her.

5 July: Another victory in the Solomons chain, at the expense of some naval loss. It was twenty-four hours after Independence Day when the invasion of the Kula Gulf began. 0045: In the midst of a sea-and-air bombardment, one of a spread of enemy torpedoes hit the destroyer *Strong*. Two other destroyers rushed through the dark to pick up the *Strong's* crew, despite being within close range of enemy shore guns on one of the islands. Enemy aircraft flew over as well and sprayed the sea— and the struggling survivors—with machine-gun fire. Bombs bounced down on the scene, as 239 officers and men got across from the sinking *Strong* to a rescue destroyer. A quarter of the crew was lost.

A sitting target for the guns ashore, the *Strong* finally sank. Many men were still swimming in the water around the ship when some of the *Strong's* depth-charges on her decks exploded. The huge blasts jolted the rescue destroyer and shocked the men in the sea. Dazed by its impact, they floundered in a state of concussion till they were hauled aboard. Some had been fatally affected by the blasts and lay inert in the water. Others were blinded by the thick oil layering the water.

The invasion of Kula Gulf cost the Americans another ship just a few hours after the *Strong* went down. As Rear Admiral Ainsworth ordered his task force to engage a new enemy group just arriving to bolster their existing squadron, three torpedoes straddled the length of the cruiser *Helena's* hull. With her bow blown off and back broken, she began to go down. The other U.S. ships continued to fire until the Japanese managed to maneuver themselves off the radar screens.

0300: "Abandon ship" sounded the pipe on the *Helena*. Soon the crew of the cruiser covered a square mile of oily water—in rafts, lifejackets, clasping onto broken bits of ship, or just floating or paddling to stay up. But they were *cheerful*, and they called out and chanted to the boats from the rescuing destroyers. They shone their torches, too, to direct the rescuers to their own particular parties.

0430: An alarm. An enemy ship was sighted on radar. The men not yet aboard boats had to be left for the time being. The enemy came to eight miles, then changed their minds, allowing the destroyers to return to their rescue mission. Another alarm. This time it meant action. An exchange of torpedoes resulted in no strikes and then, luckily, the enemy withdrew.

0600: Still another encounter. As bleary-eyed Navy men faced one more unknown dawn, the two destroyers *Nicholas* and *Radford* went on rounding up *Helena* survivors. One night in the exposed conditions was bad enough. By morning they had rescued 739 officers and men. The whole deck space of the destroyers was crammed solid, so they had to give up thoughts of taking more men aboard. They left their boats for the survivors still in the water and set off with their large human haul for Guadalcanal.

Two large groups of survivors still remained. One of these, eighty-five men altogether, clambered aboard the three motor whaleboats left for them and aimed for land, which they reached the same day. The second batch of survivors, with only life-jackets between them and ex-tinction, had a less lucky time. They received a couple of rubber boats, dropped by an Army bomber, and the injured men were hoisted onto these. That left twenty-five or so men clinging to the sides of the boats. Coated with oil, they hung on.

The whole day passed. They saw planes above but no rescuers. They were quite close to shore, really, and tried to make it during the night. But the current dragged them out again. Another day. Only thirty-six hours in the water but this was long enough. The sun and the cloying oil between them made the waiting almost unbearable. Heat and thirst. During the day, one of the injured men died. And less than two days after the sinking, several others struck out from the rafts, shouting des-perately for water. They were soon drowned. Then a case of potatoes floated past, to be grabbed by the men. These helped. But when the next day dawned, a quick count showed that more men had swum away into the night, never to return. Unknown to those left, both boats were gradu-ally being washed inshore with the tide—toward one of the myriad of islands specking the Pacific. It was tragic that the men who were lost during that night and the preceding day could only have been a mile or two from this island.

Although the island was full of enemy troops, the *Helena* men were eventually rescued by two American auxiliary vessels, escorted by four destroyers, and taking with them as a bonus one Japanese prisoner of war.

23

John Kennedy and PT-109

The life and death of John Kennedy have passed into global mythology. He was well known as the son of the U.S. ambassador to Britain, Joseph Kennedy; yet, if John had not become president of the United States, far fewer people would have remembered the story of the *PT-109*.

Kennedy joined the Navy and was assigned to Pacific duty in 1943, to Tulagi in the Solomons. Here he got his orders—to command the motor torpedo boat *PT-109*. It was April 1943 when he first set foot aboard the eighty-foot craft, which had already been on active service from Tulagi for some four months. In May Kennedy and his crew of ten were sailing out after dark on patrols for training purposes.

John Kennedy was twenty-six years old on 29 May. The next day the boat became one of a naval force sent to the Russell Islands ready for landings on New Guinea. About the middle of July *PT-109* sailed for Lumbari Island, nearer still to naval action. Almost a score of PTs were based on Lumbari; their role would involve intercepting Japanese sea movements during darkness and reporting enemy presences to bigger warships able to deal with them.

By the night of 1–2 August *PT-109* now had a total crew of thirteen men including Kennedy and formed one boat of a force assembled to attack a reported enemy group. The Japanese got through the straits they were patrolling some time after midnight, landed troops and supplies, and returned the same way a couple of hours later. The time was between 0200 and 0300.

Almost unbelievably, one of four enemy destroyers in the operation actually rammed *PT-109*, causing the stern of the boat to sink and killing two of the crew. A fuel explosion resulted in a fire around the craft. Immediately following the crash, Kennedy gave the order, "Abandon ship." The alarming fuel fire that had spread over the surrounding sea lasted little more than a quarter-hour before burning itself out. With the fire no longer a danger and *PT-109* still floating, Kennedy told the crew to board the bow portion still visible. Two or three hours elapsed while all the survivors were getting together again. Kennedy helped machinist Patrick McMahon, who had been badly scorched by the fire and explosion, and assisted another survivor, Charles Harris, to shed his heavy clothing and swim across to the bow-section of the boat.

So the survivors consisted of John Kennedy, two other junior officers, and eight crewmen. For the rest of the night, they clung to what remained of *PT-109* and kept afloat with the help of their life-jackets. They were all wearing one. Dawn: all too near an enemy-held part of Kolombangara Island, they might easily have been spotted. For this reason, and because the bow-section looked unlikely to last much longer, Kennedy decided by noon that they should try to reach an atoll over three miles distant.

Meanwhile, in the unoccupied volcanic uplands of the isle, Australian naval coastwatcher Lieutenant Evans had seen the *PT-109* bow and radioed its position to the Allies. Fighter planes were dispatched to look for any survivors.

Kennedy and the others converted a plank of wood from the boat into a float for them. Of the eleven men nine used the plank-float as a guide, while Kennedy towed Patrick McMahon. JFK breaststroked them forward slowly, with the crewman's life-jacket clenched between his teeth. This was perhaps the most medalworthy episode of the saga, since Kennedy had to go on swimming for some four hours. All eleven men reached their goal: the empty atoll, alive.

At least they were ashore. They could not drown. And McMahon did not die. Almost as soon as they were all safely ashore, Kennedy told them he intended to strike out to sea again with a light and a pistol to try to attract the attention of another PT boat. He brushed aside the others' objections and strode back into the gently lapping water at 2000. It was not deep, so he was either swimming in shallows or lurching over the cutting coral on the seabed. Needless to say, he saw no one and no one saw him. After nearly drowning during the night, he collapsed back on the atoll again. He was in no state to try again on the next night, although one of the others had a go at the same route, toward Ferguson Passage. There was really no chance of it succeeding, and the effort was no more than a gesture in the hope of seeking rescue.

Day three: Water was short, so they made the three-hour sea-trek to the nearest islet. The plank-float once more helped them get there, while Kennedy again hauled McMahon. Later on, Kennedy and Barney Ross made the short hop across to yet one more islet. The Japanese had vacated it recently, deciding not to bother to take with them some food, drink, and a small canoe. Here the two Americans met two local natives. These men had actually been dispatched by Lieutenant Evans down the hill to search for possible survivors. The two natives paddled across to the other nine Americans with victuals and water. Lennie Thom wrote a note for the natives to take back, asking for urgent help. During that

PT boat at speed, similar to Kennedy's PT-109.
Imperial War Museum

evening John Kennedy rejoined the nine, leaving Barney Ross on the other islet.

Day five now: Kennedy returned with the natives to Ross and added his own message on a coconut to Thom's for the natives to take. They must have got through quickly, because in the morning a war canoe paddled up to Kennedy and Ross. The next stage was water and food for all the survivors, followed by Kennedy accompanying the natives to Lieutenant Evans.

PT boats were at once sent speeding from Lumbazi under cover of darkness to rescue the eleven men from the *PT-109*. With the normal crew complement of these PT boats were two war correspondents. The story, of course, was how Ambassador Joseph Kennedy's son, John, had helped his ten crew members survive for five days while marooned in waters a long way behind enemy sealines and sealanes. The result was a splash story in the New York Times beneath the banners proclaiming: "Kennedy's Son Saves 10 in Pacific as Destroyer Splits His PT Boat."

The postscript to the story has lasted from then till today. John Kennedy was recommended for, and awarded, the U.S. Navy and Marine Corps Medal. No one could deny that he deserved it. His commanding officer emphasized that it was awarded "for the survival phase" of the whole affair. Cynics said later that it helped him win the presidency. It is true that the story became embellished over the years, and that John Kennedy was a controversial character. But the first week of August 1943 was an integral part of his life. And his actions during that week were all part of Kennedy the man. The war moved on.

After the death of JFK, historians and others began to reexamine and reevaluate the events of 1–2 August 1943. The overriding question has always been this: how did a slower enemy destroyer ram the faster PT boat and slice it in two without the Americans being aware of their presence? The answer must have been some sort of serious negligence by one or more of the crew. Some or all of them must have been asleep or incapable of duty. The conclusion—that the ultimate responsibility for the readiness of the craft for combat was, of course, the captain's— cannot be avoided. So John Kennedy probably felt fortunate to have avoided serious censure. Nevertheless, the mental and physical scars of the episode were bound to have remained with him permanently. Perhaps that could at least partly explain Kennedy's extreme efforts to salvage the situation by ensuring the safety of the survivors.

Midget Subs
Versus the Tirpitz

The date of the attack was 22 September 1943. All the months of training for the crews were over. The midget subs, or X-craft as they were called, prepared to tackle the *Tirpitz*. A thousand miles of rough seas heaved between the 40,000-ton prize—protected by every device conceivable—and any sort of vessel that might venture near. The *Tirpitz* lay no less than sixty miles from the sea, close under cliffs at the head of Kaafjord in northern Norway.

The overall plan included attacks on the 26,000-ton *Scharnhorst* and 12,000-ton *Lutzow* as well as the main target of *Tirpitz*. Six steel X-craft set out on their mission. They were towed by conventional submarines most of the way, and passage crews in the midgets spent a tiring eight days seeing them safely across the North Sea and up to Norway. Two men out of the three in each midget had to remain on watch for most of the twenty-four hours. Four times each day the little craft surfaced for fifteen minutes, while keeping submerged for the other twenty-three hours. The operational crews, meanwhile, got more fresh air as the full-size submarines steamed on the surface all night long. These crews included Lts. Donald Cameron and Godfrey Place.

Final orders received on the fifth day out told *X5, X6,* and *X7* to attack *Tirpitz; X8* to go for *Lutzow;* and *X9* and *X10* to aim at the *Scharnhorst.* The receipt of these orders seemed to step up the suspense and coincided with the first difficulties. At 0900 next morning *Syrtis* fired the usual underwater exploding signals to tell her small craft to surface. No response. At 0920 they hauled in the tow, which was found to have parted. *Syrtis* carried out an extensive search hour after hour, but none of the towing submarines ever saw *X9* again. The midget that *Syrtis* had been towing became the first X-craft lost. The passage crews had a job just as dangerous as the others.

The next craft to get into trouble was *X8*, whose trim seemed to be all wrong, and who was hard to handle. The crew were taken on board *Seanymph*, and *X8* was scuttled so that she should not be on the surface and endanger the rest of the operation. The only change in the plan as a result was that the *Lutzow* could not now be attacked.

By dusk on 18 September the weather relented a little and Place took Lt. Bill Whittam and the rest of the operational crew aboard *X7*. The changeover occurred outside Altenfjord, and Place borrowed the passage-crew CO's best boots, fur-lined and leather.

The other three submarines waited until the next day before they transferred operational crews. *Thrasher* was towing *X5*, *Truculent X6*, and *Sceptre X10*, so that was 5, 6, 7, and 10. The other two were gone. The crews had been transferred a night ahead of schedule, but still the midgets were being towed. The plan was for them to make their attacks and return to the big brother submarines.

Later that day *Stubborn*—towing *X7*—sighted a mine with its mooring rope caught in the midget's tow. The weapon came right along the line of the hawser until it reached the bows of *X7*. Place crawled along the casing of the midget sub and untangled it from the hawser and bows with his feet, while all the time it bobbed about on the Arctic waters. Sweat streamed down his face despite the cold. At last he managed to push it clear of the X-craft by clever kicks on its shell between the horns.

Early evening on 20 September the four little craft slipped their tows and left their guardians, who withdrew out to sea. Thus the midgets made their way into the Soroy Sound just about the ordered time, after nine days. From then on things got even more difficult and dangerous.

The two craft bound for the *Tirpitz*—6 and 7—kept pretty well together without ever encountering each other. Both craft crossed the minefield off Soroy during the night of 20–21 September. *Tirpitz* would be coming in range soon. They proceeded up the Altenfjord during the day on 21 September. Cameron's periscope on *X6* developed a defect, but the danger of blindness passed. As she crawled up the fjord at periscope depth *X7*

Lt. Donald Cameron, VC, RNR.
Imperial War Museum

Lt. B.C. Godfrey Place, VC, DSC, RN.
Imperial War Museum

saw several enemy vessels. Fortunately, visibility was fairly good so Place could dive the midget in time to avoid being seen. Even the telltale periscope trail could have ruined the whole thing if it was noticed. But no one spotted anything so outrageous, outlandish, as a pair of midget subs picking a steady course straight for the pride of the German navy.

On the port side of the fjord lay the Brattholm islands, and here at 70°N *X6* and *X7* spent the night of 21–22 September. *X10* arrived later. *X6* had to dive during the night more than once as she lay very near to the shipping lane to Hammerfest. *X7*, too, had some narrow squeaks as she tried to charge batteries while small boats chugged to and fro only a mile or so off. It would be heartbreaking if anything went wrong so near the *Tirpitz*. The only other excitement was Engine Room Artificer Whitley's successful efforts to fit a spare exhaust pipe, which he managed to do with the aid of sticky tape and chewing gum!

At last they reached the final fjord. They had negotiated all of Altenfjord. Soon after midnight *X7* left the lee of the Brattholms for

Kaafjord, off the head of the longer waterway. *X6* followed an hour afterwards. The first obstacle loomed upon them quickly: the antisubmarine net at the entrance of the fjord. It was a metal mesh, reaching almost to the bottom. But they were ready for it. Place got *X7* through the net, but Cameron had more trouble. His periscope had begun to flood soon after leaving the islands so that he could scarcely see anything up top. He made out the watery shape of a small coaster about to go through the net. This "boom" had just been opened to let the vessel through, so he daringly surfaced and put on all speed. *X6* actually swept through the antisubmarine net at early light in the wake of the enemy coaster! The midget's size—or lack of it—was certainly an advantage and the reason it was not seen.

Once through the net, Cameron dived to sixty feet and sailed by dead reckoning. He stripped the periscope but still it was imperfect. It was hardly surprising, therefore, that *X6* only barely avoided head-on collisions. Once she passed just beneath the bows of a stationary destroyer; another time, Cameron found her heading straight for the mooring buoy of a tanker half a mile from *Tirpitz*. Not a sound or a ripple must disturb the scene now. The waters of Kaafjord were glass-flat. E.R.A. Goddard had to keep all his wits about him on the wheel of *X6*. By 0705 she had reached the antitorpedo shore-net defense of *Tirpitz* and was through the boat entrance.

Meanwhile, *X7* had been forced deep by a patrol launch and been caught in a square of antitorpedo nets once used to protect the *Lutzow* but now no longer needed. For an hour or more before dawn Place pumped and blew until the craft at last shook herself free and shot up to the surface. Then a single strand of wire hooked itself across the periscope standard. By 0600 this came clear, and Place set course upfjord for the target.

0700: *X7* reached the antitorpedo net defenses. Place tried to negotiate these by diving to seventy-five feet but was caught. While she tried to extricate herself *X6* followed a picket boat through the boat gate. Breakfast was being prepared aboard the *Tirpitz* in blissful ignorance of the double danger so near at hand.

In calm, shallow water *X6* ran gently aground. She managed to free herself, but it started a stir in *Tirpitz*. In freeing the X-craft from the bottom, they broke the surface for a few seconds. A lookout aboard the battleship spotted them and reported "a long submarine-like object." His senior thought it might be a porpoise and he delayed passing on the report for five vital minutes. *X6* was now inside the range of *Tirpitz*'s guns. Again, just as the message had been conveyed to an officer, *X6* struck a rock and broke surface. She was identified, but before she could be fired on Lorimer swung her down again. She was a mere eighty yards abeam of the battleship, but the gyro was out of action and the periscope almost fully flooded. All Cameron could do was to try to fix their position by the shadow of the battleship.

Yet another five hectic minutes passed. *X6* became tangled in an obstruction hanging down from the *Tirpitz* herself. To wriggle clear *X6* had to surface once more, this time to the accompaniment of strong small-arms fire and hand grenades tossed from the deck of the ship. Cameron knew that escape was out of the question now. With the vast armament the ship carried and all the other auxiliary vessels in the fjord, *X6* could never get away.

"Smash all the secret equipment," he ordered, in case the Germans salvaged the craft. "I'm going to scuttle her."

Cameron took *X6* astern till the hydroplane guard was touching the *Tirpitz*'s hull and released the two charges, set to fire one hour later. The time was 0715. He scuttled the craft and they bailed out in turn through the wet-and-dry compartment.

In seconds they were struggling in the water near the *Tirpitz*. The German ship put out a picket boat and picked them up and also made a vain attempt to slip a tow around *X6* as she sank. Action stations had been sounded aboard *Tirpitz*, but from the state of unreadiness it was all too clear that complete surprise had been achieved. It took twenty minutes for the Germans even to prepare to shift the ship, which is a very slow time in emergency. All watertight doors were closed. Then steam for the boilers was ordered. While steam was still not up to pressure needed to sail, divers went over the side to see if they could trace the charges laid on the bottom.

Cameron, Lorimer, Goddard, and Sub-Lieutenant Dick Kendall stood in a group to one side while orders went to and fro. No one interrogated them yet, but they had been given hot coffee and schnapps after their icy dip. A human touch amid the war at sea. Cameron glanced down at his watch. It was eight o'clock. Only a quarter of an hour before the charges were due to go off. Things had not gone quite according to plan, of course, for they were not meant to be aboard *Tirpitz* on the receiving end of their own charges. They shifted a trifle uneasily from one foot to the other.

Meanwhile *X7* had stuck in the net at seventy-five feet depth—no picnic place. And they knew that *X6*'s charge would fire any time after 0800. Place decided that they must get clear as soon as humanly possible. He blew the tanks to full buoyancy and steamed full astern. She came out but turned beam-on to the net and broke surface. Then Place dived quickly.

The midget sub stuck by the bow. The depth this time was ninety-five feet. After five minutes of wriggling and blowing, she started to rise. The compass had gone haywire. Place did not know how near the shore he was. He stopped the motor, and *X7* came up to the surface. Amazingly, she must have passed underneath the nets or through the boat gate, for Place now saw *Tirpitz* straight ahead thirty yards off.

"Forty feet . . . Full speed ahead . . ."

She struck *Tirpitz* on her port side and slid quietly under the keel. Place released the starboard charge.

"Sixty feet . . . Slow astern . . ."

The port charge was released 150–200 feet further aft. It was 0730 now and *X6* had been scuttled. Place ordered 100 feet depth for *X7* and guessed they had got through the net; the compass still would not work. At sixty feet they were in the net again. Air was getting short now. Their charges would go off at about 0830, and *X6*'s any time after 0800. The situation became suddenly urgent.

X7 got entangled among first one net, then another, and a third. At 0740 her crew extricated her from one of them by sliding over the top of the net between the surface buoys. Luckily they were too close for heavy fire from the *Tirpitz*, but they were peppered with machine-gun bullets that hammered against the casing of the midget sub.

After passing over the nets they at once dived again, to 120 feet and the bottom. Then once more they tried to surface or reach periscope depth to see where they were. Their aim was now to get as far as possible from the forthcoming bangs, which could easily prove fatal to them. But in so doing, they ran into yet another net at sixty feet. Frantically frustrated, they tried to get clear.

Back aboard the *Tirpitz*, the divers returned to the vessel, having examined the hull for possible limpet mines stuck to the ship. Cameron slipped his sleeve up a fraction.

"It's o810," he breathed to Lorimer.

Then they were summoned for questioning and asked what charges they had placed, and where. Still the ship was not moved. All but an hour had elapsed. They stalled their answers, praying that the ship would not sail clear of the explosions.

o811: They prayed again that they were not directly over the charges as any eruption took place.

o812: A shattering outburst from the bowels of the fjord, below the battleship.

They were thrown off their feet by the force of it. Their own four tons of amatol had also sent up *X7*'s four tons. Eight tons of it were tearing into the *Tirpitz*. There was complete panic aboard. The German gun crew shot up some of their own tankers and small boats and even obliterated a shore position. The chaos was incredible. About a hundred men were lost, mainly through their own lack of self-control.

True, *Tirpitz* still floated, but with the force of the explosion the great ship heaved five or six feet upward and listed five degrees to port. A huge column of water streamed into the air and fell on to the decks. All the lights failed, and oil-fuel started to leak from amidships.

The surge of the explosion cracked through the water to *X7*, shaking her clear of the net. Place took her to the surface, saw *Tirpitz* still afloat, then dived deep again. The crew of *X7* gathered themselves together and took stock of the damage. Compasses and depth gauges were out of order, but little seemed wrong structurally. Nevertheless, the craft could not be controlled and broke surface several times. Each time she did so, *Tirpitz* fired on them, denting and damaging the hull more.

Place decided to abandon ship and so brought the craft to the surface. They could not use the escape chambers from a submerged position, as depth-charges were being dropped that might have killed them while they ascended from the sub. She surfaced close to a gunnery target, but before the crew could get out of the control room the gunfire sank her. Place was up on the casing so he stepped clear to the gunner target and was picked up and taken aboard the *Tirpitz*.

At about that moment, o843, *X5* was sighted 500 yards outside the nets. *Tirpitz* opened fire and claimed to have sunk her. Depth-charges were dropped, too, and nothing was ever heard of her, the third X-craft to get in sight of *Tirpitz*.

Back in *X7* it was life and death for the next two or three hours. After diving for the last time, she struck the bottom within seconds. Luckily the hatch had been shut in time. Bill Whittam took over. The diving escape sets were cut down from the stowage spot. Whittam began to flood the craft. There was no panic. They decided to use both escape hatches. Whittam and E.R.A. Whitley would use one each, and Sub-Lieutenant Bob Aitken whichever one was clear first. But they could not pass each other with their escape gear on, so Aitken was left by the wet-and-dry hatch forward.

Flooding was frighteningly slow, and it could not be sped up. The icy cold water rose gradually up their bodies, then fused an electric circuit—and the craft filled with fumes. They breathed their escape oxygen. With the craft about fully flooded, Aitken tried the forward hatch, but it would not open. He climbed back into the control room to discover that the breathing-bag was flat and the two emergency cylinders had been consumed. Whitley was dead.

In the darkness Aitken started to try to find Whittam, but as he straightened up his own oxygen bottle gave out, too. In a flash, he broke open the two emergency oxylets, which at that depth gave him only a breath or two each. He was very nearly dead; his last oxygen reserves gone, in a flooded submarine at 120 feet, with two men, both presumably dead, and the hatch still shut. All he had left in life was the breath he was still holding in his lungs. Somehow he scrambled back into the escape compartment for a last lunge at the hatch. Then he blacked out— till he opened his eyes to see a stream of oxygen bubbles as he sped to the surface. He must have opened the hatch and done his escape drill in a dream.

At 1115 Bob Aitken broke surface. A few minutes later he was drinking coffee and schnapps, wrapped in a blanket. He sat shivering still, remembering Whittam and Whitley.

Later it was learned that all three main engines of the *Tirpitz* were put out of action, as well as a generator room, lighting and electrical equipment, wireless telegraphy rooms, hydrophone station, A and C turrets, antiaircraft control positions, rangefinding gear, and the port rudder. The German naval war staff announced that she had been put out of action for months. Not until the following April was she able to limp from her anchorage, still crippled, only to await a final fate.

The six survivors of the X-craft were all made prisoners of war. All were duly decorated, Cameron and Place with the Victoria Cross. As Admiral Sir Max Horton described it, "Theirs had been a magnificent feat of arms."

Saga of the Liscome Bay

Seven to one was the ratio of Japanese to American aircraft lost in the Pacific during the winter of 1943–44: more precisely, 1,229 to 164. And a large proportion of the American air crews was saved. So the ratio in men was much higher. During nineteen major raids against fifteen enemy bases by the big carrier task forces from the Solomons to Marcus Island, and from the Marshalls to the Marianas, only one ship was lost—the escort carrier *Liscome Bay*. Yet when all is said and done, the Navy could never forget blows so brutal as the *Liscome Bay*.

A "baby flattop" is what they called escort carriers of her size. This is the story of the twenty-three minutes after she was torn to molten metal by a torpedo from a sub.

Thanksgiving Eve, 1943: The *Liscome Bay* was on her first battle assignment, covering the occupation of Makin in the Gilbert Islands. The submarine struck wholly by surprise. It was the ship's third day of the invasion and her crew had lost the tenseness that went with the beginning of an operation. They were comparatively relaxed, and only their standard occupational alertness remained. The scuttlebutt reported that the nearest enemy ships were two days away.

The torpedo came half an hour before dawn, and it was still dark when the *Liscome Bay* sank. General quarters had sounded routinely at 0505 in keeping with the strict custom of sending men to their battle stations at dawn and dusk in combat zones.

0510: The men were barely at their posts when a lookout shouted, "Here comes a torpedo."

It struck near the stern on the port side, and the havoc was instant and complete. The whole after-section broke into flames and most of the crew stationed there died. The casualty list for the *Liscome Bay* was the second largest of any U.S. Navy vessel in the war. The number of men on each baby flattop was never revealed, but they probably carried about half the 2,000 allotted to big carriers. Only 260 were saved. Ironically, many of those who died in the after-end might have been saved if they had not been called to battle stations before the attack. They would have been asleep in the crew's quarters forward.

Yeoman First Class Robert Joseph Charters had been in the Navy for six years. He arose when GQ sounded and put on his dungarees and the comfortable marine shoes he had bought before leaving San Diego. Then he set out for the small office where he stood duty watches at GQ.

The office belonged to Lt. Cdr. W. Carroll, who served the ship as first lieutenant, a detail involving the berthing of the crew and the care of all loose equipment. During battle, Carroll became damage-control officer, and it was through this post that all the damage-control parties were directed. At these times, Charters served as a talker, wearing the usual headset. Three men were usually stationed in the office during the day—Carroll; his assistant, a junior grade (jg) lieutenant; and Charters. During battle alerts, they were joined by a seaman named Gamekeeper. He manned battle phones connected to the bridge circuit.

Carroll was reading *The Virginian* when the explosion tore it from his hand. The hit was farther aft and on the opposite side of the ship, but the blast was so great that it ripped off Charters' life-jacket, dungaree shirt, battle phones, and even his marine shoes. The light went out. He remained in his stocking feet the rest of his time aboard.

Galliano, the junior grade, said to Charters, "Are you all right?"

Charters answered, "Yes," and then asked Carroll, "Are you all right?" There was no reply. He asked again. A pause, and then the commander said, "I'm all right." Galliano said, "I'm okay," without actually being asked. Flames from the hangar deck were visible overhead. Carroll felt for the doorway. "We've got to get up pressure to fight the fires," he said.

They groped outside to the passage but could not get up pressure on the hose. Charters looked at Carroll and said, "There's an awful gassy smell down here."

The officer was struggling with the valves to get up pressure and paid no attention. Finally Charters said, "This is no place for us. We better get out."

Carroll turned away reluctantly from the valves and followed Charters. Three or four more men joined them and they went forward. At the base of the burning elevator shaft, they found a warrant bosun named Hunt. Mr. Carroll said to Hunt, "Come on, Boats. Get outta here."

It was then that the others noticed for the first time that Carroll was covered with blood. He had been badly hit across the face and chest during the first explosion. The doctor happened to be in the group. He offered to dress Carroll's wounds but was refused.

They all went topside, coming out on the walkway around the flight deck. Looking back, they could see that the after-section of the ship was almost totally destroyed. All around them, 20mm and 40mm shells were exploding. Carroll told them to jump. Charters walked to the side and leaped off, unafraid of the great height and anxious only to get away from the bursting ammunition. In the water he looked back and saw that everybody had jumped except Carroll. He was walking up and down the flight deck, ordering others to jump and helping some over the side.

Back inside the ship, Bosun Hunt finally came on deck. He met Carroll again. But this time, instead of Carroll urging Hunt to go, Hunt urged Carroll to leave the ship.

"No," Carroll replied. "You go. I'm going to stay."

"I'm not going without you. I'll get a life preserver."

"No," Carroll insisted. "Go home to your wife and kids."

"If you're not going, I'm not," Hunt said. He walked across the flight deck toward the exploding ammunition, looking for an extra life-jacket.

"Come on back," shouted Carroll. "Don't go back there—I'll jump with you."

The doctor came up and joined them, and together the three of them cleared the side of the ship. Carroll's condition was getting worse. The doctor held him up while Hunt swam off to retrieve a life-raft. When Hunt came back, he asked how Carroll was. The doctor looked down at the man in his arms. "He's dead," he said.

Charters was one of the survivors of the *Liscome Bay*. He came back to the mainland and married his girl on Christmas Eve, 1943.

A rear admiral and two captains were on the ship. Rear Adm. Henry M. Mullinix was in charge of the air group operating from the *Liscome Bay* and two sister carriers in the area. One of the two captains, John G. Crommelin Jr., served as chief of staff to the admiral. The other captain was Irving D. Wiltsie, and he was actually captain of the *Liscome Bay*.

Rear Admiral Mullinix, a kind and friendly man, was in air plot when the explosion came and was badly injured. Several people saw him there with his head on his folded arms, but others reported seeing him later swimming in the flame-swept sea. He did not survive.

Captain Crommelin, one of five famous brothers who were all Navy officers, had just stepped from the shower when the torpedo hit. Naked and wet, he was badly burned. Still without clothes, he walked out onto the flight deck and directed the abandoning in his area. Later he jumped overboard himself, then swam for an hour and twenty minutes before a destroyer picked him up.

Captain Wiltsie survived the original bang. Concerned by the damage aft and the men who were stationed there, he walked toward the stern on the flight deck to inspect the area. Several officers called to him to come back, but he went on walking into erupting ammunition and smoke. He was never seen again.

Clovis Roach was a storekeeper first class. A Texan, slight and wispy in appearance with thinning blond hair, he looked as Ernie Pyle must have looked at 26. Before this he had been on the heavy cruiser *San Francisco* and he liked the security of her thick-skinned sturdiness. The *Liscome Bay*'s light metal scared him. He decided that he would go below decks only when he had to.

So at 2100 Roach went to sleep as usual in a cot on the fantail. Reveille next morning awakened him twenty minutes before general quarters. Roach went down to the galley and bakeshop, where he talked with his buddies among the cooks and bakers. He munched a coffee ring, drank a cup of coffee, and shot the breeze about who was on duty the night before. Several of the men were complaining about the lack of action. Roach replied, "I've seen it calm like this before. Something'll happen. It always does when it's calm."

GQ sounded and he headed forward to his battle station. He was wearing dungarees, a hat, regular Navy oxfords, and carrying his life-

preserver under his arm. Roach's battle station was in the forward issue room and it was his duty to hand out emergency issues of flight and
engine gear during battle. But the forward issue room was two decks
down, and because of his aversion to being below decks he didn't go
there. He went instead to sickbay, two decks above the issue room but
astride the sole passage leading below. It had become his habit to stay
there during GQ unless he spotted someone heading below with a request. Then he would accompany the man below, issue the requested
items, and come back up to sickbay. Roach's statement on the subject
was very succinct: "As long as it's necessary to stay below I'll stay there,
but if it's not, I won't."

Five men had battle stations in sickbay: the doctor, a chief pharmacist's mate, and three other pharmacist's mates. They were there when
Roach arrived. Roach went into the treatment room with one of the
others. He sat on the table and the mate sat on a chair by a bulkhead.
While they were talking about their mission against Makin and specu-
lating on the success of the operation against Tarawa farther south, the
torpedo went off. The bulkhead behind the treatment table blew inward,
hitting Roach on the back and knocking him ten feet through the door.
He yelled, "There may be another one."

Then he hit the deck again. Another explosion followed, somewhat
less violent than the first, and Roach got to his feet. So did the others,
and in the general melee of voices they all established that they were
still alive. That was something. Roach groped his way back into the treatment room, searching for his life-jacket. He found it in the dust and
rubble on the deck.

The men looked down the passages leading from sickbay. Both were
blocked by debris and flames from the hangar deck. Roach also looked
down the hatch leading to the forward issue room. It was utterly im-
passable. He went back and tried the port and starboard passages again.
No success.

The list of the ship, the smoke and flames, and the lack of any communication made it obvious that it was time to get out, if a way could
be found. Roach spoke up: "I'm going to try working my way forward
along the port passageway to the first-division compartment. Anybody
want to come?"

Without waiting for an answer, he started forward. He could hear
others following him, but he did not look back. All the bulkheads were

blown in. He climbed and crawled around them. He squirmed through a hole so small that he scraped off a shoe. Finally there was only one man behind him. Together they made it through the first-division compartment. They found it slightly damaged and empty and they knew there must be a way out. To Roach it seemed the first clear sign that he might be a survivor. Following a trail of fresh air, he climbed two ladders and came out eventually on the high—or starboard—side of the ship. The flames and smoke were curling up the flight deck, so he knew he couldn't abandon ship there. He went down to the port side. By the light of the flames he could see heads bobbing about in the water. No rafts were visible, but someone behind him said, "There are three rafts and a floater-net way out there."

Always a lone operator, Roach left the others on the deck, climbed down the anchor chain, and dropped six feet into the water. He took off his remaining shoe and started to swim, but his life-jacket held him back as flames whipped around the bow. Only a change in the wind saved him from burns or worse. He swam out to the floater-net and climbed on with about forty others. Someone shouted in a hoarse cry, "There she goes."

Roach looked back to see the flames quenched as the ship slid beneath the waves. That was the end of the *Liscome Bay*. But not the end of Roach. He was a survivor. In the specific and the general sense.

January—December 1944

The D-day Armada

The D-day invasion was the most massive amphibious assault in the whole of history: 132,000 troops were transported from southern England to northern France, to a fifty-mile strip of the Normandy shore. Nearly 7,000 ships and craft took them there. The Americans landed to the west on Utah and Omaha beaches. The British and Canadians landed to the east on Gold, Juno, and Sword. Airborne landings supported both flanks. Ten thousand Allied troops were either killed or wounded, or one in every thirteen men.

D-1. Sunrise silhouetted landing craft and warships as they started out to sea. Some were already on their way: Forces U, O, and G from the west, Force J from the Portsmouth area, Force S from east of Portsmouth. They came from Falmouth, Fowey, Plymouth, Salcombe, Dartmouth, Brixham, Torbay, Portland, Weymouth, Poole, Southampton, Solent, Spithead, Shoreham, Newhaven, Harwich, and the Nore. All with one purpose: to liberate Europe.

But first came the Channel. The wind gusted and whipped the waves to five feet and more. Men gripped their stomachs, gritted their teeth. The winds stood at WSW with a force of 16–20 MPH. It fell at times, but then the gusts returned.

The Red Crosses of a field ambulance unit brought reality to a scene described by the naval commander, Adm. Bertram Ramsay, as unreal because of the absence of enemy activity. Someone would need these on the next day. Meanwhile, barrage balloons fluttered over the con-

*DUKWs launched from larger craft were invaluable
for amphibious support.* Imperial War Museum

voys. Tank landing craft plowed a line-astern course, escorted by a bevy
of larger ships.

All through that morning they sailed from west, north, and east. The
first rendezvous? Area Z, a circular zone, eight miles in diameter and twenty-
five miles south of Portsmouth and Hayling Island. From here on, they
would follow one of the swept channels in a due southerly direction. Area
Z was at once christened "Piccadilly Circus" by the Royal Navy.

So that the start of the ten approach channels should be precisely
positioned, ten special buoys had been laid, timed to transmit signals
between 1400 and 2200 on six successive days from 4 June. The system
proved to be completely successful. As the ships assembled at Area Z,

the men ate stew, followed by plum pudding. And the flat-bottomed tank landing-craft pitched and rolled to the tide.

After lunch began the biggest, most majestic minesweeping operation of the war. As many as 300 sweepers moved south in perfect formation. Twelve flotillas of large minesweepers and many more smaller ones literally swept all before them in a broad twelve-channel front. This was fifteen miles wide at the start and thirty miles wide at the southern end. The crews of destroyers, corvettes, and others watched fascinated as the groups of sweepers, in immaculate drill-like lines, moved back and forth down the vital channels. Cold-blooded courage accompanied the crews of the sweepers, and the periodic punctuation of their purpose by violent explosions seemed detached from the peaceful pattern of ships on sea.

The sweepers found fewer fields than they expected. There was reason to think that the Germans would have laid a line right across from the Cherbourg peninsula to Le Havre, but this did not materialize. The credit for foiling the enemy's definite intention went to the Air Forces and the Navy. Air attacks had unknowingly delayed the arrival of mine supplies by their blanket bombing of French railways. And when the mines finally reached Le Havre, the Royal Navy and Coastal Command intercepted the flotilla of ships sent specially from Brest to lay them. They dealt with every minelayer except one.

Since the sweepers encountered less interruption than was anticipated, they were ahead of schedule and actually within sight of the invasion coast long before dark. Two flotillas were level with Le Havre by sunset and so close that some of them could see individual houses on the Vierville coastline, destined to be the location of the Omaha landings, now less than twelve miles off. Yet no guns fired on them. Although the enemy was prepared for invasion, they discounted this week in view of the poor weather. And on this day of all others, the Luftwaffe flew only a single mission in the west—and this was far from the invasion scene. General Eisenhower, as supreme commander, could hardly have hoped for such luck.

But it was not all due to luck. While the fleet was still assembling at Area Z, the elaborate coverplan, Operation Fortitude, went into action. For days now the Allied Air Forces had been hammering the French coast from Cap Gris Nez to Le Havre. Even until D-1, twice the tonnage of bombs was being dropped in the Pas-de-Calais area as in Normandy.

There is no doubt that this deceptive bombing did its job, so that by D-1 the enemy had no idea that invasion was imminent, and even if they had, all the signs pointed to the Pas-de-Calais. To underline this, dummy paratroops were dropped in three main areas, to cause confusion about the real destination of airborne forces soon to be in France.

But the main diversions were over the sea, near the Straits of Dover. The Allies wanted to conceal the ultimate direction of the fleet moving mainly eastward up the channel. This force would not reach Area Z till dark, when its change of route south would not be noticed. An amazing radar operation, designed to deceive the enemy into believing the assault to be aimed farther east, accomplished this goal. The twofold task was, first, to jam enemy warning stations in the actual area to be invaded—Cherbourg and Le Havre—and second, to mislead the Le Havre–Calais stations into reporting that the fleet was sailing toward this sector.

Thirty-four small ships and over a hundred aircraft undertook this strange mission. Following in the wake of the minesweepers, the vessels aimed for Cap d'Antifer, north of Le Havre, towing as many barrage balloons as they could to simulate big ships on enemy radar screens. Then, when they were within radar range, they sailed slowly up toward Calais. Bombers then flew around overhead, dropped tinfoil by the bundle, one each minute. These strips of paper would give the Germans false radar readings. The aircraft made endless orbits, slowly nearer the coast, to suggest a convoy of ships sailing across the Channel well to the north of the actual D-day landfall. Similar diversions off Boulogne also helped toward the eventual state of surprise achieved. With a phantom fleet off Dover, craft ostensibly on obscure courses up the Channel, dummy paratroops, and jamming on radar, the confusion was complete before the end of D-1.

The armada slowly turned south and the men took their last look at England as St. Catherine's Point, on the southeast tip of the Isle of Wight, merged into the horizon. Nothing now but ships and sea till the next day. And no one knew what that held in store for anyone.

Darkness. Exactly as planned, all the forces moving east from Devon and the west generally veered round to starboard. Every ship and craft was on the move at last. Apart from the thousands of landing craft themselves, Operation Neptune needed eight battleships and monitors, twenty-two cruisers, ninety-three destroyers, 450 escorts and minesweepers, and 360 motor launches, motor torpedo boats, and kindred craft.

Past now were camouflage and concealment. Landing craft had emerged from their rivers and creeks, and the first sections of the floating breakwater were on their way, too. The weather was keeping to the forecast of rough on Monday and better on Tuesday for D-day. Force U met stormy seas, and their commanding officers battled on through them all, spending a total of seventy hours on their bridges, or nearly three days and nights without sleep. Out of the 128 tank landing craft in the Group U 2A of this force, only seven failed to take part in the actual assault, owing to engine trouble as well as the weather. Fully 95 percent participated.

Still all was anticlimax. The quiet before the storm. The realization slowly came to Admiral Ramsay that utter tactical surprise was being achieved. Was it possible that thousands of landing craft and all their attendant ships could cross the Channel without the Germans knowing?

The sullen oily sea of the grey day dissolved into a black mass of surging liquid. By 0200 Force U, nearly 1,000 ships strong, was arranging in order undetected off the Cotentin Peninsula, only twelve miles northeast of the Utah landing beaches. Overhead they heard the friendly drone of aircraft carrying airborne troops to precise points on that peninsula—or so they hoped. Gradually the 30,000 men and 3,500 vehicles approached the shore. E-boats due to patrol the Seine Bay turned back toward Cherbourg because of bad weather. The radar jamming of enemy stations was succeeding, for the coastal batteries still remained silent.

Also twelve miles offshore, in channels 3 and 4, Force O for Omaha halted at 0251–0300 to lower their landing craft from the parent vessels that had borne them across so far. The sea swirled below the craft as they hit it with a jolt. Many of the men were sick long before the assault. The sea swamped some of the craft almost as soon as they were on their own, and several sank. Men drowned, dragged down by the weight of the gear and the rough rollers. Others were hauled to safety. Luckier landing craft shipped gallons of water, and only bailing with tin hats saved the men from the fate of the drowned. One battle against sinking, the next to beat seasickness, and soon the Germans to face.

Casualties were light in the assault craft, but the special tanks met a mass of tragedies. Because of the state of the sea, one battalion of tank landing craft could not launch its amphibious vehicles. The other one risked twenty-nine, but a number of these sank at once, four miles out to sea. Some were swamped during the long run-in. And of all twenty-nine, only two were to reach the shore. Men struggled to get free, but many died.

Even the troops in ordinary landing craft were chilled, cramped, and weakened by sickness—the worst way possible to await an assault that to many would be a baptism of battle. Because of the danger of enemy shore batteries, the lowering positions from the motherships had been fixed for the Western Task Force at ten to eleven miles from the shore. The distance also put them outside the area known to be mined. This long haul to the shore contributed to the tragic losses sustained by the Americans.

Proceeding in parallel along channels 5 to 10, Forces S and J stole still farther inshore before reaching their agreed lowering positions. Seven to eight miles out they prepared for the final assault. Over to the left, Le Havre still slumbered. The waves were four feet now, and the 15-MPH wind helped to drown any sounds of the approaching invaders.

Clouds thickened through the night. Now the eastern forces were within range of the heavy guns of Le Havre. Force S, the 3rd British Division with all its supporting units, anchored uneasily at this assembly point, not knowing if the enemy radar was working or not. In fact, it was not.

Craft near enough to notice could see the reassuring silhouettes of escort warships, *Warspite* and *Ramillies*. The first false dawn etched masts and funnels in the sky. Then, as faint light sprinkled over the fleet, a squadron of aircraft flew low over the area, laying an enveloping smokescreen to the east. The black fog blanketed the whole force from Le Havre just at the critical moment of bombardment.

The first fighting. Four E-boats and some armed trawlers headed out of Le Havre just as Bombarding Force D arrived on the eastern flank. They were spotted against the land, and the order went at once to the aircraft: "Make smoke."

The aircraft flew in low over the sea, and laid their screen in seconds, but from behind it the enemy fired a group of torpedoes. *Warspite* and *Ramillies* were able to track these, which went right between the two warships. Suddenly the sound of a hit, followed by flames licking and lashing the deck of the Norwegian destroyer *Svenner*. The Allies opened fire and soon sank one of the trawlers and damaged another. The attack was not renewed. So this hit-and-run raid was the German navy's total effort on D-day. Fire gripped the destroyer as she slipped lower in the waterline. Slowly she sank amid acrid smoke.

Then a dull, droning soulless sound, but with the regular beat of engines. Ships' motors bringing the armada in right on time. Heaving low over the horizon, they advanced. LCAs, LCIs, LCTs, LCFs, LSSs, LCGs; landing ships and headquarters ships; DUKWs and minecraft. Up to forty ships in a column, with the lines reaching right away to port and starboard. Closer, closer, till anticipation was about to become actuality. Men crouched low just above the outline of their landing craft. A host of heads bent on a purpose as proud as any in history.

Thousands of men—like Cpl. George Andy, Royal Marines, coxswain of LCA 786 and age nineteen. Seven miles out in the tideway his assault landing craft lost its steering wheel while being lowered from the parent ship. The crew's duty was to get the thirty-two soldiers ashore, and in such a sea only one way existed to do so. Tandy slipped over the stern and stood with one foot on the rudder-guard, guiding the rudder with the other. With sickening frequency the sea hoisted him high in the air and then plunged him back into the troughs. For four and a half hours Tandy stuck it, through mines and everything else. Numbed, bruised, bewildered—but still alive.

In the chilly dawn waters, this landing craft symbolizes Operation Overlord, the invasion of Normandy. Imperial War Museum

As LCA 786 and all the others crept toward the coast, the battle-ships braced themselves for the attack. Terrific tension, as the angles of their guns slowly widened to the exact elevation. Thin fingers poised, pointing to land—and the day of reckoning, deliverance. D-day.

Out of the morning mist broke a barrage of sound. The concerted crescendo of almost 1,000 guns. Across the sea the shells whistled and whined to the Normandy shore, and the decks of the ships shuddered with the quivering recoil. The starter's gun. Here was history about to be made, as cloudy columns of smudgy smoke rose in a green-black blot along the fringes of France. Men's hearts were in their mouths, or throats, or stomachs. A glance at a watch, muted mutterings, a prayer.

The Americans were due to land on Omaha and Utah. Over at Omaha the morning made the Utah landings seem like a beach party—almost. Going back a few hours, here "hell" was the only word for the time from 0300 onwards, indeed, from 0251, when the headquarters ship *Ancon* anchored in the transport area thirteen miles offshore.

The assault was to be delivered by the 1st U.S. Infantry Division, with the 116th Regiment attached from the 29th U.S. Infantry Division. The 29th Division were due to follow up and take over the western sector of the area.

The wind force of ten to eighteen knots caused havoc. Waves here were up to six feet high, while on the beach the breakers measured three to four feet. At 0300 the assault infantry units began loading into their small craft, lowered from parent ships. Some were immediately swamped, and so the pattern was set: a battle against the elements and the enemy.

Then came the tragedy of the first twenty-nine amphibious tanks on the left flank: floundering, foundering, sinking, in the watery wild-ness before dawn. Launched at H-50 minutes, 6,000 yards out, they began within minutes to suffer the crippling damage of broken struts, torn canvas, and engine trouble from water flooding the engine com-partment. The remaining three tanks of the battalion could not be launched because the ramp of their LCT was damaged.

As landing craft came within a few miles of the shore, they passed men from the sunken tanks, those who were not already drowned strug-gling in life-preservers and on rafts. Over on the right flank, the DD tanks could not be launched ahead of the assault at all, owing to the sea and the fate of the first thirty-two. So the landing craft carrying the infantry had to plod and toss toward the shore without this vital advantage of vanguard support.

Right from departure, spray drenched the assault craft. Most of them started to ship enough water to necessitate the use of pumps, which were incapable of carrying the load. The troops' only option was to bail themselves out with their helmets, which at least occupied their hands and minds.

Ten out of the 180–200 landing craft used in the early waves were swamped—some almost as soon as they were lowered, others nearer the beach. But nearly all the men were saved by naval craft or passing ships. So from the outset the troops were drenched and, in addition, became cramped, seasick, scared, and weakened, the worst possible way of starting strenuous and dangerous action on an alien shore.

The Omaha assault gradually got more chaotic, so that by 0600 craft were coming in anything from a few hundred yards to a mile off course. The weather made navigation over thirteen miles inevitably inaccurate. The strong onshore wind whipped the tide higher than it would have been normally, so the underwater obstacles were awash sooner than anticipated and hidden deeper every minute. By then, many men had been seaborne in their landing craft for three hours and had reached a low ebb of efficiency.

H-35 minutes brought the bombers on the scene. From 0555 to 0614 this force of Liberators added another dramatic dimension and disappointment to the hard-tried troops. In their anxiety not to hit any advance craft coming in near the coast, the bombers missed the beach defenses and obstacles altogether.

The concentrated naval barrage had broken five minutes earlier, at 0550. The battleships *Texas* and *Arkansas* poured some 600 rounds of heavy shells ashore and then came the cruisers, destroyers, and support fire. The aim was to neutralize not only the beach defenses but positions that could lay flanking fire on the invasion points. But, as with the air assault, the cloud prevented accurate rangefinding, and the ships had to err on the side of overshoot. It was to prove a costly margin of safety.

The Liberators droned away into the distance. Sixteen more minutes to go. The naval shells burst behind the beaches as the time ticked by on thousands of wristwatches. More mortars from the shore. And any minute the men had to tumble out of the craft to face the next stage. The navigational side-slip went on. There was no point on relying on anyone else now. Some of the tank landing craft failed to keep their position in such intensely difficult conditions.

Nearer, nearer, now, advanced the first forces on Omaha. 0627. The overpowering pounding from the ships reached its crescendo, then suddenly stopped, dead on schedule. There was just one thought in the mind of every man. Just three more minutes, just a few hundred yards of water. And then?

0628: Leading craft, 440 yards out, came under heavy fire from automatic weapons and artillery ashore. The beaches were unscarred by the air bombardment.

0629: Men crouched down in their landing craft, clenched their teeth and hands, and waited as that last sixty seconds circled away. Right away on the west flank, directly in front of an opening at Vierville, tank landing craft came in. The LCT carrying one company commander was sunk just offshore. Five officers were killed or wounded.

Eisenhower, Montgomery, and other Allied officers discuss plans at their headquarters near Portsmouth.
Imperial War Museum

Eight of one company's sixteen tanks landed and started to fire from the water's edge. An amphibious tank hit an underwater obstacle in the murky morning and exploded. This was due to the fast-flooding tide. Nearby, a landing craft suffered the same fate from a direct hit before its occupants had even begun the battle. For them it was over.

One of six assault landing craft carrying the leading company in the assault on the western sector foundered and started to sink. Well out of their depth, the men had to jump. Rangers passing in another craft saw them leaping from the LCA and being dragged down by their loads. Assault waves were coming in late, by four to six minutes.

0635: A 970-yard strip of hell on the beach was designated Dog Green. The remaining five craft had stopped short of the beach, grounding 100 yards out on sand barriers. The enemy's automatic weapons had range, and the fire was actually beating on the ramps before they were lowered. Or else bullets whipped into the surf just ahead of ramps.

Ramps down. Sixteen steps to who knew what? Some of the Yanks clattered down and fell waist-deep into the water. Others found themselves up to their necks. Their heads were targets for the fire from shore. From two particular points the enemy hit with awful results.

As the range of the ramps attracted a convergence of fire, some of the men dived over the sides or kept under the water for as long as they could. Stiff, weak, loaded, they trudged in through the shallows, the uneven footing making their progress all the slower. Like a nightmare.

As if this were the signal for which the enemy had waited, all boats came under criss-cross machine-gun fire. . . . As the first men jumped, they crumpled and flopped into the water. Then order was lost. It seemed to the men that the only way to get ashore was to dive headfirst in and swim clear of the fire that was striking the boats. But, as they hit the water, their heavy equipment dragged them down and soon they were struggling to keep afloat. Some were hit in the water and wounded. Some drowned then and there . . . but some moved safely through the bullet-fire to the sand and then, finding they could not hold there, went back into the water and used it as cover, only their heads sticking out. Those who survived kept moving forward with the tide, sheltering at times behind underwater obstacles, and in this way they finally made their landings.

Within ten minutes of the ramps being lowered, A Company had become inert, leaderless and almost incapable of action. Every officer and sergeant had been killed or wounded. . . . It had become a struggle for survival and rescue. The men in the water pushed wounded men ashore ahead of them, and those who had reached the sands crawled back into the water pulling others to land to save them from drowning. In many cases only to see the rescued men wounded again or to be hit themselves.

Within 20 minutes of striking the beach A Company had ceased to be an assault company and had become a forlorn little rescue party bent upon survival and the saving of lives.

This was only the start. The rest of D-day lies beyond the scope of a story of the war at sea. The British landed with tanks. The Canadians and French played their part. The U.S. Rangers, too. And the Americans eventually got off Omaha. Then the Allied navies brought the amazing artificial Mulberry Harbors across the Channel to assist the buildup after the initial invasion. And as the armies advanced, only sunken hulks remained as reminders of the splendor and the pain of D-day, 6 June 1944.

The USS Rích:
D-day and After

The USS *Rich* helped "put 'em ashore" in France. In other words, it was D-day for a DE (destroyer escort). One of the crew was D. J. Lawrence, who remembered it all.

It was the morning of 6 June. The *Rich* had steamed hard to get on station from her Irish port. She scythed swiftly through the sharp swell that was running in the Channel on D-day. All around were the heterogeneous display of invasion craft inching through the gloom. Overhead came the continuous drone of aircraft engines as the Allied air forces bombed targets inland. The dull crump of their bombs could be heard far out to sea. Embracing the *Rich* were heavier ships, the big battlewagons whose guns thundered in unison with the crash of the bombs. Closer in still, the cruisers added their own distinctive din.

The German shore batteries were far from silenced. Splashes from their enormous shells hid the *Quincy* at times, as she herself was dropping her own salvos on the beach. As a precaution, a heavy smokescreen was laid between the marauding forces and the shoreline. The *Corry* was in too close and she alone was denied the protection being afforded the main force. The big shells from the Nazi batteries splashed all around her as she took desperate avoiding action. The guns eventually found their target and a heavy-caliber shell hit the little DD. They broke her back. She was the only ship of size to fall to the German marksmen.

All of 6 and 7 June the story was the same for the *Rich*. Everybody at general quarters all night; steady steaming; and watchful eyes turned skywards looking for the absent Luftwaffe. It was the night of 7 June when the klaxon for action stations sounded, all too late.

The AA guns all around opened up for the first time. Men on deck who saw the whole thing swore afterwards that the German bomber was trailing a string of blue lights that seemed to serve no purpose except to distract the gunners. "They trailed out like the lights on a Christmas tree," said GM/c Fox, who was handling No. 3 gun. "I should have had him. I was still cursing my bad luck the next day."

The aircraft swept in low and released a bomb that fell just astern of the little destroyer escort. It felt like it was going to lift us clear out of the water.

The second bomb burst almost alongside and the third caught the French destroyer ahead of the *Rich* squarely on the stern. There was a blinding blue flash as the Frenchman went up. She totally disintegrated . . . we were horror-struck.

It was 0830 on 8 June. The *Rich* received orders to move in to the beach and stand by the *Glennon,* which had been mined. "All hands to general quarters." We had no premonition of the danger to come; everybody had been told that the beachhead was firmly established and that the invasion forces were even at that moment pressing inland.

I was at G2 in the fire-room. The Joe pot was going as usual and we were more or less relaxing. I had just made an entry in the log at nine o'clock when the explosion came. She lifted out of the water and then fell violently back again. I remember the coffee pot flying across the room. Everything was crashing and flying around, including floor plates. One of them in the engine room flew right up and was hurled into the condenser. Then all the lights went out. That was terrible. Everything total darkness and we could hear the hiss of superheated steam . . .

The word *superheated* can conjure up dreadful pictures. But any blackgang man will know the chill feeling when below-decks is suddenly plunged into darkness. Even a normal lighting breakdown will cause everyone to stand still in their places until the emergency supply comes on. Walking into heavy machinery can be a painful experience. But under the conditions that just enveloped the *Rich*, the blackgang knew from the dread sound of steam that out there somewhere in the darkness was a thin finger so hot it could strip flesh to the bone.

I got hold of a flashlight, and soon found that the port steam gauge glass was broken. The sound of the free steam was coming from here. The fire-room crew isolated the gauge from the steam line and lit off No. 2 boiler hoping to raise the steam pressure—which had fallen to 300 lb.

The lights had by now come back on. The force of the explosion had tripped the generators out. We really didn't have time to think about what damage had occurred or what in hell was happening topside. No sooner had the lights come on again than we were thrown to the deck by the second explosion. Again we were thrust into darkness and this time there was no relief because the lights never did come on again.

We could hear the steam hissing again. We found that this time it was the starboard gauge and we set about isolating this as well. The chief groped his way into the fire-room, and when he checked out the damage, ordered the men topside.

We needed no second bidding and headed for the ladder. We could feel the *Rich* taking on a list even as we climbed. It was now that the third explosion came, this one the heaviest of all. The *Rich* had sailed into the center of a Nazi minefield. It wasn't charted, and most of the men thought that the bomber trailing the Christmas tree lights had been responsible.

A guy named Bateman was just going up through the hatch when that explosion threw him clear to the overhead. He got a gash right across his head. Balack had secured his evaporators before starting up the ladder and he too was hurled across the deck and badly bruised. We made our way up through the gloom, and the shambles of what had been the machine shop. It was like going through tangled barbed wire on a dark night. You needed to take a real hold on your nerves and not panic. It was that bad. The spare boiler tubing had come down from the overhead and lay twisted into a maze like a gigantic metal spider web. Ammo from the 20mm clipping room lay all over the place. There were tools, boxes, pipes, spare parts . . . all jumbled up and leaning at crazy angles and in dangerous positions. But somehow we got through and out onto the deck.

Now for the first time we men from the engine room had some idea of what had happened. The entire stern of the *Rich* had just been blown off. We could see no smoke or fire. We just heard the slow and deadly hiss of steam from No. 1 fire-room. The ship's body was grotesquely broken and twisted. There could be no doubt about it—we were finished. The starboard side had been thrust upward a good three feet above the rest of the deck. The mast had smashed down across the flying bridge, trapping several men there.

The ship was settling, going down slowly by the bow. In a matter of seconds a PT boat chugged alongside and other rescue craft soon appeared, ready to take off the wounded. There was no sign of panic among those of us who were all right, we were too busy caring for the wounded.

We could feel the ship going down under our feet. We had only one thought and that was to care for those needing help. Everyone did something. Some hurried about the ship administering morphine to those worst injured. Others got the wounded onto stretchers and over the side to the waiting PT boat. When the supply of stretchers ran out, volunteers went down into the darkness of the officer quarters and brought back mattresses to serve instead.

I found the gunnery officer, Lieutenant Fraser, who had a bad injury to his head. Fraser told me to go and see if the captain was all right. When I got to the bridge I found that the rangefinder had been blown off its base and had fallen to the deck. This and the blast had between them injured a great number of men. The skipper was alive but had sustained leg injuries. The executive officer, Lt. Cmdr. Pearson, USNR, was severely injured but refused to move. He just said: "There are others worse off than me—tend to them first."

Ensign Cunningham had a broken leg but kept going in spite of being in terrible pain. He insisted on helping others down from the shattered bridge. And so it went on, all through the stricken ship. Every man was his own hero that terrible morning. None was more prominent than his fellows. Everyone was filled with that quiet heroism that will take over a ship's company when they know she is dying from her wounds.

I reported back to the gunnery officer. By now water almost covered the main deck, and he realized that the end could not be far away. Lt. Fraser made sure that the depth-charges were set on "safe," so that when the *Rich* made her final plunge the water pressure would not automatically set off the hydrostatic pistols in the ash-cans. If the charges went up, it would mean the inevitable death of all those men in the water and fatal damage to the surrounding ships.

Almost all the wounded had been transferred by now, but some could not be moved. Others were still trapped by the rangefinder and the fallen mast on the bridge. The last moments came . . .

The *Rich* hung on as though reluctant to give up its hold on life and to take those of her crew still trapped to the watery grave. She began to roll. Her buoyancy almost gone, she was awash and well down on the port side. The rescue craft that had tied up alongside now cast off. They began to put distance between themselves and the dying vessel so as not to be caught by her as she turned over. Two or three men on the flying bridge went off at the last moment, the ship revolving beneath their feet. Using the top part of the bridge as a boost, they dived into the water that was fast rising to meet them.

Lt. Cmdr. Pearson still refused to allow himself to be moved in favor of others. It had become too late to help him now. He went down with the ship . . .

Those in the water turned on their backs as they swam, to watch the last throes of their gallant little ship. Their beloved *Rich* went down slowly, gracefully, with dignity, her colors still flying.

The rescue craft swarmed back to pick up those who had escaped at the last moment and got most of them out of the water in a matter of minutes. Those who lost their lives and went down with the *Rich* were those men killed outright in the three explosions that tore the ship apart. The survivors were taken to England, and most of us returned to the States shortly afterwards.

Nothing in the short life of the *Rich* emblazoned her name across Navy records. She was a small ship of the fleet who performed at times a monotonous and seemingly unimportant task. Yet it is the sum of such tasks when well done that makes all the difference between success and failure in war. So it was for the *Rich.*

George Bush and
the Flying Casket

Autumn 1943: U.S. Navy pilot Ens. George H. W. Bush was training for
future action in torpedo bombers. After finishing his flight training, Bush
was assigned to the USS *San Jacinto,* a light aircraft carrier. Now it was
spring 1944 as the *San Jacinto* sped west over the watery vastnesses of
the Pacific Ocean. Bush would be piloting a TBM Avenger, designed to
carry and drop a 2,000-pound torpedo or similar bombload. It was called
"low and slow" by some of the pilots, and "flying casket" by other people.
But Bush rather fancied the idea of diving almost to water level and then
gliding along to release his torpedo.

Bush's first sight of fatalities came one day after he had landed safely
on the carrier. Another pilot crashed into one of the ship's gun-positions.
Bush saw all four of the gun crew killed before him. Some of the Avengers' early assignments were shielding land forces as they fought from island to island. Or the Avengers glide-bombed specific enemy strongpoints
on land. On still other occasions, they searched for submarines, and in this
role they carried depth-charges ready to be dropped.

Bush was one of the pilots providing low-altitude screening for the
Americans when they hit Guam and Saipan, often flying through frightening ack-ack counterattack. He said later, "We could see the troops
going ashore and the big guns from the battleships firing over them. All
I could do was count my blessings that I was up there instead of down
below."

In Europe D-day came and went. Mid-June now in the Pacific, as the enemy instigated air attacks on the U.S. ships grouped off Guam, Saipan, and other Mariana Islands. The *San Jacinto* inevitably formed one of the prime aims for the 300-strong air armada. The carrier's fighters took off first to counter the threat, but the order went for the Avengers to fly off, too, to avoid any danger of their being bombed while on their own flight deck.

As Bush was about to be catapulted into the air, he suddenly saw that the Avenger had oil-pressure trouble. The launch went ahead, but the engine faltered in only a minute or two. George was carrying his normal crew complement of two others and a weapon-load weighing 2,000 pounds. Bush guided and coaxed the Avenger over the wavetops, hauled the nose upwards, and then the tail just grazed the sea. The nose went forward almost gracefully and the crew of three moved rapidly from wing to raft. They began quite a frantic paddle motion, thinking of the depth-charges still aboard the sinking Avenger. At a predetermined depth, the weapons went off without harming the trio. They were saved by a U.S. destroyer and duly returned to their carrier. Just a microcosm in the whole sea war.

Through the midsummer months, the same pattern of operations followed: either attacking enemy land targets on the islands or seeking Japanese submarines. June, July, August. On 1 September 1944 Bush and the rest of his Avenger squadron had as their target an enemy radio-communications post on one of the Bonin Islands. They were getting nearer to Japan itself now—only five hundred or so miles. Ack-ack opposition interfered with the attack, which was only partially successful. The Avenger pilots learned that the enemy radio still transmitted, so it proved no surprise when they received word that they would be resuming their attack on the following day.

Bush's radioman/gunner was Jack Delaney. A pal of Bush's, gunnery oficer Ted White, asked if he could accompany them on the raid. White received permission from their commanding oficer and the three of them catapulted off promptly on time. The Avenger was one of four from the carrier, escorted by a squadron force of protective fighters. The Avengers had their full complement of bombs for the attack, four Avengers each with four bombs adding up to 2,000 pounds per plane, a dangerous load to be carrying as they flew slowly into really shaking shellfire from the ground.

*George Bush flew fifty-eight missions as a USN pilot. When he
and the other two crew had to abandon their Avenger in the
Pacific, Bush was the only one to survive.* Imperial War Museum

The squadron commander flew one of the opening pair of Avengers. They dropped their loads through the ground firing and observed strikes on a transmitting tower, as well as hitting other adjacent targets. Then Bush and the fourth Avenger prepared to go in. Bush commenced the dive prior to dropping but almost at once received an alarming physical impact. An ack-ack shell tore at the Avenger's engine. Fire threatened the wings of the bomber and the usual acrid smoke thickened around the cockpit. Bush continued the dive course; the four bombs were released and scored hits on the radio station; and then they pulled away, fast.

Bush swung around in the direction of open water, as he knew the Avenger was doomed. Over the bomber's intercom he told White and Delaney, "Bail out. Bail out."

Bush did not get an answer, so he put the bomber on as level a heading as he could, and bailed out himself. But in so doing, he pulled the cord of his parachute before he was fully free of the plane. The parachute became enmeshed in the tail of the Avenger and Bush hit his head on the tail. By some stroke of fortune, the parachute wrenched itself free under the wind pressure and took Bush with it. The descent was too quick but did not injure him. Bush shook the harness of the parachute off him and managed to strike out toward the life-raft. Once aboard the raft, he looked all around the seascape engulfing the small craft, but he could not see either of the other two air crew. He paddled strongly to try to keep the raft away from the island they had been attacking. He did not want to end up as a prisoner of war in Japanese hands.

Bush had hit his head badly on the plane's tail and it was still bleeding after an hour or more. He went on paddling by instinct and after a couple of hours he felt really ill. Head hurting, arms aching, sick after swallowing seawater. "It seemed just the end of the world," he said later. At that stage, he did not know if there was going to be any "later."

Bush needed a minor miracle. It appeared in the form of a moving dot that increased in size by the second. The other Avenger crews in the attack had, in fact, spotted his raft and radioed his position back to base. The message reached the U.S. submarine *Finback*. The dot that Bush was watching turned out to be *Finback*'s periscope. Like some revelation, he watched while the conning tower of the submarine heaved onto the surface, and soon the whole mammal-like bulk dripped itself glossily dry. It only took a few minutes for the *Finback* crew to get Bush on board before the craft vanished once more below the surface.

Only one of the crew had been spotted bailing out of Bush's Avenger, but his parachute failed to deploy properly. The second man must have gone down with the plane. He may have been killed or injured but in either case he was never seen again. The loss of his two air crew has always been a sadness to George Bush.

That was not quite the end of the story. *Finback* had picked up three other USN air crew from the sea and the four fliers had to remain submerged in *Finback* for about a month. They even experienced being depth-charged by an enemy bomber. Bush said later, "That depth-charging got to me. It just shook the boat, and those guys would say, 'Oh, that wasn't close.'"

It was actually almost two months before Bush got back to *San Jacinto,* in the end of October. U.S. assault troops were landing on Leyte. Bush now had a new Avenger aircraft, which he flew on further air strikes aimed at shore installations in the Philippines, as well as enemy shipping off the coast. He went on flying until nearly Christmas, when he was sent home. His flying log read as follows: "1,228 hours airborne; 126 carrier landings; 58 combat missions." George Bush married Barbara Pierce on 6 January 1945. Neither of them knew that one day they would be living in the White House, Washington, D.C.

Dace, Darter, and Leyte Gulf

It was 23 October 1944; the tomblike silence that reigned in the *Dace*'s conning tower was suddenly shattered by a series of explosions.

"Depth-charges. Depth-charges," one of the men yelled.

"Depth-charges, my eye," said the captain. "Those are *Darter* torpedoes, and she's getting her licks into the Japanese fleet."

The explosions the *Dace*'s crew had heard were indeed caused by the *Darter*, the opening shots in the Battle of Leyte Gulf. It was the greatest naval engagement of the war, and a stunning victory for the Allied forces.

But to go back to dawn of that day. There was a faint glow in the east as the radarman saw the *Darter* disappear from the radarscope. She had submerged. The *Dace* continued northward, feeling alone and naked in the wide expanse of Palawan Passage. Minutes later the diving alarm broke the stillness of the tropical dawn. The *Dace* slid beneath the sea in the most fateful dive of her career.

Neither the *Darter* nor the *Dace* had long to wait. The Japanese, suspecting nothing, had finally come into range and were promptly greeted by a salvo of torpedoes from the *Darter*. A series of rapid explosions told the *Dace* that the *Darter* had made a successful attack.

"It looks like the Fourth of July out there," exclaimed the captain. "One is burning," he continued. The men in the *Dace* hung onto the captain's words as he described what he saw. but they were not out there to record a major event in world history for posterity. They were there to work and soon had no time for unnecessary talk.

"Here they come," said the Old Man. "Stand by for a setup. Bearing, mark. Range, mark. Down scope. Angle on the bow, ten port."

The number of hits that they scored largely depended upon the fire-control officer and his assistant, and they had to work fast and efficiently, Ranges, bearings, angles on the bow followed in quick succession as the problem developed.

The captain singled out the third ship in line—the biggest he could see. They thought it was a battleship, though it turned out to be a heavy cruiser. Their fire-control problem had been solved, and with the captain's words, "Let the first two go by, they are only heavy cruisers," they began to fire. Six torpedoes sped from the forward tubes. Almost immediately these began to strike home. One, two, three, four explosions. Four hits out of six fired.

The offensive phase was over. Now it was time to start running, and they frittered away no time in doing so. The sixth torpedo had hardly left its tube when they were told to dive. On their way down, they heard a crackling noise that started very faintly but soon became overpowering, like the sound cellophane makes when crumpled. Those experienced in submarine warfare knew that a ship was breaking up, but the noise was so close, so loud, so gruesome, that they came to believe that it was not the enemy ship but the *Dace* that was doomed. Anxious seconds elapsed as they awaited the reports from the compartments that all was secure. They finally came. The *Dace* was all right. But then a new and terrifying thought gripped them. Could the ship be breaking up on top of them? They were making full speed in an attempt to clear the vicinity of the attack, but that crackling noise still sounded all around them; they couldn't escape it. Relief came with a rush. They were leaving the noise astern. They had not only hit but sunk a major Japanese warship.

Their elation was short-lived, however. They had just settled down at their running depth when a string of depth-charges exploding close announced the arrival of Japanese destroyers. At first the *Dace* thought that they had made a mistake, for they had not expected this attack.

They thought that the destroyers would concentrate on the *Darter* and leave them alone. Another string, just as loud as the first one, exploded close aboard. There was no mistake. The Japanese were after the *Dace* and they were very close. The boat was being rocked consid-

U.S. submarine Dace. *U.S. Navy*

erably. Lightbulbs were shattered; locker doors were flying open; wrenches were falling from the manifolds.

Finally the attack let up, and the *Dace* began to work her way back to the scene of the attack. At the time, of course, they could not know that the *Darter* had sunk an *Atago*-class cruiser and damaged a second heavy cruiser. But as they continued northward they sighted masts. The Jap cruiser crippled by the *Darter* was lying dead in the water, guarded by two destroyers and two aircraft. The *Dace* tried to get in another attack during the day but was unsuccessful because of the effective defensive screen. The men were not too concerned, however, as they had the cruiser in view at all times, and they knew they could team up with the *Darter* that night to finish her off. They surfaced before the *Darter*. The navigator got a fair fix. The *Darter* surfaced; they made contact and began to lay plans for finishing the crippled cruiser.

The enemy ship still had some life left in her. With the two destroyers she got under way on a southwest course at a modest speed of six knots. The submarines began their attempts to polish her off, but soon realized that it was not going to be easy. The *Dace* went in and out, trying to draw them away, but to no avail. Finally they realized that the only hope of success was in a submerged attack. *Dace* was discussing the possibility when they received a dispatch from the *Darter:* "WE ARE AGROUND."

The captain of the *Dace* was faced with a difficult decision: either continue in his attempts to sink the cruiser or go to the rescue of the *Darter.* His decision was not reached hastily, but everyone on board was happy when it was announced. They were to go to the assistance of the *Darter.* It was hard to give up pursuing a ship that they knew would probably sink with one torpedo hit, but it would have been doubly hard to abandon their comrades to death on the dangerous shoals of Palawan Passage.

About an hour and a half later they were within a stone's throw of the *Darter.* So high that even her screws were out of the water, she looked rather like a vessel in dry dock. It would be hard to get close to her. They decided to approach from the stern and slowly began to close her. The current took charge and they had to make a second approach. The captain of the *Darter* was worried about the daring of the *Dace.* He kept telling the *Dace*'s captain to stay out a bit, not to come so close, to beware of the reef. They paid no heed and continued to close until they could pass over their bowlines. By the use of that line and by the use of the engines, they were able to keep away from the reef, now only fifty yards away to starboard.

The fact that the *Darter* could never get off the reef was obvious from the outset. As soon as the bowline went over, the transfer of personnel began. In the darkness, gnome-like figures on the deck of *Darter* went down her side into the rubber boats awaiting them below. Minutes later they reappeared at the side of the *Dace,* where willing hands hoisted them aboard. There was little conversation. It was a grim and distressing task. There were only two six-man rubber lifeboats available and it was slow work. They had started the operation at about 0200 and it was not before 0439 that the captain of the *Darter,* the last man to leave the ship, climbed over the side of the *Dace.*

They got away from the site as fast as possible, for not only were they in fear of the reef but the captain of the *Darter* had set demolition charges on his ship. So there was good reason to set the submarine's annunciators at full speed and keep them there until they were safe.

The allotted time for the charges to go off drew near. With blinking eyes, they saw the second hands of watches circle to zero time. They braced themselves for the stillness to be broken by a terrific explosion.

But only a ridiculously low and inoffensive pop came from the *Darter.* What had happened? Something had obviously gone wrong, and the *Darter,* instead of exploding, was very much in evidence still on the reef.

They took position on her beam and fired two torpedoes, one at a time. Both exploded on the reef without as much as rocking *Darter.* This confirmed the fear that she was too high on the reef. They had two more torpedoes; the *Dace* went directly astern of *Darter* and fired. The story was repeated. Both torpedoes went off against the reef. It was now 0530. The first streaks of light were beginning to appear. What to do next? They had to destroy that ship, and there was only one thing to do—hit her with the gun.

"Crew, man the gun," was passed over the system. Almost immediately the deserted deck became alive with men as the gun crew prepared the weapon for action. Soon they were scoring hits on the *Darter* and beginning to feel easier in their minds about the whole undertaking. Suddenly a cry came from the conning tower: "Plane contact—six miles."

"Clear the deck. Diving alarm. Take her down."

The instinct of self-preservation took charge of them. Their twenty-five-inch conning-tower hatch, the only way to get into the *Dace,* attracted everyone as if it had been a magnet. Some walked down; others slid down; still others were pushed down. Some came down feet first, others headfirst, and even sideways. The officer of the deck managed to close the hatch bare seconds before the boat went under the surface.

They all braced themselves for the explosion that they felt sure would follow the alarm. They didn't have long to wait, but for the second time that day an awaited loud bang resolved itself into a distant pop. Once again they wondered what had happened. An unknown enlisted man said: "That dumb, stupid pilot. He bombed the *Darter!*"

He was right. The Japanese pilot had sighted two submarines on the surface. He saw one of the submarines diving and he could not tell that the *Darter* was aground, so he decided to go for *Darter* instead of *Dace.* They all agreed he had made an excellent choice and they hoped he had been able to do what they had failed to achieve earlier that morning with their torpedoes and guns.

But later, when they came up to periscope depth to see, they discovered that the Japanese pilot was a bad shot. There sat the *Darter,* still on the reef, looking lonely and exposed. Above it circling low was the enemy aircraft. The *Dace* had to move on, since they knew it would not be long before the Japanese sent a surface ship to reconnoiter and board the *Darter.*

Still reluctant to abandon the *Darter* permanently, the *Dace* sneaked back that night. Warily they got closer and closer, when the radar operator heard the sound of echo ranging. It was a single ping, clearly defined. They could not take the chance that a Japanese submarine was lying there waiting for them, so once and for all they turned and cleared the vicinity at full speed.

Although they had lost the *Darter,* all of her crew had been saved. And they had accomplished their mission of giving warning to the American fleet at Leyte Gulf; they had sunk two heavy cruisers and damaged a third. For all this, the price was only one deserted sub and a few cuts and bruises. It was worth it.

The invasion of the Philippines used every type of warfare known in 1944: land and amphibious forces, surface and subsurface ships, and a huge umbrella of air cover. The islands on which the assault was made formed a maze of channels and the two with the best exits to the Pacific proper were San Bernardino Strait in the north, between Luzon and Samar Islands, and Surigao Strait in the south, between Leyte and Mindanao.

One of the precautions taken against an enemy stab from the west was to post submarines on the opposite side of the archipelago. And so, the morning of 23 October, before daylight, the *Darter* and *Dace* flashed the word to the invasion forces that a strong enemy fleet was plowing northeast into Philippine waters.

The naval stage was set for the Battle of Leyte Gulf.

24 October: Now on the alert, thanks to the submarine service, the carrier air forces extended their searches. They soon found two large enemy fleets steaming eastward: two battleships, two heavy cruisers, two light cruisers, and ten destroyers. In spite of damage from air attack the enemy persisted in its course to the strait, which met Leyte Gulf at its mouth. Soon it would encounter a surprise reception committee.

Meanwhile, the patrol parties met a larger enemy force made up of five battleships, seven heavy cruisers, and twice that number of destroyers. Like the other force, these ships were hit on their way through the Sibuyan Sea, to such effect that they turned around and gave up the attempt to force the San Bernardino Strait.

While these carrier strikes continued against the two large enemy fleets, the American vessels were being hit by hundreds of land-based planes. During these attacks from a hundred airfields, the light carrier USS *Princeton* was hit and set on fire so severely that she had to be destroyed. Among the attackers was one group of carrier-based aircraft flying in from the north, so search groups from the Third Fleet took off to try to track down their carriers. At 1540 two more enemy forces were detected coming down from the northern tip of Luzon to join the battle: two battleships, four carriers, one heavy cruiser, three light cruisers, and six destroyers. The Third Fleet veered to meet them.

The Americans aiding and protecting the Leyte landings were now the target for three converging naval groups totaling no fewer than nine battleships, four carriers, thirteen heavy cruisers, seven light cruisers, and thirty-odd destroyers.

Shortly after midnight the small torpedo boats reported the approach of the enemy's battered southern strength. The little ships hit two of them with torpedoes, but they still came on. Three hours later U.S. destroyers found the enemy ships coming through in two columns at twenty knots. The destroyers attacked, accompanied by the bigger American ships. The enemy was caught in the narrow waters of a strait. It was also caught in the fire of five battleships they had reckoned as lost at Pearl Harbor—the *West Virginia, Maryland, Tennessee, California,* and *Pennsylvania.* Five sturdy states of the good old USA!

The Japanese columns slowed indecisively and fatally to twelve knots. Shell after shell from the U.S. battleships burst either on or around them, so that they changed their minds again and tried to reverse course and escape. In this heavyweight slugging match before dawn, the Americans sank a battleship, several cruisers and five destroyers.

25 October: In the morning, the "wings over the Navy" finished off a second battleship and crippled a cruiser. All this with only a single patrol torpedo boat sunk.

While the southern prong of the enemy attack was being virtually obliterated by surface action, the northern one was located by air in the night. Although it was trying to get away by course-changing, the Americans kept it tagged. The enemy carriers were found with few planes on their decks. The aircraft sent out against the Yanks the previous day had had to land on Luzon to refuel before they could return to their carriers. In fact, twenty-one of these homing planes were intercepted by the

U.S. naval air arm fighter-cover as the big ships attacked the enemy on the surface. In any case, the enemy planes could not have landed amid that storm of bomb-burst and shell-scorch. Three of the four Japanese carriers were already on their way to the bottom and the flight deck of the fourth looked so much like a flat sieve that no plane could find a hole-free strip for landing. More U.S. cruisers and destroyers caught this fourth carrier as it hobbled home and they torpedoed it to the bottom off the Philippines.

While all this went on, Admiral Halsey diverted some of the Third Fleet units south at top speed because a group of American escort carriers—the baby flattops—operating in support of the Leyte landings were in danger from superior enemy power. Superior meaning larger, not better.

25 October: The antisub patrol of these escorts detected the surviving elements of the enemy which had been attacked in the Sibuyan Sea and forced to flee westward. No small ships, these, but four battleships, seven cruisers, and nine destroyers.

Strongly silhouetted in the early sunlight, the escort carriers sustained shattering fire from the enemy. Converted merchantmen, the carriers headed off into the east wind and launched aircraft to attack the enemy ships. But the greater speed and gunpower of the Japanese swiftly allowed them to close the gap. This was the one phase of the Battle of Leyte Gulf that went against the United States.

Tropic rain deluged down at 0725 as the destroyer USS *Noel* was hit. Some of the crew were killed, but that did not stop her from firing her torpedoes two minutes later. Then another pair went eight minutes later still. Then she tried to withdraw, with her director platform devastated, but as she valiantly and vainly pressed between battleships and cruisers her end became inevitable. Her guns went on firing. But more firing came from the huge bulks of the enemy ships on each side of her. The *Noel* was literally a mass of molten metal. Men lay dead. Whole decks were ripped in jagged hunks. A few minutes more and she sank. Captain Kintberger went down with her, together with Screen Cdr. William D. Thomas and 253 men. Fifteen wounded died later. In one stroke 268 American families would never see their sons, husbands, brothers again. That was the real meaning of war.

Then suddenly the enemy hauled away. They broke off the battle with a final, harmless spread of torpedoes before steaming over the northern horizon at high speed, trailing oil from pierced hulls as they went.

It is not too difficult to understand their retreat. The Japanese admiral received word of the destruction of the southern force in Surigao Strait, the route of the northern force, and the destruction of its carriers. He had to get back through the San Bernardino Strait or face annihilation. Furthermore, although he may not have known it, the Americans had a battleship and cruiser force in Leyte Gulf to protect transports and landing craft from enemy ships. This force had wiped out the enemy southern group before daylight in the south. And it was still available, almost intact, to prevent the entrance of the enemy's central force.

The vanguard of the returning Third Fleet units caught a straggling destroyer before it reached the strait and sank it with one spread of "fish." Air groups, too, sank one or two more of the desperate fugitives.

Meanwhile, at the scene of the attack on the carriers, the Japanese went on with their harassment from land-based aircraft. They accounted for a second American escort carrier, but the Battle of Leyte Gulf was a clear victory for the Americans. The enemy fleet would now need more than they had to meet the forthcoming final drives against their empire.

So to sum up the respective losses after the battle: The Americans lost one light carrier, the USS *Princeton;* two escort carriers, the USS *Saint Lô* and USS *Gambier Bay;* two destroyers, the USS *Johnston* and USS *Noel;* one destroyer escort, the USS *Samuel B. Roberts;* and some smaller craft. The Japanese lost two battleships; four carriers; six heavy cruisers; two light cruisers; and many destroyers. By its very scale, the victory reduced future casualties in the war at sea.

January—August 1945

30

Luzon and Iwo Jíma

The war was approaching its climax. Before that climax came, two more names would be inscribed in history—Luzon and Iwo Jima. The adventures of a single ship sum up the whole drama of those two epic battles: the USS *Lunga Point*. This escort carrier took her name from that night of 30 November 1942, known officially as the Battle of Tassafaronga, but better remembered as the Battle of Lunga Point. It marked the last major attempt by the Japanese to reinforce their troops on Guadalcanal, and thus it was the turning point of the Solomons campaign.

The invasion of Luzon, scheduled to begin on 9 January 1945, involved the largest number of ships in a single operation so far in the Pacific.

4 January: The *Lunga Point* was cruising just west of Panay Island when her men went to general quarters at 1705. They had hardly manned their guns when a Zero peeled off at 6,000 feet and made his dive on the carrier from dead ahead. By 1716 the Zero was no more, crashing seventy-five yards astern with a tremendous bang. Other enemy planes buzzed about and fatally hit a sister carrier, the USS *Ommaney Bay,* but luckily a destroyer was able to pick up most of her crew.

Next day, the log of *Lunga Point* read:

0812: steaming as before. 0817: dogfight reported bearing 023° T. 27 miles. 0818: manned all gun stations. 0820: general quarters sounded. 0824: one enemy plane shot down by a CAP [Combat Air Patrol].

It was Lieutenant (jg) Ramey who "tallyhoed" the enemy pilot and shot him down, so to mark the first success by the squadron he ate the traditional steak and cake for dinner. The log had not yet finished for the day, however:

> 1216: steaming as before. 1445: received orders for OTC to arm four VTs with torpedoes. 1327: four VTs ready to fly with torpedoes and four FM2s with rockets, to intercept reported Japanese destroyers.

Two enemy destroyers had been seen off Luzon twenty miles away, and *Lunga Point* planes went in for the attack with two or three other squadrons. The result was that the two Japanese destroyers were no more, without any loss of U.S. aircraft. A retaliation raid hit several other U.S. vessels.

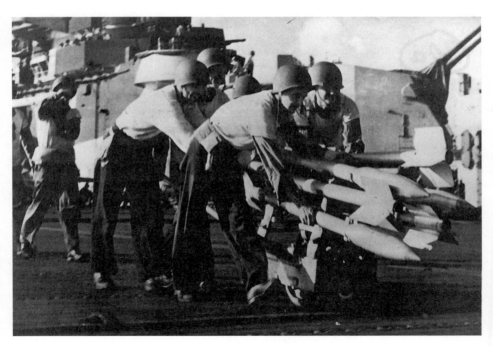

Torpedoes being loaded before the attack on Formosa.
Imperial War Museum

February 1945: *Lunga Point*'s narrowest escape occurred during the Iwo Jima operations. All hands seemed to have a premonition that they were about to undergo an attack. Tangible tension could be felt throughout the ship. Then it happened.

Just at dusk, a group of kamikaze bombers launched an aerial torpedo onslaught. The planes could not even be seen until just within range of the *Lunga*'s guns. They shot the first one down and he fell in flames to starboard, about 200 feet from the ship. The second was hit but turned and flew low over the carrier's stern. It ended up in the sea.

They hardly had time to reload their guns when the third and fourth came straight toward them in suicide attacks. The Japanese made easy targets for the baby flattop's guns, which shot them down quickly. One of them burst into a frightening mushroom of fire as it struck the sea 300 feet off. The fourth blazed across the flight deck after shearing off his starboard wing and landing wheel as he hit the after-part of the bridge. The plane sprayed gasoline dangerously all over the deck, actually setting fire to it before bouncing into the water and exploding on the port beam.

Several sailors in the port gun batteries were burned by the plane's scorching fuselage. Fire parties quickly extinguished the flight deck, and first aid treated the men's burns. Meanwhile, the bombers had gone but had dropped three torpedoes that whistled by the *Lunga Point* perilously near her bows. The significance of these misses was brought home to everyone on board as they watched their sister ship *Bismarck Sea* go down from an exactly similar attack just 2,000 yards away.

Iwo Jima created conditions for heroism among the Navy fliers on *Lunga*. Lt. Bud Foster had accompanied other planes on a direct support hop over Iwo Jima in his Wildcat fighter and a part of his mission was to drop a napalm fire bomb on his target. When he got there, however, he found that the bomb release proved faulty and he could not get rid of the weapon.

After completing the rest of his mission, Foster returned to their operating area and called the captain to tell him of the situation. Should he get out or try to land on the *Lunga*? The skipper told Lt. (jg) Max Palena, the aviation ordnance officer, to report to the bridge, where they went into a detailed discussion of the release system of the bomb racks. They decided to help Foster to get rid of the stubborn bomb. To do so,

Navy pilot about to take off for the Formosa attack.
Imperial War Museum

they put him through almost every conceivable maneuver including flying "on his back," but even this failed to shake off the bomb.

The captain then called Admiral Durgin over the TBS (transmission between ships) and asked him for advice. It was a difficult decision. If Foster bailed out, he would probably be picked up unharmed but they would have lost a precious plane. If they brought him in, Foster—and others—might die as a result. Even the ship itself might be sunk. Durgin left it up to the captain, saying, "Do what you think best. Good luck."

The captain and Palena then considered the possibility of the bomb's fuse being armed and the chances of the bomb being released by the impact of a landing. To check whether or not the bomb was armed, the captain got one of the torpedo bomber pilots to fly wing-on to Foster, as close as possible, to see if the arming wire was still secured to the fuse and that the bomb was secured to the rack. The pilot did this and sent the reply, "Affirmative."

The captain asked Foster by radio: "Do you want to try to land aboard?"

Foster radioed back: "If you think it advisable, I'll land aboard, Captain."

Foster knew his life was at stake. For ten minutes he tried to shake off the bomb, but it was no good. Foster came into the landing circle. All planes were taken below to the hangar deck except two, for which no room could be found. All fire parties manned their stations and everyone took a long breath. Some of them even prayed. Foster first made a pass at the ship, flying close to the bridge, so that the captain and Palena could see that the bomb was still secure. Then the captain ordered Foster in to land.

Commander Eastwold and Lieutenant (jg) Palena were the only ones on the flight deck when Foster came in with a very good landing. Now no one breathed. The Wildcat touched down. For a fleeting instant the bomb remained intact on the plane. Then the impact of the arresting gear loosened it. The bomb bounded down the deck toward the parked planes. If it had hit them, it might have gone off, throwing liquid fire all over the ship, or even sinking her.

Palena was standing near the bridge block, and as the bomb slid beneath the third barrier he jumped out after it and caught it between the barrier and one of the planes. He straddled the bomb and yelled, "Somebody give me a wrench!"

A big pipe wrench appeared, but it was actually too big. Seconds later AOM2/c Olup, one of Palena's ordnance men, ran across the flight deck with a small wrench for him to use in removing the fuse. As Palena was working on it, the executive officer stood beside fire parties. Palena knew that it might go up. Seconds seemed interminable as he withdrew the fuse. Then, suddenly, out it came. They threw the bomb over the side and all was well.

Okínawa and
the Kamíkazes

Easter Sunday, 1 April 1945: "Love Day" was D-day for Okinawa. Beautiful weather for the East China Sea. Cloudless skies, smooth jade water, promise of a sparkling spring morning, with a hint of gardenia in the air. At home church bells would be ringing for sunrise services. But to the men in Operation Iceberg the day was just 1 April. The struggle for Okinawa would be the final fling, and both on land and at sea that meant a bloody battle. As the Japanese saw their ancient empire crumbling, they fought with frenzy.

Before dawn: The Iceberg forces had taken their position off the Okinawa coast. Marked for the landings were beaches below Cape Zampa on the west shore. For five days these had been softened up in the usual fire-and-iron manner by bombing and shore bombardment. Whole teams of underwater demolition men went in to dynamite obstacles and cut away snares. A force of seventy-five minesweepers and forty-five auxiliary craft combed the entire perimeter of the island's southern coast. During all these activities Okinawa's shore guns were quiet. Not a shot was fired. The silence was sinister.

The invaders did not know that General Ushijima had concentrated his forces in southern Okinawa on a line across the island. Nor did they know that this line, with ancient Shuri Castle as its keystone, contained a system of deep tunnels and limestone caves reinforced with ferroconcrete that were almost invulnerable to air attack and naval barrage.

But the Iceberg leaders did not know that Okinawa was an enemy Gibraltar, and that its capture would be resisted to the last. And that meant to the last man.

To subdue and secure this Nansei Shoto bastion, Adm. Chester Nimitz had allocated some 1,450 U.S. vessels manned by well over half a million men. Operating at the southern end of the Nansei Shoto chain, a British carrier force under Vice Adm. Sir B. M. Rawlings added its own weight to the armada.

Directly off Okinawa, Admiral Turner's amphibious force contained 1,213 ships carrying 182,000 assault troops under command of Gen. Simon Bolivar Buckner. A total of 318 combatant vessels were on the Iceberg front. Several European invasions had covered wider fronts, but the hauls were relatively short compared with these trans-Pacific lifts. Forces and supplies came from America, Hawaii, Espíritu Santo, Guadalcanal, and other distant bases. Iceberg employed the largest fleet yet assembled in naval history—over forty carriers, eighteen battleships, scores of cruisers, submarines, minesweepers, landing craft, patrol vessels, salvage vessels, and auxiliaries. More than 148 American destroyers and destroyer escorts were in the armada that fought the Okinawa campaign.

From a naval standpoint, the story of the campaign is the story of those DDs and DEs that bore the brunt of the sea-air battle. Allied carrier groups stood far offshore; bombardment groups came and went. On blockade duty U.S. submarines met practically no opposition. But the destroyer forces were in there fighting for days and weeks on end. The "small boys" got the man-size job at Okinawa and they put up a giant-size effort to accomplish that job.

Most of the destroyers and escorts worked as radar pickets or patrol vessels. Covering the approaches to Okinawa they mounted guard at radar picket stations positioned in a ring encircling the island or patrolled the convoy approaches and served as antisubmarine and anti-aircraft guards on a perimeter that circled the transport area. These ships constituted Task Flotilla 5, under command of a veteran destroyer man, Commo. Frederick Moosbrugger. Twenty-three destroyers worked with the fire-support groups that bombarded the Okinawa beaches in the interval between dawn and H-hour of D-day.

0830: The troops began to land on the six-mile stretch of Hagushi foreshore. There was virtually no opposition. By nightfall on 1 April the advance guards had seized the Yontan and Kadena airfields. About

50,000 soldiers and Marines went ashore. "Love Day" had been practically bloodless. But by the morning of 2 April, Buckner's troops were clashing with the outposts of the Shuri Line. During the next three days the land battle steadily developed. And on 6 April the kamikaze hurricane had broken over the sea in full fury.

Down from Kyusho and the upper Mansei Shoto islands came the planes. Some were new, and some had been modernized, but many were old-timers—aged and battle-scarred, rigged especially for suicide jobs, and carrying just enough gas for a one-way trip. As they approached Okinawa on 6 April, many of these pilots were shot down by intercepting planes. However, about 200 broke through the screen. Not to live, but hoping to die, weaving and skidding, barrel-rolling and looping, they descended on the Iceberg forces at Hagushi Beach.

At Okinawa the shore was afire. The sky was afire. The sea was afire. Plane after plane screeched into the sea, downed by destroyer gunners fighting for their lives. One ship after another was blasted by the aviators, welcoming death for the glory of the god-emperor. Destroyer *Mullany* was hit. *Newcomb* was hit. *Leutze* was hit. *Howarth* was hit. *Hyman* was hit. *Morris* was hit. *Haynsworth* was hit. Destroyer escort *Fieberling* was hit. *Harrison* was scorched by a near-miss. And to climax this inferno, two destroyers, the USS *Bush* and *Colhoun*, went flaming and exploding to the bottom.

12 April: Franklin D. Roosevelt died in Warm Springs, Georgia. The kamikazes continued to come, about 200 strong. With them also came the mosquito-sized Oka planes. The noonday sky was blue, and sunshine flecked the sea with silver-gold. Then, all in a breath, the sky was spattered with shrapnel bursts and the seascape was gouged by explosions, smudged with smoke, streaked with oil, and littered with debris.

Seventeen times the suicide pilots struck, flinging themselves on the American ships. The *Tennessee* was struck. The *Idaho* was struck. As usual, it was the destroyers who were in the vortex of the kamikaze tornado. DE *Whitehurst* was hit. And so were the *Stanly, Riddle, Cassin Young, Rall, Purdy,* and the *Mannert L. Abele.*

The *Abele* was hit twice by two suicide pilots. The first came screaming at her about 1445. Plunging through fusillades of ack-ack fire, the plane smashed into the destroyer's starboard side. The blast wiped out the after-engine room, hurling men and machinery skyward. Sixty sec-

3 Mannert L. Abele. *U.S. Navy*

onds later, what was believed to be a Baka (small rocket) smashed into the ship's starboard side, blowing up the forward fire room.

The double blasting broke the ship's back, and with her starboard side done for she was soon swamped. *Abele's* captain, Cdr. A. E. Parker, had the satisfaction of knowing that the destroyer's guns had shot down two of the kamikazes. But that was small compensation for the loss of a new destroyer. The vessel's main deck was awash almost immediately after the Oka assault. Three minutes later, she went down.

A Japanese plane dropped a bomb squarely in the center of a large group of swimming survivors, and those who lived through this found themselves struggling in a sludge of oil and blood. Lt. (jg) John E. Hertner, ship's medical officer, worked valiantly on the wounded in the rafts and the water. Seventy-three of the destroyer's crew were lost.

Rescue vessels were on hand. It was no easy task to get the injured and exhausted men aboard. At the last, two swimmers were unable to make it. Ship fitter Arthur G. Ehrman, USNR, dived back into the sea from the deck of a rescue ship and helped them both aboard safely.

16 April: Another nightmare day. The carrier *Intrepid* was damaged by a suicide plane, and the destroyer *McDermut,* working in the flattop's screen, was badly slashed by friendly antiaircraft (AA) fire. Destroyer *Laffey* was hit by a kamikaze. DE *Bowers* and destroyer *Bryant* were also hit. Destroyer *Pringle* was struck—fatally—again by kamikaze.

0900: The *Pringle* was under Lt. Cdr. J. L. Kelley Jr. She was patrolling radar picket station no. 14 with destroyer-minelayer *Hobson* and two landing craft when her radar registered an aerial blip (or "pip" in U.S. parlance). Lookouts sighted the bandit a moment later. This time it was a Zeke making a shallow dive; *Pringle's* AA batteries paved the aircraft's way with fire. The Zeke suddenly skidded, turned over on a broken wing, and plunged into the sea.

0910: Three Vals came winging across the seascape. Skimming the waterline, they began to stunt around *Pringle,* dipping and weaving and alternately opening and closing the range at distances between 1,000 and 9,000 yards—batlike tactics calculated to baffle the destroyer's gunners.

Although the wild maneuvering drew a steady fire that wore loaders and hot-shell men to a frazzle, *Pringle's* gunners were not entirely baffled. One of the outside Vals flew smack into a shell splash and crashed. But the middle Val got in. Suddenly peeling off to make a shallow dive, the kamikaze rushed at the ship. On the bridge Kelley tried to swing the vessel away. The destroyer could not make it. There was a crash as the plane bored into the ship's superstructure just behind the no. 1 stack. Either a pair of 500s or a 1,000-pound bomb ripped into the ship's interior. The resultant blast uprooted both smokestacks, wrecked the superstructure from pilothouse to no. 3 gunmount, gutted the vessel's midships area, and buckled her keel.

With all power instantly lost, the *Pringle* drifted for a moment, paralyzed. Then her contorted hull broke in two. Bluejackets and officers smeared with oil, grease, and some blood struggled out of the sinking wreckage and into the water. The sea swiftly closed over her. *Pringle* was gone.

Valiant rescuers—the destroyer-minelayer *Hobson* and the two landing-craft that had been on station with *Pringle*—were immediately on the job. Before noon, most of the destroyer's 258 survivors clambered onto rescue craft. Almost half of these were suffering from burns, fractures, shock, or minor injuries. But they considered themselves the lucky ones. Sixty-two of their shipmates were now dead.

Bush, Colhoun, Mannert L. Abele, and now the *Pringle*—four destroyers downed by kamikazes off Okinawa in three weeks. After the loss of the *Pringle,* Adm. Raymond Spruance reported to Admiral Nimitz:

> The skill and effectiveness of enemy suicide air attacks and the rate of loss and damage to ships are such that all available means should be employed to prevent further attacks. Recommend all available attacks with all available planes, including Twentieth Air Force, on Kyushu and Formosa fields.

Nimitz agreed. All available planes were mustered, and all available attacks were made on the designated airfields. But the lair of the kamikazes was hard to find. The Japanese Special Attack Corps, brooding in secret nests in the home islands, the Nansei Shoto, and on Formosa, kept them flying— and kept them dying. Seven more destroyers were damaged by kamikazes before April was out. And another was struck by a suicide speedboat.

As the Battle of Okinawa raged into May, all hope of a quick windup to Operation Iceberg was lost. It expired in the crash of shells and bombs ashore where the Shuri Line sprawled across the terrain like the wake of a forest fire. And it expired in the island's seething coastal waters, where the transport areas were fouled with oil and debris and where the destroyer picket line fought constant death from the sky.

Bad weather grounded the kamikazes for an odd day or two—long enough to give exhausted sailors a chance to catch their breath. But any break in the storm clouds, any lift in the rain, and down they swooped again. May brought no relief to the destroyer men off Okinawa. Alert followed alert. Lookouts, radar watch, all hands, waited tensely for the next raid or a surprise assault the next moment. It was a rare exception when any attack failed to develop.

A case in point was the *Morrison.* The familiar pips moved across the radar screen, and the Corsairs covering the station were coaxed in to meet the approaching planes. The Corsairs shot down two of the enemy, but they were unable to block the main onslaught. The kamikazes broke through the CAP defense, singled out their target, and launched a multiple, coordinated suicide attack.

Morrison's gunners, and those on her companion ships, hurled a concentrated fusillade at the planes. Proximity bursts and direct hits brought down a couple. But four kamikazes roared in through the barrage, the sniper shots, and machine-gun volleys, straight for the destroyer.

They struck *Morrison* one at a time at two-minute intervals. The first knocked out some of her guns; the second added wrack to ruin; the third and fourth strikes were delivered upon a staggering, half-dead ship. At least two of the planes were carrying big bombloads. The blasts ripped up the destroyer's superstructure and tore out her vitals. A mass of twisted metal, spouting smoke and flame, *Morrison* started the inevitable descent. There was no time to abandon. The ship sank so swiftly that most of the men below decks were lost. Only those topside thrown or washed off the ship were saved. By 0840 the *Morrison* was under the sea.

One of the landing craft, LCS 21, picked up the survivors after they had been in the water about two hours. Out of a total complement of 331 men, only 179 were recovered. And 108 of those rescued were wounded. Only seventy-seven of the *Morrison's* company escaped injury in the kamikaze raid.

When the Okinawa battle stormed into the second week of May, both the Japanese and Americans were fighting with the utmost fury. Iceberg was costing the U.S. Navy more effort, more suffering, more casualties than any previous invasion operation in its history. At Okinawa the Navy was paying the highest death toll of all the services. A whole flotilla of landing craft, minecraft, and other small vessels lay buried in the offshore shallows. Eight destroyers were on the bottom beneath the picket line. Although no warship larger than a destroyer had been sunk, scores of vessels limped out of the area mutilated and disabled by damage. Processions of the lamed and maimed crawled to the Philippines, to Guam, and to other sanctuaries; the anchorage at Kerama Retto was crowded with these cripples.

9 May: The war in Europe was over but here another kamikaze victim was claimed: the DE *Oberrender* went down.

28 May: Kamikazes delivered yet another all-out onslaught on the picket line. During all four weeks of this month, the only letup had come when rain grounded the planes. During this period the following were damaged by the hell-bent attackers: destroyers *Hudson, Evans, Hugh W. Hadley, Bache, Douglas H. Fox, Stormes, Braine,* and *Anthony,* as well as destroyer escorts *England* and *John C. Butler.*

Skippered by Cdr. R. L. Wilson, the destroyer *Drexler* was standing radar picket duty. On station with her was the destroyer *Lowry* and two picket support craft. *Drexler* had totaled fifteen days as an Okinawa radar picket, and she was only too well acquainted with the prospects.

This day the kamikazes flew over the line in swarms. Some 115 were reported "splashed." Influence-type ammunition, "double-banking," and CAP cover were exterminating more and more of the aerial suiciders, but not enough to save the *Drexler*. Six kamikazes broke through the screen shielding the *Drexler-Lowry* group. This death squad made a highly coordinated thrust on *Drexler*. Riddled by the destroyer's fire, two of the planes plunged into the sea, and two failed to strike the ship. But the remaining two, power-diving, rammed the destroyer. The blast of the second strike opened *Drexler*'s deck to the sky and threw her over on her beam. She never returned to an even keel.

Tons of water sluiced into her torn hull, swamping her lower compartments. Deeper and deeper her beam went under, until she was lying on her side in the sea. Forty-nine seconds after the final suicide strike, the ship rolled over with a great heave and went down. Nearly all hands below decks were imprisoned. Those topside were either flung or managed to jump from the ship as she capsized. About 170 officers and men were picked up, fifty-one of them wounded. But 158 men and eight officers died with their ship. The Navy's destroyer men were taking it in Iceberg. Four more DDs were to go down before the Okinawa campaign was over.

1 June: Victory for the Americans on Okinawa was at last dimly in sight. Over Shuri Castle, citadel of the defense line, a tattered Stars and Stripes now waved. Some 50,000 Japanese lay dead in the crumbled fortifications of the Shuri Line. The troops of General Buckner were slugging relentlessly forward, while General Ushijima retreated to a position in the south to make a last suicide stand.

On 27 May Admirals Spruance and Marc Mitscher had relinquished sea-air commands to Admirals Halsey and McCain. The naval forces at Okinawa were now designated "Third Fleet," but they were the same battle-scorched ships and combat-weary men that had been there from the beginning of Operation Iceberg.

4 June: The kamikazes struck in a series of eighteen raids. They were shot down in flocks; no ships were damaged.

Crew abandon the sinking USS William D.
Porter. *U.S. Navy*

5 June: The kamikaze storm was reinforced by a tempest of nature
that played havoc with the American fleet. Swirling out of the ocean east
of Formosa, a rampaging typhoon smote the Okinawa front and caught
Halsey's heavy ships steaming northward to strike at Kyushu. In this
cataclysm of wind and water, the bow was torn from the cruiser *Pitts-
burgh*, the carrier *Hornet* was damaged, and about a score of ships
suffered injury. In the wake of the typhoon, kamikazes struck the battleship *Mississippi* and cruiser *Louisville*.

7 June: The raids continued and more enemy pilots died.

10 June: The kamikazes got another ship, the *William D. Porter*.
Captained by Cdr. C. M. Keyes, she was a veteran ship with old hands
on her bridge and at her guns, and she gave a good account of herself
in this, her last battle.

The kamikaze showed up early in the forenoon watch. As it hove
into near view, it turned out to be a Val. The *William D. Porter* and the

four LCS "pallbearers" with her splotched the air and the Val with ack-ack, but still it came on. The kamikaze struck the sea close aboard and blew up with a blast. The tremendous concussion had the effect of a mine exploding. It crushed the underside of *Porter*'s hull and opened her stern to the flood. The inrush could not be stemmed and the entire after-part of the ship was swamped.

Moving up alongside, the four "pallbearers" joined in the destroyer's battle for buoyancy. All available pumping facilities were rushed into action. Everything that could be done was tried, but the flood could not be controlled. As the deck went sodden underfoot and the stern settled deeper in the sea, Commander Keyes ordered the vessel to be abandoned. Fortunately the men had time to go overside with care. The wounded were handled gently, and those with minor injuries—sprains, lacerations, burns—did not have to endure long immersion in saltwater. None of the sixty-one wounded were lost. And the entire crew was removed from the *William D. Porter* before she finally sank. The time: 1119. She was the eleventh destroyer lost at Okinawa. Her crew was the only one to come through without a fatality.

By the third week in June, the battle for Okinawa was drawing to a bitter end. General Buckner's forces were closing in on Ushijima's tattered remnants, standing in the craggy hills of southern Okinawa with their backs to the sea.

21 June: Japanese resistance collapsed in a horror of banzai charges and hara-kiri. By evening the carnage was ended. Under a flutter of white flags, Japanese officers walked across the fields of the dead to surrender their long swords. From foxholes and covers, the remaining enemy emerged from catacombs. They had no stomach for hara-kiri. The surrender of this riddled and skeletal garrison is generally regarded as the last act of the Okinawa campaign. Officially the island had fallen. Operation Iceberg was over. The war went on . . .

Brítísh Mídget Sub Versus Japanese Cruíser

26 July 1945, noon: Lt. Ian Fraser and Leading Seaman James (Mick) Magennis set out in their midget sub *XE3*. Their target: one of two 10,000-ton Japanese heavy cruisers, the *Nachi* and *Takao*, lying in the Johore Strait near Singapore Island. In the event, *XE3* attacked the *Takao* and the sister sub *XE1* went for the *Nachi*.

As the midget subs set out, the Japanese warships were at anchor. Although they had not been to sea for some time, they were in a position to shell the Singapore Causeway across the straits, which could have been dangerous to any Allied forces approaching the island by that route.

Operational submarines towed the two *XE*s from their starting point, Brunei Bay in Borneo. HM Submarine *Stygian* towed *XE3*. Telephonic touch broke down and the only means of communication between the parent and child submarines was by walkie-talkie sets used when the two vessels surfaced.

A passage crew occupied *XE3* during the four days of the outward tow. They were lucky in having good weather because, as the commander-in-chief of the British Pacific Fleet stressed afterwards, the task of the passage crew is a hard one. The towing speed at times reached eleven knots, yet all the while moisture had to be mopped up and every scrap of equipment kept at maximum efficiency. The whole operation depended on their success. Needless to say, both *XE1* and *XE3* were turned over to the operational crews in perfect condition.

Lt. I. E. Fraser, VC, DSC, RNR.
Imperial War Museum

Leading Seaman J. J. (Mick) Magennis, VC.
Imperial War Museum

This change-over from the passage crew was effected at 0600 on 30 July. Seventeen hours later, the tow was slipped at the dead of night, leaving *XE3* alone at sea in a spot forty miles from the *Takao*'s anchorage. "Operation Struggle" it had been named. Now the struggle really started. With the commander of *XE3*, Ian Fraser, were in fact *three* other crew: Sub-Lt. W.J.L. (Kiwi) Smith of the Royal New Zealand Volunteer Reserve; Engine Room Artificer Charles Reed; and Leading Seaman Mick Magennis.

Fraser fortunately stood only five feet four inches, so he was much happier upright in a midget sub's five-and-three-quarter-feet headroom than a much taller man. He had had plenty of practice, but this was his first real X-craft operation.

Throughout the rest of that night, he sat on the casing looking through binoculars as the sub slipped softly through the waters on the tropical surface. He left the safe "swept" channel on purpose, to avoid enemy listening gear at their posts, and navigated through a known minefield. In the middle of the night, as he dangled his legs and looked through the glasses, he suddenly saw the dark outline of a tanker with an armed escort proceeding toward Singapore Straits. He scrambled to his feet, vanished below, shut the lid behind him, and uttered one word: "Dive."

"The safest thing for us to do, Kiwi," he told the first lieutenant, "is to sit on the bottom for as long as it takes this little Oriental procession to pass."

Thirty minutes later, he came to periscope depth for a peep around. They were safe from the ships but not from the minefield; only then did he notice that the craft had become entangled with a mine that had not exploded.

31 July, mid-morning: No one knew then that the war would be over in another fortnight. Fraser sighted the trawler that acted as a guard vessel at the submarine net boom. Magennis was preparing his gear for "bailing out" quickly and cutting a way through the wire netting.

"Don't bother," Fraser called. "It looks as if the gate has been left open by some kind soul."

Even so, the navigational job was difficult. Fraser had to take *XE3* along the side of the guard vessel, shifting the midget sub at a snail's speed. The water was shallow and the sun shone deep down almost to the bottom. The sub slithered through this clear liquid, visible to anyone who looked down from the enemy ship. Luckily, no one did.

Fraser navigated at periscope depth through several miles of narrow channels where steady sea traffic came and went. Keen pilotage from Fraser, level depth-keeping by Smith, and alert steering from Reed were all necessary. A few minutes after noon, Fraser said simply, "There she is."

The *Takao* lay ahead. She was a very heavy cruiser, carrying eight 8-inch guns. One shell from any of these would wipe out *XE3* and all its crew. Fraser lowered the periscope. Two hours passed and they got closer to the cruiser. They still remained unseen.

1400: Fraser went into the attack. He took a quick peep through the periscope and then dropped on the double! Twenty yards off through the lens was a cutter full of Japanese sailors, "liberty men" going ashore for the afternoon. *XE3* dived. The cutter passed. Fraser continued blind. He knew where the cruiser lay, but how deep was the water? He wondered if he could get *XE3* underneath her. As it transpired, *Takao* was in very shallow water for such a substantial ship. *XE3* went in with her keel scraping the bottom of the sea.

This was going to be difficult, the more so since the method of attack would be different from the *Tirpitz* attack by midget subs. Even on the seabed Fraser could not find enough water. *XE3* came to the cruiser's plating and hit it hard and true with a metallic thud. They wondered if the Japanese had heard it. Fraser brought the craft astern again, and by a series of trials—and errors—he discovered that the Japanese ship lay almost aground at either end, but with some water under her amidships.

The clock ticked towards 1500. By plying back and forth parallel to the *Takao,* and occasionally hitting her hull, *XE3* at last found a spot halfway under the cruiser. This was hardly a pleasant place to be, with ten thousand tons of enemy shipping on top. Fraser wedged *XE3* between the hull and the seabed, although he knew that she might become more tightly squeezed if the tide fell much lower.

Magennis had the job of getting outside the craft to attach limpet mines to the hull of the *Takao.* These would go off in due course and hole her. That was the theory. He went into the chamber, flooded it, and then found that the external hatch only opened a quarter of the normal amount. Only a matter of inches, in fact.

Mick Magennis deflated the breathing apparatus, exhaled until his chest was as small as possible and squeezed through the hatch. Then he began to unload the limpet charges from the port container on the outside of the sub. But as he did so, a stream of oxygen bubbles escaped from his equipment, which must have been damaged while he was wrestling with the hatch. Anyone seeing the bubbles reach the surface would have been more than suspicious.

He took the first limpet mine from its container and prepared to place it against the hull of the ship. It was supposed to stay there by magnetism, but the cruiser's hull was so thick with barnacles, and the *Takao* lay at such a slope, that the magnets would not work. Magennis scraped a little patch free and then secured the charges in pairs. For half an hour he swam, scraped, carried, and tied, securing them with a line under the ship's keel. It was an exhausting job, far more so since his supply of oxygen slowly but steadily went on leaking.

He could well have placed just one or two and then returned to *XE3;* instead, he attached the entire half dozen over a length of forty-five feet of the hull. He got back exhausted to the wet-and-dry hatch, struggled through it, shut it, dried out the chamber, and collapsed into the control room. His hands had been torn to pieces with vicious lacerations from the barnacles. They brought him a drink and sat him down in a bunk, wrenching his diving apparatus off him.

XE3 had done its job. She could make her getaway. But still the hazards hung about her. All she had to do was to get rid of the starboard side-cargo, the large explosive charge, and the port limpet-container—and then back out. But *Takao* had closed her hold on the tiny adversary and would not let her free. A terrifying time.

For nearly an hour, *XE3* went full astern, full ahead, and did everything conceivable to the tanks. But it was no good. It looked as if they would die as soon as the charges fired: killed with their own explosives. The waiting was nerve-wracking. All of them sweated, but the sub just would not budge. Then suddenly, without any warning, she shot astern right out of control, careered toward the surface, and sent a splash of spray upwards only fifty yards from the *Takao*. So quickly did it happen that somehow it was not seen from the enemy warship. A second later the bow was tilted down and hurtled back to the bottom. Fortunately, this was not far, as they lay in a mere fifteen feet of clear water. They bumped aground and water began to come into the midget sub.

Fraser realized that the limpet-container had not released itself, which accounted for the craft being hard to handle. He knew that they had no hope of escaping until it was cleared. As he was an experienced diver Magennis at once volunteered to leave *XE3* again and free the container, despite his exhaustion, the oxygen leak in his set, and their lying in such shallow water.

Fraser said he would go, but Magennis was insistent. So he set out, complete with a big spanner and not much else. Seven minutes elapsed. It was hard work to get the container free from the attachment bolts, but he managed it finally. The container rolled a little way from the craft. Magennis groped back to the wet-and-dry hatch and returned safely aboard and into the control room for the second time. Now they could get away; they were still only yards from the charges.

Under control again, *XE3* sailed a yard or two below the surface, farther and farther from the scene. Through the minefields, the listening hydrophone positions, the loop-detector circuit, the net boom. Fraser glanced at his watch. It read 2130. It was still the same day and he felt tired, but they had gotten clear, out of range of any retaliation, and far beyond earshot. Had they not been, two minutes later they would have heard an explosion rend the dusk of the Straits.

The charges went off, ripping a sixty-foot-long by thirty-foot-wide hole in the hull of the *Takao*. Her turrets were put out of action; her range-finders were damaged; several compartments were flooded; and altogether she was immobilized.

On and on the *XE3* plowed, at periscope depth now and again. Finally they sighted *Stygian*. They had been on duty without sleep for fifty-two hours. Reed was at the helm for thirty hours without a break and they had been submerged for sixteen hours nonstop during the attack. For this action Fraser and Magennis were awarded the Victoria Cross.

The Final Victory

While the U.S. Third Fleet and British Task Force 37 were striking at the very heart of Japan—Tokyo's airfields—the cruiser *Indianapolis* set sail from San Francisco on a top-secret mission. We return to that a little later . . .

24 July 1945: By this time, the Allied fleets were in virtual command of all the waters washing the diminishing Japanese empire. The fliers of the Third Fleet found some of the remnants of the enemy navy at anchor in Kure Harbor. U.S. Navy planes pulverized them around the clock with bombs, bullets, and rockets. Hit after hit rent and wrecked the Japanese warships trapped in the harbor below. Then night fighters and torpedo planes intensified the onslaught.

In two days the Third Fleet sank or damaged tonnage totaling a quarter of a million and got 130 planes, while losing only thirty-two of their own. Some of these pilots were saved, however. Ens. Herb Law, flying from the ship *Belleau Wood,* was one of them.

Law was badly hit in the left leg while attacking an airfield, and his plane started smoking ominously. He was too low to bail out, but he somehow landed and escaped from the agonized aircraft. As he tried to bandage his bleeding leg, a woman ran out of the bushes and fired at him from ten yards but missed. She ran off for help, and the enemy soon found him. They took off his clothes, bound him, and gave him no food or water for three days. He was beaten with clubs, fists, and leather straps, and, in general, used as a judo guinea pig. Yet he survived to tell his story.

28 July: The Navy fliers returned to the scene of the shambles at Kure and finished off all the ships they could see. There was an air of

After Hiroshima, the second atomic bomb dropped on Nagasaki. The plume rose to 20,000 feet—nearly four miles high. Then the Japanese surrendered. The fight for the sea was finally won. U.S. Navy

expectant inevitability about those last few days of July. Throughout 28 July, too, Navy planes focused their fire on the battleship *Haruna,* which stayed afloat for a few hours, but at last gave up and sank in shallow water. The crowning disgrace to the Japanese was to see her turrets still sticking above the waterline. By nightfall, the emperor's navy no longer existed as a serious fighting force. Only a few stray submarines and other small craft still survived in the open sea. That night, more planes pitched into the important port of Hamamatsu. And the scene was set for the climax to the whole of World War II.

We return to the *Indianapolis,* which left San Francisco the day the Third Fleet planes were raiding Tokyo. The ship sailed out under the Golden Gate at 0836 with a big box on board that contained the main nuclear parts of an atomic bomb.

Tests of the bomb had just been completed at the time of the Potsdam peace conference, then in progress in Europe. President Harry S. Truman got news of its success while he was there. The Allies agreed to use it only if the Japanese refused to give in.

The wake of the *Indianapolis* spread quickly westward from Frisco to Pearl Harbor. After refueling, she surged on again, to Tinian, anchoring in the harbor there at about 1100 on 26 July. The vital part of the bomb

USS Indianapolis. *U.S. Navy*

Arrival of the Japanese on the USS Missouri. *U.S. Navy*

was unloaded, and two days later the rest of the nuclear components for both the Hiroshima and Nagasaki bombs arrived by air.

29 July: Her part played, the *Indianapolis* sailed unescorted out of Tinian on her way from Leyte to Guam. The famous cruiser made the usual zigzag course during the day until darkness fell, then straightened up for a normal night. But by one of those million-to-one chances, a solitary submarine of the shattered Japanese fleet happened to be lying on the surface, actually at right angles to the course which the *Indianapolis* was plying, and at exactly the right range for firing torpedoes. The captain of the submarine waited in the gloom of the first few minutes of 30 July, until the cruiser sailed into the trap.

The sub torpedoes were aimed forward and hit the bow area twice. The great cruiser began to settle by the bow. With all her complex communications struck, it was hard to give orders. Soon afterwards, Capt. Charles B. McVay III was compelled to issue the final order: "Abandon

The surrender is signed. U.S Navy

ship." In the nightmare of that night, no SOS signal went out from her radio. It was four days before the pilot of a Ventura reconnaissance plane chanced to see the oil slick from the sunken ship and the dots of many men's heads kept afloat by their life-jackets. Eventually, 316 men were rescued after this tragedy. The *Indianapolis* had done her duty. The war moved into its final phase.

6 August: The crews of the three B-29s scheduled to drop the first atomic bomb went aboard their aircraft in the middle of the night after a tropical rainstorm. The *Enola Gay,* the bomb-carrying plane, took off first and climbed up to 4,000 feet. The bomb commander assembled the nuclear weapon slowly and with infinite care. Then they all ate breakfast while the B-29 throbbed on toward Iwo.

Dawn: They met the other two aircraft and together they climbed to 10,000 feet, where the weather was better. They had been in the clouds most of the time till then, and the rain had spattered the screens. But otherwise it still seemed to all a quiet, uneventful flight, except that they were carrying the means of ending the war in a single flash of fission. They did not talk much now.

Before climbing, they had armed the bomb. Now the bombers gained altitude. Navigation was right—to the minute and the mile.

They saw Hiroshima huddled far below. The weather was clear, yet with a slight haze. One of the two escorting B-29s circled to come in some miles behind the bomb-dropper. Their task was to take pictures. The other bomber stayed on their beam. Only four minutes more. Then three, then two. The bombardier gazed through his periscope, motionless. 1½ minutes. After that he did not touch the bombsight once.

They were coming in high and fast now. The second hands of their watches jerked around to zero and a hush spread through the plane. The sky seemed still, horizons muted. Then the bomb fell, within fifteen seconds of the exact moment they had planned six months earlier.

The B-29 turned sharply to try to get as far as possible from the stupendous shock wave that would soon be rising. They lived through a strange ninety seconds more while the bomb dropped and the historic mushroom-shaped cloud rose.

A flash in the firmament. The bomb burst vividly, vehemently. A ball of fire from the flashpoint, growing each semi-second. The plane was banking at that moment and snapped like a tin roof. They looked at each other apprehensively. Then they heard the sound. A sharp crack and crash followed by a long roll like thunder.

They circled around only a mile above the primeval holocaust, taking pictures of the cloud boiling before their eyes. Black smoke, and orange, blue, gray. That was all they saw, for the dust hid the whole city. They could not speak, only watch, hypnotized.

Suddenly it was over for them, as the breeze caught the ball, breaking it into a raging, ragged, billowing cloud. They headed for home. It was a long, seven-hour haul and most of them slept some of the time. They had been awake for a day and a half.

Mid-afternoon: Back at Tinian, the three B-29s buzzed down and landed. The Japanese had refused to surrender. Now 70,000 of them were killed by the bomb, and as many injured. Three days later came the second atomic bomb, on Nagasaki. The next day the Japanese cabinet agreed to surrender. World War II was over. The Allied navies had helped win it.

About the Author

John Frayn Turner was born in Portsmouth, England, and served with the British Royal Navy. He is the author of twenty-five books, mostly modern histories and biographies, including *Invasion '44,* his comprehensive account of D-Day. Mr. Turner's other books include *Service Most Silent, Periscope Patrol,* and *A Girl Called Johnnie.* His biography *Douglas Bader* was the *London Evening Standard's* book of the week.

Mr. Turner worked for a decade on Royal Air Force publicity and has flown numerous test flights of new aircraft as well as accompanying the Red Arrows aerobatic team. A managing editor of five magazines, Mr. Turner has been a theater and music critic for many years.

The Naval Institute Press is the book-publishing arm of the U.S. Naval Institute, a private, nonprofit, membership society for sea service professionals and others who share an interest in naval and maritime affairs. Established in 1873 at the U.S. Naval Academy in Annapolis, Maryland, where its offices remain today, the Naval Institute has members worldwide.

Members of the Naval Institute support the education programs of the society and receive the influential monthly magazine *Proceedings* and discounts on fine nautical prints and on ship and aircraft photos. They also have access to the transcripts of the Institute's Oral History Program and get discounted admission to any of the Institute-sponsored seminars offered around the country.

The Naval Institute also publishes *Naval History* magazine. This colorful bi-monthly is filled with entertaining and thought-provoking articles, first-person reminiscences, and dramatic art and photography. Members receive a discount on *Naval History* subscriptions.

The Naval Institute's book-publishing program, begun in 1898 with basic guides to naval practices, has broadened its scope to include books of more general interest. Now the Naval Institute Press publishes about one hundred titles each year, ranging from how-to books on boating and navigation to battle histories, biographies, ship and aircraft guides, and novels. Institute members receive significant discounts on the Press's more than eight hundred books in print.

Full-time students are eligible for special half-price membership rates. Life memberships are also available.

For a free catalog describing Naval Institute Press books currently available, and for further information about subscribing to *Naval History* magazine or about joining the U.S. Naval Institute, please write to:

Membership Department
U.S. Naval Institute
291 Wood Road
Annapolis, MD 21402-5034
Telephone: (800) 233-8764
Fax: (410) 269-7940
Web address: www.navalinstitute.org